THE KEY

STUDENT STUDY GUIDE

Mathematics 20-3

THE KEY student study guide is designed to help students achieve success in school. The content in each study guide is 100% curriculum aligned and serves as an excellent source of material for review and practice. To create this book, teachers, curriculum specialists, and assessment experts have worked closely to develop the instructional pieces that explain each of the key concepts for the course. The practice questions and sample tests have detailed solutions that show problem-solving methods, highlight concepts that are likely to be tested, and point out potential sources of errors. **THE KEY** is a complete guide to be used by students throughout the school year for reviewing and understanding course content, and to prepare for assessments.

Copyright © 2018 Castle Rock Research Corporation

Rao, Gautam, 1961 –
THE KEY STUDY GUIDE – Mathematics 20-3 Alberta
ISBN: 978-1-77044-632-8

    1. Science – Juvenile Literature. I. Title

Publisher
Gautam Rao

Published by
Castle Rock Research Corporation
2000 First & Jasper
10065 Jasper Avenue
Edmonton, AB T5J 3B1

    10 9 8 7 6 5 4 3 2 1

CASTLE ROCK
RESEARCH CORPORATION

Dedicated to the memory of Dr. V. S. Rao

THE KEY

THE KEY consists of the following sections:

KEY Tips for Being Successful at School gives examples of study and review strategies. It includes information about learning styles, study schedules, and note taking for test preparation.

Class Focus includes a unit on each area of the curriculum. Units are divided into sections, each focusing on one of the specific expectations, or main ideas, that students must learn about in that unit. Examples, definitions, and visuals help to explain each main idea. Practice questions on the main ideas are also included. At the end of each unit is a test on the important ideas covered. The practice questions and unit tests help students identify areas they know and those they need to study more. They can also be used as preparation for tests and quizzes. Most questions are of average difficulty, though some are easy and some are hard—the harder questions are called *Challenger Questions*. Each unit is prefaced by a ***Table of Correlations***, which correlates questions in the unit to the specific curriculum expectations. Answers and solutions are found at the end of each unit.

KEY Strategies for Success on Tests helps students get ready for tests. It shows students different types of questions they might see, word clues to look for when reading them, and hints for answering them.

Practice Tests includes one to three tests based on the entire course. They are very similar to the format and level of difficulty that students may encounter on final tests. In some regions, these tests may be reprinted versions of official tests, or reflect the same difficulty levels and formats as official versions. This gives students the chance to practice using real-world examples. Answers and complete solutions are provided at the end of the section.

For the complete curriculum document (including specific expectations along with examples and sample problems), visit https://education.alberta.ca/programs-of-study.

THE KEY Study Guides are available for many courses. Check www.castlerockresearch.com for a complete listing of books available for your area.

For information about any of our resources or services, please call Castle Rock Research at 1.800.840.6224 or visit our website at http://www.castlerockresearch.com.

At Castle Rock Research, we strive to produce an error-free resource. If you should find an error, please contact us so that future editions can be corrected.

CONTENTS

KEY Tips for being Successful at School

KEY TIPS FOR BEING SUCCESSFUL AT SCHOOL

KEY FACTORS CONTRIBUTING TO SCHOOL SUCCESS

In addition to learning the content of your courses, there are some other things that you can do to help you do your best at school. You can try some of the following strategies:

- **Keep a positive attitude**: Always reflect on what you can already do and what you already know.

- **Be prepared to learn**: Have the necessary pencils, pens, notebooks, and other required materials for participating in class ready.

- **Complete all of your assignments**: Do your best to finish all of your assignments. Even if you know the material well, practice will reinforce your knowledge. If an assignment or question is difficult for you, work through it as far as you can so that your teacher can see exactly where you are having difficulty.

- **Set small goals for yourself when you are learning new material**: For example, when learning the parts of speech, do not try to learn everything in one night. Work on only one part or section each study session. When you have memorized one particular part of speech and understand it, move on to another one. Continue this process until you have memorized and learned all the parts of speech.

- **Review your classroom work regularly at home**: Review to make sure you understand the material you learned in class.

- **Ask your teacher for help**: Your teacher will help you if you do not understand something or if you are having a difficult time completing your assignments.

- **Get plenty of rest and exercise**: Concentrating in class is hard work. It is important to be well-rested and have time to relax and socialize with your friends. This helps you keep a positive attitude about your schoolwork.

- **Eat healthy meals**: A balanced diet keeps you healthy and gives you the energy you need for studying at school and at home.

HOW TO FIND YOUR LEARNING STYLE

Every student learns differently. The manner in which you learn best is called your learning style. By knowing your learning style, you can increase your success at school. Most students use a combination of learning styles. Do you know what type of learner you are? Read the following descriptions. Which of these common learning styles do you use most often?

- **Linguistic Learner:** You may learn best by saying, hearing, and seeing words. You are probably really good at memorizing things such as dates, places, names, and facts. You may need to write down the steps in a process, a formula, or the actions that lead up to a significant event, and then say them out loud.

- **Spatial Learner:** You may learn best by looking at and working with pictures. You are probably really good at puzzles, imagining things, and reading maps and charts. You may need to use strategies like mind mapping and webbing to organize your information and study notes.

- **Kinesthetic Learner:** You may learn best by touching, moving, and figuring things out using manipulatives. You are probably really good at physical activities and learning through movement. You may need to draw your finger over a diagram to remember it, tap out the steps needed to solve a problem, or feel yourself writing or typing a formula.

SCHEDULING STUDY TIME

You should review your class notes regularly to ensure that you have a clear understanding of all the new material you learned. Reviewing your lessons on a regular basis helps you to learn and remember ideas and concepts. It also reduces the quantity of material that you need to study prior to a test. Establishing a study schedule will help you to make the best use of your time.

Regardless of the type of study schedule you use, you may want to consider the following suggestions to maximize your study time and effort:

- Organize your work so that you begin with the most challenging material first.

- Divide the subject's content into small, manageable chunks.

- Alternate regularly between your different subjects and types of study activities in order to maintain your interest and motivation.

- Make a daily list with headings like "Must Do," "Should Do," and "Could Do."

- Begin each study session by quickly reviewing what you studied the day before.

- Maintain your usual routine of eating, sleeping, and exercising to help you concentrate better for extended periods of time.

CREATING STUDY NOTES

MIND-MAPPING OR WEBBING

Use the key words, ideas, or concepts from your reading or class notes to create a mind map or web (a diagram or visual representation of the given information). A mind map or web is sometimes referred to as a knowledge map. Use the following steps to create a mind map or web:

1. Write the key word, concept, theory, or formula in the centre of your page.

2. Write down related facts, ideas, events, and information, and link them to the central concept with lines.

3. Use coloured markers, underlining, or symbols to emphasize things such as relationships, timelines, and important information.

The following examples of a Frayer Model illustrate how this technique can be used to study scientific vocabulary.

Definition	Notes
• Perimeter is the distance around the outside of a polygon.	• Perimeter is measured in linear units (e.g., metres, centimetres, and so on).

Perimeter

Examples	Non-Examples
• The length of a fence around a yard • The distance around a circle (circumference)	• The area of grass covering a lawn • The size of a rug lying on a floor

Definition	Notes
• A cube is a solid 3-D object with six faces.	• A cube is different from other shapes because it has six equally-sized square faces, eight vertices, and twelve equal edges.

Cube

Examples	Non-Examples
	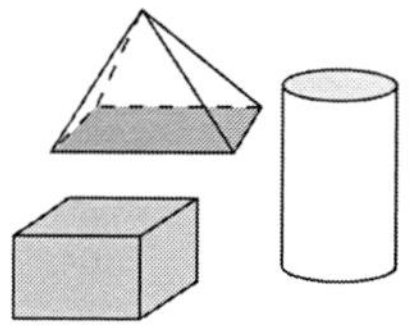

INDEX CARDS

To use index cards while studying, follow these steps:

1. Write a key word or question on one side of an index card.

2. On the reverse side, write the definition of the word, answer to the question, or any other important information that you want to remember.

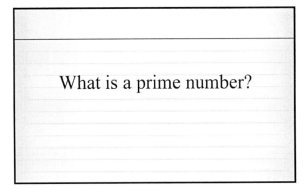

SYMBOLS AND STICKY NOTES—IDENTIFYING IMPORTANT INFORMATION

Use symbols to mark your class notes. For example, an exclamation mark (!) might be used to point out something that must be learned well because it is a very important idea. A question mark (?) may highlight something you are not certain about, and a diamond (◊) or asterisk (*) could highlight interesting information that you want to remember. Sticky notes are useful in the following situations:

• Use sticky notes when you are not allowed to put marks in books.

• Use sticky notes to mark a page in a book that contains an important diagram, formula, explanation, or other information.

• Use sticky notes to mark important facts in research books.

MEMORIZATION TECHNIQUES

- **Association** relates new learning to something you already know. For example, to remember the spelling difference between dessert and desert, recall that the word *sand* has only one *s*. So, because there is sand in a desert, the word *desert* has only one *s*.

- **Mnemonic** devices are sentences that you create to remember a list or group of items. For example, the first letter of each word in the phrase "Every Good Boy Deserves Fudge" helps you to remember the names of the lines on the treble-clef staff (E, G, B, D, and F) in music.

- **Acronyms** are words that are formed from the first letters or parts of the words in a group.
  For example, RADAR is actually an acronym for Radio Detecting and Ranging, and MASH is an acronym for Mobile Army Surgical Hospital. HOMES helps you to remember the names of the five Great Lakes (Huron, Ontario, Michigan, Erie, and Superior).

- **Visualizing** requires you to use your mind's eye to "see" a chart, list, map, diagram, or sentence as it is in your textbook or notes, on the chalkboard or computer screen, or in a display.

- **Initialisms** are abbreviations that are formed from the first letters or parts of the words in a group. Unlike acronyms, an initialism cannot be pronounced as a word itself. For example, BEDMAS is an initialism for the order of operations in math (Brackets, Exponents, Divide, Multiply, Add, Subtract).

KEY STRATEGIES FOR REVIEWING

Reviewing textbook material, class notes, and handouts should be an ongoing activity. Spending time reviewing becomes more critical when you are preparing for a test. You may find some of the following review strategies useful when studying during your scheduled study time:

- Before reading a selection, preview it by noting the headings, charts, graphs, and chapter questions.

- Before reviewing a unit, note the headings, charts, graphs, and chapter questions.

- Highlight key concepts, vocabulary, definitions, and formulas.

- Skim the paragraph, and note the key words, phrases, and information.

- Carefully read over each step in a procedure.

- Draw a picture or diagram to help make the concept clearer.

KEY STRATEGIES FOR SUCCESS: A CHECKLIST

Reviewing is a huge part of doing well at school and preparing for tests. Here is a checklist for you to keep track of how many suggested strategies for success you are using. Read each question, and put a check mark (✓) in the correct column. Look at the questions where you have checked the "No" column. Think about how you might try using some of these strategies to help you do your best at school.

KEY Strategies for Success	Yes	No
Do you attend school regularly?		
Do you know your personal learning style—how you learn best?		
Do you spend 15 to 30 minutes a day reviewing your notes?		
Do you study in a quiet place at home?		
Do you clearly mark the most important ideas in your study notes?		
Do you use sticky notes to mark texts and research books?		
Do you practise answering multiple-choice and written-response questions?		
Do you ask your teacher for help when you need it?		
Are you maintaining a healthy diet and sleep routine?		
Are you participating in regular physical activity?		

Measurement

MEASUREMENT

Outcome		Practice Questions	Unit Test Questions	Practice Test
Table of Correlations				
20M	Measurement			
20M.1	Solve problems that involve SI and imperial units in surface area measurements and verify the solutions.	1, 2, 3, 4, 5, 6, 7, 8, 9, 10, 11, 12, 13	1, 2, 3, 4, 5, 6, 7, 8, 9, 10, 11, 12, 13, 14	20, 21, 22
20M.2	Solve problems that involve SI and imperial units in volume and capacity measurements.	14, 15, 16, 17, 18, 19, 20, 21, 22, 23, 24, 25	15, 16, 17, 18, 19, 20, 21, 22, 23, 24, 25, 26	23, 24, 25, 26

20M.1 Solve problems that involve SI and imperial units in surface area measurements and verify the solutions.

UNDERSTANDING SURFACE AREA OF 3D OBJECTS

The surface area of any 3D object is the sum of the areas of all its faces. The faces can be flat or curved.

When calculating the surface area of an object, it can be helpful to imagine what the net of the object would look like.

A net helps you see all the faces of the object at once. The curved faces now become flat faces and can be easily identified as 2D shapes.

Look at the following rectangular prism as an example:

Rectangular Prism

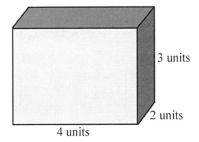

3 units

2 units

4 units

This is the net for this rectangular prism:

Net of Rectangular Prism

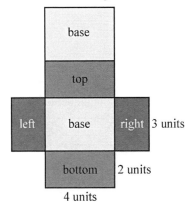

3 units

2 units

4 units

The same process can be applied to a triangular prism:

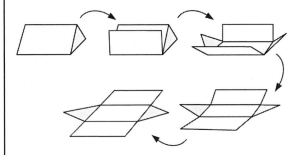

A net illustrates the fact that, even though surface area is only calculated using 3D objects, surface area is a 2D measure itself. Like area, surface area is measured in square units or units^2.

The following list highlights the relationship between the net, bases, and lateral faces of the most common 3D objects. In each case, the area of all of the faces is calculated and added up to determine the surface area of that object.

SURFACE AREA OF RECTANGULAR PRISM

The surface area of a rectangular prism is the sum of its two rectangular bases and four rectangular lateral faces.

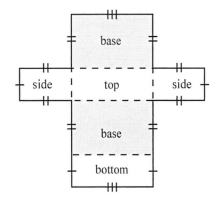

SA = base + base + top + bottom + side + side

SURFACE AREA OF TRIANGULAR PRISM

The surface area of a triangular prism is the sum of its two triangular bases and three rectangular lateral faces.

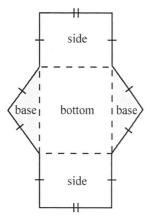

SA = base + base + bottom + side + side

SURFACE AREA OF CYLINDER

The surface area of a cylinder is the sum of its two circular bases and one rectangular lateral face.

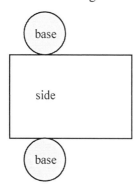

SA = base + base + side

SURFACE AREA OF TRAPEZOIDAL PRISM

The surface area of a trapezoidal prism is the sum of its two trapezoidal bases, the top face, bottom face, and two congruent side faces.

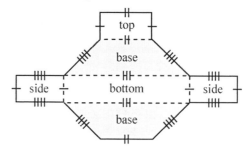

SA = base + base + top + bottom + side + side

20M.1 Solve problems that involve SI and imperial units in surface area measurements and verify the solutions.

DRAWING NETS AND CONSTRUCTIONS OF 3-D OBJECTS

A solid three-dimensional (3-D) shape is made out of two-dimensional (2-D) shapes joined together. If the three-dimensional shape is flattened out, the two-dimensional drawing that results is called a **net**. A net is a pattern that when folded makes a three dimensional figure.

The following nets are the most common types of nets you will come across.

Rectangular Prism	
Solid	**Net**
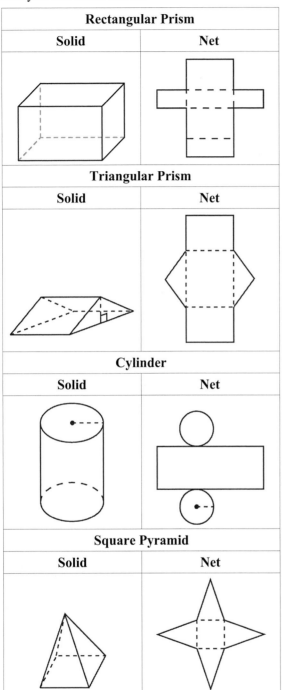	

Triangular Prism	
Solid	**Net**

Cylinder	
Solid	**Net**

Square Pyramid	
Solid	**Net**

In order to draw a net, imagine that you are flattening out the shape. Draw the front, top, back, bottom, and side views. If measures are required, label those accordingly on the net.

Example

Draw the net of the rectangular prism below.

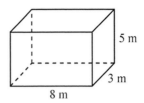

Solution

A rectangular prism is made up of four rectangles that join the two rectangular bases.

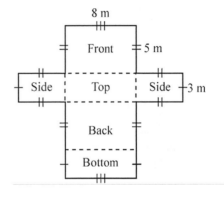

Example

Draw the net of the cylinder.

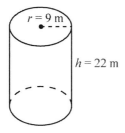

Solution

A cylinder is made up of one rectangular face that goes around two circle bases.

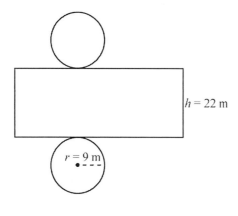

When constructing a 3-D shape from a net, imagine that you are cutting the net and gluing the edges together.

Example

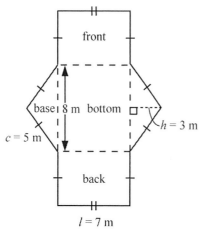

Construct a 3-D shape using the given net.

Solution

Imagine that you are gluing the ends of the net together.

When all the edges meet up, the following shape is formed:

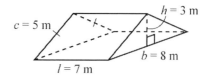

20M.1 Solve problems that involve SI and imperial units in surface area measurements and verify the solutions.

CALCULATING THE SURFACE AREA OF RIGHT RECTANGULAR PRISMS

A right rectangular prism is a three-dimensional object with six rectangular faces. A prism is called a right prism if, when placed on one of the bases, the top base of the prism is directly above the bottom base of the prism.

A cube is a special type of rectangular prism in that all the sides are the same length.

An example of a right rectangular prism is given.

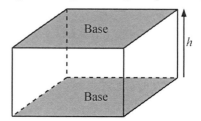

If the rectangular prism is flattened out, the two-dimensional drawing that results is called a **net**.

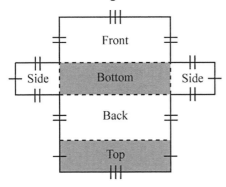

The net is used to calculate the surface area of right rectangular prisms. The **surface area** of a rectangular prism is the sum of the areas of all the faces.

To calculate the surface area of a rectangular right prism, follow these steps:

1. Draw the net of the rectangular prism.
2. Calculate the area of each face.
3. Add the areas of the faces.

Example

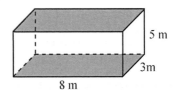

Calculate the surface area of the given right rectangular prism.

Solution

Step 1

Draw the net of the shape.

A right rectangular prism is made up of four rectangular faces (front, bottom, back, and top in the diagram) that join the two rectangular bases (sides).

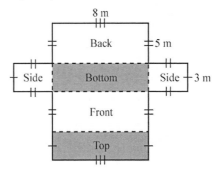

Step 2

Calculate the area of the faces.

Looking at the net, there are some faces that are the same size:

- Top and bottom
- Front and back
- Sides

Find the area for one face, and multiply it by 2 because the measures of the two faces are the same.

$A_{\text{top and bottom}} = 2(l \times w)$
$= 2(8 \text{ m} \times 3 \text{ m})$
$= 2(24 \text{ m}^2)$
$= 48 \text{ m}^2$

$A_{\text{sides}} = 2(l \times w)$
$= 2(5 \text{ m} \times 3 \text{ m})$
$= 2(15 \text{ m}^2)$
$= 30 \text{ m}^2$

$A_{\text{front and back}} = 2(l \times w)$
$= 2(8 \text{ m} \times 5 \text{ m})$
$= 2(40 \text{ m}^2)$
$= 80 \text{ m}^2$

$SA_{\text{right rectangular prism}}$
$= A_{\text{top and bottom}} + A_{\text{sides}} + A_{\text{front and back}}$
$= 48 \text{ m}^2 + 30 \text{ m}^2 + 80 \text{ m}^2$
$= 158 \text{ m}^2$

Often, practical problems require similar approach.

Example

Ann wants to paint the walls and door of her basement all one colour. The room is 3 m long, 3.5 m wide, and 2.5 m high. There are no windows.

On average, the cost of painting is $1.49 for each square meter painted. How much will it cost to paint the walls?

Solution

First, calculate the total area requiring paint, and then calculate the cost of the paint.

Step 1

Draw the net of the shape.

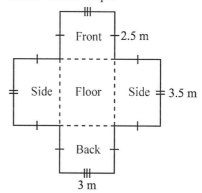

Because Ann is only painting the walls, you only need to calculate the front, back, and sides of the right rectangular prism.

Step 2

Calculate the area of the faces.

Looking at the net, there are some faces that are the same size:

- Front and back
- Sides

Find the area of one face, and multiply it by 2 because the measures of the two faces are the same.

$$A_{\text{front and back}} = 2(l \times w)$$
$$= 2(3 \text{ m} \times 2.5 \text{ m})$$
$$= 2(7.5 \text{ m}^2)$$
$$= 15 \text{ m}^2$$

$$A_{\text{sides}} = 2(l \times w)$$
$$= 2(3.5 \text{ m} \times 2.5 \text{ m})$$
$$= 2(8.75 \text{ m}^2)$$
$$= 17.5 \text{ m}^2$$

$$SA_{\text{walls}} = A_{\text{front and back}} + A_{\text{sides}}$$
$$= 15 \text{ m}^2 + 17.5 \text{ m}^2$$
$$= 32.5 \text{ m}^2$$

Ann will need to paint 32.5 m^2.

Step 3

Calculate the cost of the paint.

Multiply the total surface area by $1.49 /m^2.

32.5 m^2 × $1.49 / m^2 = $48.43

It will cost Ann $48.43 to paint her room.

_____

Example

Andrew wants to wrap a gift for a friend. The box the gift is in has a length of 12.5 cm, a width of 11.5 cm, and a height of 4 cm.

What is the minimum amount of gift-wrapping Andrew needs to cover the box if there is no overlap?

Solution

The surface area of the box must be determined.

Step 1

Draw the net of the shape.

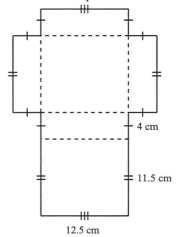

4 cm

11.5 cm

12.5 cm

20M.1 Solve problems that involve SI and imperial units in surface area measurements and verify the solutions.

SOLVING PROBLEMS INVOLVING THE SURFACE AREAS OF RECTANGULAR PRISMS

To find the surface area of a rectangular right prism, follow these steps:

1. Draw the net of the rectangular prism.
2. Calculate the area of each face.
3. Add the areas of the faces.

Step 2

Calculate the area of the faces.

Looking at the net, it can be seen that the following faces are the same size:

- Top and bottom
- Front and back
- Sides (left and right)

Find the surface areas of the given pairs of faces. This requires the surface area of one face to be calculated and then multiplied by 2 in order to calculate the areas of both faces.

$$A_{\text{front and back}} = 2(lw)$$
$$= 2(12.5 \times 4)$$
$$= 2(50)$$
$$= 100 \text{cm}^2$$

$$A_{\text{sides}} = 2(lw)$$
$$= 2(11.5 \times 4)$$
$$= 2(46)$$
$$= 92 \text{ cm}^2$$

$$A_{\text{top and bottom}} = 2(lw)$$
$$= 2(11.5 \times 12.5)$$
$$= 2(143.75)$$
$$= 287.5 \text{ cm}^2$$

Step 3

Calculate the surface area.

Add the areas of the faces.

$$SA_{\text{rectangular prism}}$$
$$= A_{\text{front and back}} + A_{\text{sides}} + A_{\text{top and bottom}}$$
$$= 100 \text{ cm}^2 + 92 \text{ cm}^2 + 287.5 \text{ cm}^2$$
$$= 479.5 \text{ cm}^2$$

The surface area of the box is 479.5 cm^2.

20M.1 Solve problems that involve SI and imperial units in surface area measurements and verify the solutions.

CALCULATING SURFACE AREA OF RIGHT TRIANGULAR PRISMS

Prisms are 3-dimensional geometric shapes with flat sides *(polyhedrons)* with two congruent (identical) and parallel faces called bases connected by rectangular faces. A prism is called a **right prism** if, when placed on one of the bases, the top base of the prism is directly above the bottom base of the prism. The number of sides on the base determines the number of rectangular faces in the prism. The shape of the base determines the name of the prism.

Poly means many, and *hedra* means faces.

These are right triangular prisms with three rectangles. The bases are triangles. This (or any similar) right prism can be sliced parallel to the base. Each cross-section will be in the shape congruent to the bases. Imagine slicing the right prism repeatedly starting at one base and continuing until the other base is reached. It will appear that the cross-section base is "moving" perpendicular to the rectangular faces. The base moves perpendicular to rectangular faces a distance h.

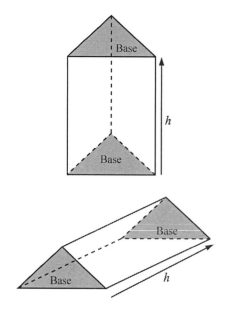

Three-dimensional shapes are shown in different forms. The solid shape is what you see when you have something like a child's building block. Each of the outside surfaces is called a **face**.

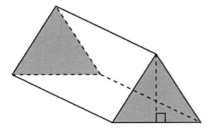

If the three-dimensional shape is flattened out, the two-dimensional drawing that results is called a **net**.

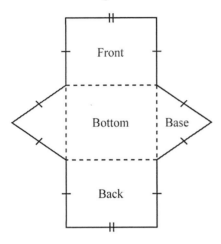

Nets are used to calculate the surface area of different objects. The **surface area** of a three-dimensional solid is the combined area of all the faces.

To calculate the surface area of a right triangular prism, follow these steps:

1. Draw the net.
2. Calculate the area of the faces.
3. Add all areas of the faces.

Example

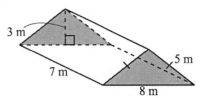

Calculate the surface area of the given right triangular prism.

Solution

Step 1

Draw the net of the shape.

A right triangular prism is made up of three rectangles, which may or may not be the same size, joined to two triangular faces.

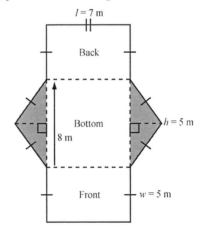

Step 2

Calculate the area of the faces.

Looking at the net, there are some faces that are the same size:

- Front and back (triangular bases)
- Sides (rectangular faces)

For faces that are equal, find the area for one face, and multiply it by the number of times that face repeats.

There is only one bottom. The area of the bottom is:

$$A_{\text{bottom}} = l \times w$$
$$= 7 \times 8$$
$$= 56 \text{ m}^2$$

There are two equal rectangular faces:

$$A_{\text{rectangular sides}} = 2(l \times w)$$
$$= 2(7 \times 5)$$
$$= 2(35)$$
$$= 70 \text{ m}^2$$

There are two triangular bases:

$$A_{\text{triangular sides}} = 2\left(\frac{bh}{2}\right)$$
$$= 2\left(\frac{8 \times 3}{2}\right)$$
$$= 2(12)$$
$$= 24 \text{ m}^2$$

Step 3

$$SA_{\text{right triangular prism}}$$
$$= A_{\text{triangular sides}} + A_{\text{rectangular sides}} + A_{\text{bottom}}$$
$$= 24 + 70 + 56$$
$$= 150 \text{ m}^2$$

Surface area problems such as the one above have many applications. Consider the following example.

Example

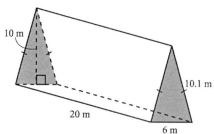

A greenhouse is often built with transparent walls (sides) to let sunlight in on top of soil where plants grow. A particular greenhouse manufacturer uses acrylic glass to construct greenhouses in the shape of a right triangular prisms with dimensions as shown in the diagram.

How much acrylic glass is needed to construct each structure shown above?

Solution

Step 1

Draw the net of the shape.

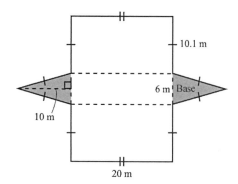

Step 2

Calculate the area of the faces.

Since no acrylic glass is required to make the floor of the greenhouse, you only need to calculate the front, back, and side faces of the right triangular prism.

Looking at the net, there are some faces that are the same size:

- Front and back (triangle bases) Note: Even though the prism does not stand on one of the triangles, traditionally the non-rectangular sides of prisms are called "bases" as described in the introduction to this lesson.
- Sides (rectangle faces)

Find the area for one face, and multiply it by 2 because the measures of the two faces are the same.

$$A_{\text{triangular bases}} = 2\left(\frac{bh}{2}\right)$$
$$= 2\left(\frac{6\text{ m} \times 10\text{ m}}{2}\right)$$
$$= 2(30\text{ m}^2)$$
$$= 60\text{ m}^2$$
$$A_{\text{rectangular faces}} = 2(l \times w)$$
$$= 2(20\text{ m} \times 10.1\text{ m})$$
$$= 2(202\text{ m}^2)$$
$$= 404\text{ m}^2$$

Step 3

$$SA_{\text{greenhouse}} = A_{\text{triangular bases}} + A_{\text{rectangular faces}}$$
$$= 60\text{ m}^2 + 404\text{ m}^2$$
$$= 464\text{ m}^2$$

Each greenhouse will require 464 m^2 of acrylic glass.

20M.1 Solve problems that involve SI and imperial units in surface area measurements and verify the solutions.

SOLVING PROBLEMS INVOLVING THE SURFACE AREA OF A TRIANGULAR PRISM

To solve problems involving the surface area of a right triangular prism, follow these steps:

1. Draw a net that represents the problem.
2. Calculate the areas of the faces.
3. Add the areas of all the faces.

Example

Johnathon drew a sketch of the water trough he wants to make out of sheet metal.

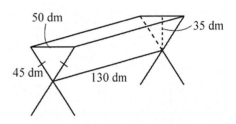

How much material is needed to make the water trough?

Solution

Step 1

Draw the net of the shape.

A triangular right prism is made up of three rectangles, that may or may not be the same size, joined to two triangular faces. In this triangular right prism, one of the faces is not shown.

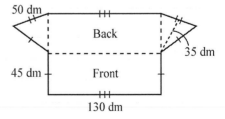

Step 2

Calculate the area of the faces.

Looking at the net, there are some faces that are the same size:

- Front and back (rectangular faces)
- Sides (triangular faces)

Find the area for one face, and multiply it by 2 because the measures of the two faces are the same.

$$A_{\text{front and back}} = 2(l \times w)$$
$$= 2(130 \times 45)$$
$$= 2(5\ 850)$$
$$= 11\ 700$$

$$A_{\text{triangles}} = 2\left(\frac{bh}{2}\right)$$
$$= 2\left(\frac{50 \times 35}{2}\right)$$
$$= 2\left(\frac{1\ 750}{2}\right)$$
$$= 2(875)$$
$$= 1\ 750$$

Step 3

Calculate the total area of the triangular right prism.

$$SA_{\text{water trough}} = A_{\text{front and back}} + A_{\text{triangles}}$$
$$= 11\ 700 + 1\ 750$$
$$= 13\ 450\ \text{dm}^2$$

Johnathon needs $13\ 450\ \text{dm}^2$ of sheet metal to make his water trough.

Solution

────────────

20M.1 Solve problems that involve SI and imperial units in surface area measurements and verify the solutions.

CALCULATING THE SURFACE AREA OF A RIGHT TRAPEZOIDAL PRISM

A right trapezoidal prism is a three-dimensional object with six rectangular faces. A prism is called a right prism if the top base of the prism is directly above the bottom base of the prism when it is placed on one of the bases.

An example of a right trapezoidal prism is shown.

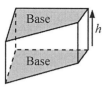

If the right trapezoidal prism is flattened out, the two-dimensional drawing that results is called a **net**.

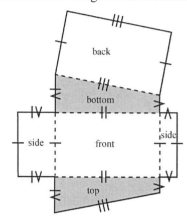

The net is used to calculate the surface area of right trapezoidal prisms. The **surface area** of a right trapezoidal prism is the sum of the areas of all the faces.

To calculate the surface area of a right trapezoidal prism, follow these steps:

1. Draw the net of the shape.
2. Calculate the area of each face.
3. Add the areas of the faces.

Example

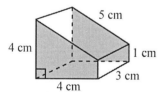

Calculate the surface area of the given right trapezoidal prism.

Solution

Step 1

Draw the net of the shape.

A right trapezoidal prism is made up of four rectangular faces (front, bottom, back, and top in the diagram) that join the two trapezoidal bases (sides).

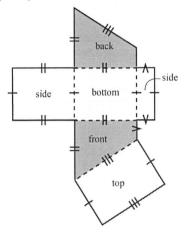

Step 2

Calculate the area of each face.

Solve for the area of each face by applying the appropriate formula.

$$A_{\text{front and back}} = h\left(b_1 + b_2\right)$$
$$= (4)(4 + 1)$$
$$= 4 \times 5$$
$$= 20 \text{ cm}^2$$

$$A_{\text{top}} = lw$$
$$= 5 \times 3$$
$$= 15 \text{ cm}^2$$

$$A_{\text{bottom}} = lw$$
$$= 4 \times 3$$
$$= 12 \text{ cm}^2$$

$$A_{\text{small side}} = lw$$
$$= 3 \times 1$$
$$= 3 \text{ cm}^2$$

$$A_{\text{large side}} = lw$$
$$= 4 \times 3$$
$$= 12 \text{ cm}^2$$

Step 3

Add the areas of the faces.

$$SA_{\text{right trapezoidal prism}}$$
$$= A_{\text{front and back}} + A_{\text{top}} + A_{\text{bottom}} + A_{\text{small side}} + A_{\text{large side}}$$
$$= 20 + 15 + 12 + 3 + 12$$
$$= 62 \text{ cm}^2$$

The surface area of the right trapezoidal prism is 62 cm^2.

20M.1 Solve problems that involve SI and imperial units in surface area measurements and verify the solutions.

DEVELOPING THE SURFACE AREA FORMULA FOR A CYLINDER

Surface area is the total area of all the faces, or surfaces, of a three-dimensional object. Surface area is measured in square units, or units^2.

Cylinders are three-dimensional figures with two congruent and parallel circular bases connected by a curved rectangular face. In a right cylinder, the parallel circular bases are perpendicular ($\perp$) to the curved rectangular face (side).

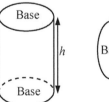
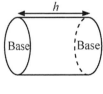

When a cylinder is flattened out, the two-dimensional shape that results is called a **net**.

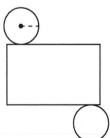

From the net, you can see that a cylinder is made up of two circles and a rectangle.

The surface area of a cylinder is the sum of the areas of all the faces.

To develop the surface area formula for a cylinder, start with the base, which is a circle. This is a two-dimensional shape. To calculate its area, use the formula for the area of a circle, $A_{circle} = \pi r^2$.

Since there are two circles, multiply the area of a circle by 2 to get the combined area of both circles.

$A_{circles} = 2\pi r^2$

The remaining face of the cylinder is a rectangle. The area of a rectangle is equal to length times width, or $A_{rectangle} = l \times w$.

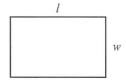

Since the rectangle wraps around the bases, which are circles, the length of the rectangle is equal to the circumference of the circle, $C = 2\pi r$, and the width of the rectangle, w, is equal to the height of the cylinder, h.

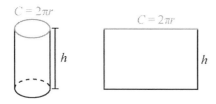

Therefore, the area of the rectangular face is $A_{rectangle} = 2\pi r \times h = 2\pi rh$.

This means that the formula for the surface area of a cylinder is $SA_{cylinder} = A_{circles} + A_{rectangle}$, or

$SA_{cylinder} = 2\pi r^2 + 2\pi rh$.

20M.1 Solve problems that involve SI and imperial units in surface area measurements and verify the solutions.

CALCULATING THE SURFACE AREA OF CYLINDERS

Cylinders are three-dimensional objects with two congruent and parallel circular bases connected by a curved rectangular face. In a right cylinder, the parallel circular bases (circles) are perpendicular ($\perp$) to the curved rectangular face (side).

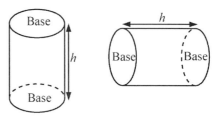

When a cylinder is flattened out, the two-dimensional shape that results is called a **net**.

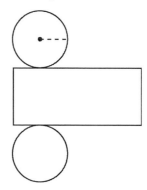

The net is used to calculate the **surface area** of a cylinder. The surface area of a cylinder is the sum of the areas of all the faces.

To calculate the surface area of a cylinder:

1. Draw the net of the cylinder.
2. Determine the radius or diameter of both circles.
3. Calculate the area of the two circles and the rectangle.

Example

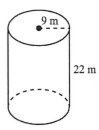

9 m

22 m

Calculate the surface area of the cylinder.

Solution

Step 1

Draw the net of the cylinder.

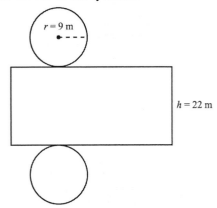

$r = 9$ m

$h = 22$ m

Step 2

Determine the diameter of the cylinder.

$d = 2r = 2 \times 9 = 18$ m

Step 3

Calculate the area of the two circular bases and the rectangle.

First, calculate the area of one of the circular bases.

$$A_{circle} = \pi \times r^2$$
$$= 3.14 \times 9^2$$
$$= 3.14 \times 81$$
$$= 254.34 \text{ m}^2$$

Multiply the area of the circular base by two because the measure of each of the circular bases is the same.

$$A_{circles} = 2 \times 254.34$$
$$= 508.68 \text{m}^2$$

To calculate the area of the rectangle, you need to know its length and width. Let the length (l) equal the height (h) of the rectangular part of the cylinder, which is 22 m. Since the width of the rectangle is equal to the circumference of the circle, calculate the circumference of the circle.

$$C = \pi d$$
$$= 3.14 \times 18$$
$$= 56.52 \text{ m}$$

Now that you have both the length (height) and width of the rectangular part, you can calculate the area of the rectangle.

$$A_{rectangle} = h \times w$$
$$= 22 \times 56.52$$
$$= 1\ 243.44 \text{ m}^2$$

Step 4

Add the area of the two circular bases to the area of the rectangle.

$$SA_{cylinder} = A_{circles} + A_{rectangle}$$
$$= 508.68 + 1\ 243.44$$
$$= 1\ 752.12 \text{ m}^2$$

Use the same process to solve surface area problems in everyday life.

Example

In ceramics class, Jean is going to glaze the outside of a cylindrical vase she is making. The vase is 30 cm tall and 15 cm across.

How much glaze will she require if each bottle of glaze covers 400 cm^2?

Solution

Step 1

Draw the net.

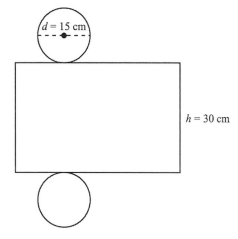

Step 2

Calculate the radius.

$$r = \frac{d}{2} = \frac{15}{2} = 7.5 \text{ cm}$$

Step 3

Calculate the area of the faces.

Because a vase is open at the top, you only need to calculate the area of one circle and the rectangle.

$$A_{bottom} = \pi \times r^2$$
$$= 3.14 \times 7.5^2$$
$$= 3.14 \times 56.25$$
$$= 176.625$$

$$A_{side} = h \times \pi d$$
$$= 30 \times 3.14 \times 15$$
$$= 1\ 413$$

$$SA_{vase} = A_{bottom} + A_{side}$$
$$= 176.625 + 1\ 413$$
$$= 1\ 589.625 \text{ cm}^2$$

Divide the surface area of the vase by the surface area that one bottle of glaze will cover in order to determine the number of bottles she will have to buy.

$$1\ 589.625 \div 400 = 3.974\ 062$$

Since Jean cannot buy part of a bottle, she will need to buy 4 bottles of glaze to cover the vase.

20M.1 Solve problems that involve SI and imperial units in surface area measurements and verify the solutions.

SOLVING PROBLEMS INVOLVING THE SURFACE AREA OF CYLINDERS

To solve problems involving the surface area of a cylinder, follow these steps:

1. Draw the net of the cylinder.
2. Calculate the radius.
3. Calculate the area of the circular base.
4. Calculate the area of the rectangle.
5. Calculate the total surface area of the desired shape.

Example

A pool manufacturer wants to make a circular pool that has a diameter of 7.5 m and a height of 1.5 m.

How much material will it take to make the pool, expressed to a tenth of a metre?

Solution

Step 1

Draw the net of the shape.

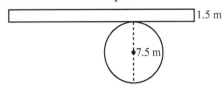

Step 2

Determine the radius or diameter.

$$r = \frac{d}{2} = \frac{7.5}{2} = 3.75 \text{ m}$$

Step 3

Calculate the area of base. The base of the pool is a circle.

Use the formula for area of a circle and solve.

$$\begin{aligned} A_{\text{circle}} &= \left(\pi \times r^2\right) \\ &= \left(3.14 \times 3.75^2\right) \\ &= \left(3.14 \times 14.0625\right) \\ &= 44.156\,25 \end{aligned}$$

Step 4

Calculate the area of the rectangle.

The formula for the area of a rectangle is $A = l \times w$. Length (l) in the rectangular part of the cylinder is equal to the height (h). When the rectangle is unrolled, the width (w) is the same distance as the circumference.

Rewrite the area formula for the rectangle as follows:

$$\begin{aligned} A_{\text{rectangle}} &= l \times w \\ &= h \times \text{circumference} \\ &= h \times \pi d \end{aligned}$$

Substitute in the values and solve.

$$\begin{aligned} A_{\text{rectangle}} &= h \times \pi d \\ &= 1.5 \times 3.14 \times 7.5 \\ &= 35.325 \end{aligned}$$

Step 5

Calculate the total area of the pool.

$$\begin{aligned} A_{\text{pool}} &= A_{\text{circle}} + A_{\text{rectangle}} \\ &= 44.156\,25 + 35.325 \\ &= 79.481\,25 \text{ m}^2 \end{aligned}$$

It will take 79.5 m² of material to make the pool.

If the surface area of a cylinder is being calculated where there are no missing parts, steps 3, 4, and 5 can be combined into one step to make the formula for calculating the surface area of a cylinder.

$$SA = \left(2 \times A_{\text{circle}}\right) + A_{\text{rectangle}}$$
$$SA = 2\pi r^2 + 2\pi rh$$

20M.1 Solve problems that involve SI and imperial units in surface area measurements and verify the solutions.

CALCULATING SURFACE AREA OF PYRAMIDS

Pyramids are made up of a base and triangles that meet at a single point called a vertex. The name of a pyramid is based on the shape of its base; for example, a pyramid with a square base is called a square-based pyramid and a pyramid with a six-sided base is called a hexagonal pyramid.

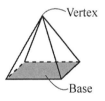

Example

Calculate the surface area of the given square-based pyramid.

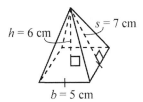

Solution

A square-based pyramid is made up of four equal triangles that join to one square base.

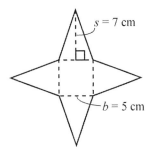

The area of the base is a square. The formula for the area of a square is l^2, and since the length of each side of the base is b, the area of the square base is b^2.

The formula for the area of a triangle is $\dfrac{bh}{2}$.

In a square-based pyramid, the base of each triangle is referred to as b. The height is referred to as the slant height (s).

Therefore, the area of the four equal triangles can be written as follows:

$$A_{\text{four triangles}} = 4\left(\frac{bh}{2}\right)$$
$$= 4\left(\frac{bs}{2}\right)$$
$$= \overset{2}{4}\left(\frac{bs}{\underset{}{2}}\right)$$
$$= 2(bs)$$

The surface area of the whole pyramid is defined by the surface area of the square base and the surface area of the four triangular lateral faces.

Square Base	Lateral Faces
b^2	$2(bs)$

Therefore, the surface area of the given square-based pyramid can be found as follows:

$$SA_{\text{pyramid}} = A_{\text{base}} + A_{\text{lateral faces}}$$
$$= (b^2) + 2(bs)$$
$$= (5^2) + 2(5 \times 7)$$
$$= (25) + 2(35)$$
$$= 25 + 70$$
$$= 95 \text{ cm}^2$$

Example

Draw the net for the given square-based pyramid, and calculate its surface area.

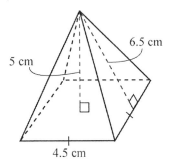

Solution

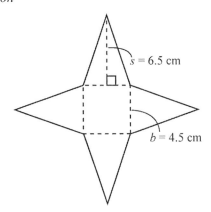

$$SA_{\text{square-based pyramid}}$$
$$= (b^2) + 2(bs)$$
$$= (4.5^2) + 2(4.5 \times 6.5)$$
$$= (4.5 \times 4.5) + 2(4.5 \times 6.5)$$
$$= (20.25) + 2(29.25)$$
$$= 20.25 + 58.5$$
$$= 78.75 \text{ cm}^2$$

20M.1 Solve problems that involve SI and imperial units in surface area measurements and verify the solutions.

Solving Problems Involving the Surface Area of Pyramids

The surface area, *SA*, of a pyramid can be determined by applying the formula $SA = A_{base} + A_{lateral\ faces}$, where A_{base} is the area of the base and $A_{lateral\ faces}$ is the area of the lateral faces.

Example

A company that manufactures glass ornaments is planning to produce hollow, enclosed glass ornaments in the shape of a square-based pyramid. The company has these two possible designs in mind.

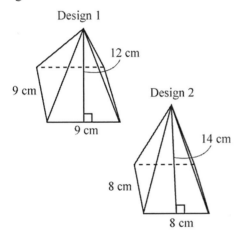

If the company plans to produce 2 000 glass ornaments and the cost to produce each ornament is \$0.04/cm^2, how much will the company save in production costs if they choose Design 2 rather than Design 1?

Solution

The surface area, *SA*, of a pyramid can be determined by applying the formula $SA = A_{base} + A_{lateral\ faces}$.

Step 1
Determine the area of the base of the pyramid in Design 1.
Since Design 1 has a square base, the area, *A*, of the base in this design can be determined by applying the formula $A = s^2$, where *s* is the side length of the base.
$A = s^2$
Substitute 9 for *s*.
$A = 9^2$
$A = 81\ cm^2$

Step 2
Determine the area of the lateral faces of the pyramid in Design 1.
Each of the four lateral faces in Design 1 is triangular. The area, *A*, of a triangle can be determined by applying the formula $A = \frac{1}{2}bh$, where *b* is the base of the triangle and *h* is the height of the triangle. Since Design 1 has four congruent lateral faces, the area of the lateral faces can be determined with the formula $A = 4 \times \left(\frac{1}{2}bh\right)$.

Substitute 9 for *b* and 12 for *h*.
$A = 4 \times \left(\frac{1}{2} \times 9 \times 12\right)$
$A = 4 \times 54$
$A = 216\ cm^2$

Step 3

Determine the surface area of the pyramid in Design 1.

In the formula $SA = A_{base} + A_{lateral\ faces}$, substitute 81 cm^2 for A_{base} and 216 cm^2 for $A_{lateral\ faces}$.

$SA = A_{base} + A_{lateral\ faces}$
$SA = 81\ cm^2 + 216\ cm^2$
$SA = 297\ cm^2$

Step 4

Determine the cost to produce 2 000 ornaments if Design 1 is chosen.

Since the surface area of one ornament is 297 cm^2 and 2 000 ornaments are to be produced at a cost of $0.04/cm^2, the cost would be $297 \times 0.04 \times 2\ 000 = \$23\ 760$ if Design 1 is chosen.

Step 5

Determine the area of the base of the pyramid in Design 2.
$A = s^2$
$A = 8^2$
$A = 64\ cm^2$

Step 6

Determine the area of the lateral faces of the pyramid in Design 2.

Substitute 8 for b and 14 for h in the formula $A = 4 \times \left(\frac{1}{2}bh\right)$.

$A = 4 \times \left(\frac{1}{2}bh\right)$
$A = 4 \times \left(\frac{1}{2} \times 8 \times 14\right)$
$A = 4 \times 56$
$A = 224\ cm^2$

Step 7

Determine the surface area of the pyramid in Design 2.

In the formula $SA = A_{base} + A_{lateral\ faces}$, substitute 64 cm^2 for A_{base} and 224 cm^2 for $A_{lateral\ faces}$.

$SA = A_{base} + A_{lateral\ faces}$
$SA = 64\ cm^2 + 224\ cm^2$
$SA = 288\ cm^2$

Step 8

Determine the cost to produce 2 000 ornaments if Design 2 is chosen.

Since the surface area of one ornament is 288 cm^2 and 2 000 ornaments are to be produced at a cost of $0.04/cm^2, the cost would be $288 \times 0.04 \times 2\ 000 = \$23\ 040$ if Design 2 is chosen.

Step 9

Determine how much the company would save in production costs if Design 2 is chosen over Design 1.

The company would save
$\$23\ 760 - \$23\ 040 = \$720$ in production costs if Design 2 is chosen.

――――――――――――――――

20M.1 Solve problems that involve SI and imperial units in surface area measurements and verify the solutions.

CALCULATING THE SURFACE AREA OF A CONE

A cone is a three-dimensional object with a circular base and a curved lateral face.

For the given cone, h is the height of the lateral face, r is the radius of the circular base, and s is the slant height of the lateral face.

If the three-dimensional shape is flattened out, the two-dimensional drawing that results is called a **net**.

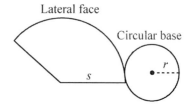

Lateral face

Circular base

The surface area of a right cone can be determined by adding the area of the base and the area of the lateral face. The area of the lateral face can be found by multiplying the circumference of the base by the slant height of the cone and dividing by 2.

$$SA = A_{\text{base}} + A_{\text{lateral face}}$$
$$= \pi r^2 + \frac{2\pi rs}{2}$$
$$= \pi r^2 + \pi rs$$

To calculate the surface area of a cone, follow these steps:

1. Draw the net.
2. Calculate the areas of the faces.
3. Add all the areas of the faces.

Example

Calculate the surface area of the given cone.

Solution

Step 1
Draw the net for the given cone.

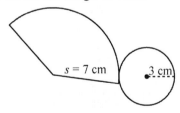

Step 2
Calculate the surface area.

The total surface area of the cone is determined by adding the areas of the circular base and the lateral face.

$$SA_{\text{cone}} = A_{\text{base}} + A_{\text{lateral face}}$$
$$= \pi r^2 + r\pi s$$
$$= (3.14 \times 3^2) + (3 \times 3.14 \times 7)$$
$$= (3.14 \times 9) + (3 \times 3.14 \times 7)$$
$$= 28.26 + 65.94$$
$$= 94.2 \text{ cm}^2$$

Therefore, the surface area of the cone is 94.2 cm².

20M.1 Solve problems that involve SI and imperial units in surface area measurements and verify the solutions.

CALCULATING THE SURFACE AREA OF A SPHERE

The surface area of a sphere can be found using the formula $SA = 4\pi r^2$, in which r is the radius of the sphere.

r = radius

Example
An image of a sphere is given.

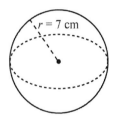

$r = 7$ cm

The surface area of the given sphere is _____ cm².

Solution

Use the formula $4\pi r^2$ to calculate the surface area of the sphere.

$$SA_{\text{sphere}} = 4\pi r^2$$
$$= 4 \times 3.14 \times 7^2$$
$$= 4 \times 3.14 \times 49$$
$$= 615.44 \text{ cm}^2$$

Example
An image of a sphere is given.

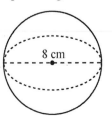

8 cm

The surface area of the given sphere is _____ cm^2.

Solution

Step 1

Find the radius of the sphere.

$r = \dfrac{d}{2}$

$\quad = \dfrac{8}{2}$

$\quad = 4$ cm

Step 2

Determine the surface area of the sphere.

Use the formula for the surface area of a sphere.

$SA_{\text{sphere}} = 4\pi r^2$

$\qquad\quad = 4 \times 3.14 \times 4^2$

$\qquad\quad = 4 \times 3.14 \times 16$

$\qquad\quad = 200.96$ cm^2

20M.1 Solve problems that involve SI and imperial units in surface area measurements and verify the solutions.

CALCULATING SURFACE AREA OF 3D COMPOSITE FIGURES

Three-dimensional (3-D) composite figures are made of two or more shapes put together. To calculate the surface area of a 3-D composite figure, find the outside surface area of each shape and then add the surface areas together.

Example

A composite figure with labelled lengths is shown.

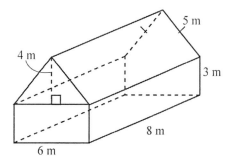

The surface area of the given composite figure is _____ m^2.

Solution

To find the surface area of this shape, calculate the area of the outside faces.

Because this is a solid shape, find the area of each face, and then add them together.

Step 1

Break the figure into two shapes: a rectangular prism and a triangular prism.

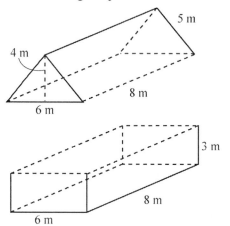

Step 2

Determine the surface area of the outside sides of each shape.

Rectangular prism: There is no top to this figure because the triangular prism sits on top of it.

$$l = 8 \text{ m}$$
$$w = 6 \text{ m}$$
$$h_{\text{rectangular prism}}(h_r) = 3 \text{ m}$$
$$\begin{aligned} A_{\text{lateral faces}} &= 2(lh_r) \\ &= 2(8 \times 3) \\ &= 2 \times 24 \\ &= 48 \text{ m}^2 \end{aligned}$$

$$\begin{aligned} A_{\text{bottom}} &= lw \\ &= 8 \times 6 \\ &= 48 \text{ m}^2 \end{aligned}$$

$$\begin{aligned} A_{\text{bases}} &= 2(wh_r) \\ &= 2(6 \times 3) \\ &= 2 \times 18 \\ &= 36 \text{ m}^2 \end{aligned}$$

$$\begin{aligned} SA_{\text{rectangular prism}} &= 48 + 48 + 36 \\ &= 132 \text{ m}^2 \end{aligned}$$

The surface area of the outside faces of the rectangular prism in the given figure is 132 m^2.

Triangular prism: There is no bottom to this figure because it sits on the rectangular prism.

$$l = 8 \text{ m}$$
$$b = 6 \text{ m}$$
$$h_{\text{triangular prism}}(h_\Delta) = 4 \text{ m}$$
$$w_{\text{rectangular faces}}(w_r) = 5 \text{ m}$$
$$\begin{aligned} A_{\text{rectangular faces}} &= 2(lw_r) \\ &= 2(8 \times 5) \\ &= 2 \times 40 \\ &= 80 \text{ m}^2 \end{aligned}$$

$$\begin{aligned} A_{\text{triangular bases}} &= 2(\frac{bh_\Delta}{2}) \\ &= bh_\Delta \\ &= 6 \times 4 \\ &= 24 \text{ m}^2 \end{aligned}$$

$$\begin{aligned} SA_{\text{triangular prism}} &= 80 + 24 \\ &= 104 \text{ m}^2 \end{aligned}$$

The surface area of the outside faces of the triangular prism is 104 m^2.

Step 3

Find the surface area of the composite figure.

$$SA_{\text{composite figure}} = SA_{\text{rectangular prism}} + SA_{\text{triangular prism}}$$
$$= 132 + 104$$
$$= 236 \text{ m}^2$$

Example

Find the surface area of the given composite object. _____ cm^2

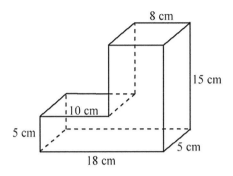

Solution

Step 1

Break the object into two rectangular prisms: one on the left and one on the right.

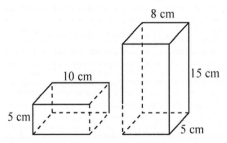

It could also be broken into one on top and one on the bottom.

Step 2

Determine the surface area of the outside faces of the left prism.

There are five faces—front and back, top and bottom, and left side. There is no right side because it is attached to the other prism.

$$A_{\text{front/back}} = 2(lh)$$
$$= 2(10 \times 5)$$
$$= 100 \text{ cm}^2$$

$$A_{\text{top/bottom}} = 2(lw)$$
$$= 2(10 \times 5)$$
$$= 100 \text{cm}^2$$

$$A_{\text{left side}} = wh$$
$$= 5 \times 5$$
$$= 25 \text{ cm}^2$$

$$SA_{\text{left prism}} = A_{\text{front/back}} + A_{\text{top/bottom}} + A_{\text{side}}$$
$$= 100 + 100 + 25$$
$$= 225 \text{ cm}^2$$

The surface area of the outside faces of the left rectangular prism is 225 cm².

Step 3

Determine the surface area of the outside faces of the right prism.

There are six faces—front and back, top and bottom, right, and a partial left side.

$$A_{\text{front/back}} = 2(lh)$$
$$= 2(8 \times 15)$$
$$= 240 \text{ cm}^2$$

$$A_{\text{top/bottom}} = 2(lw)$$
$$= 2(8 \times 5)$$
$$= 80 \text{cm}^2$$

$$A_{\text{right side}} = wh$$
$$= 5 \times 15$$
$$= 75 \text{ cm}^2$$

$$SA_{\substack{\text{right} \\ \text{prism}}} = A_{\substack{\text{front/} \\ \text{back}}} + A_{\substack{\text{top/} \\ \text{bottom}}} + A_{\substack{\text{right} \\ \text{side}}} + A_{\substack{\text{left} \\ \text{side}}}$$
$$= 240 + 80 + 75 + 50$$
$$= 445 \text{ cm}^2$$

The surface area of the outside faces of the right rectangular prism is 445 cm².

Step 4

Find the surface area of all outside faces of the composite object.

$$SA_{\substack{\text{composite} \\ \text{figure}}} = SA_{\substack{\text{left} \\ \text{prism}}} + SA_{\substack{\text{right} \\ \text{prism}}}$$
$$= 225 + 445$$
$$= 670 \text{ cm}^2$$

Other 3-D figures have one or more pieces missing. To find the surface area of this type of figure, it is important to think of surface area as anything that air can touch.

Example

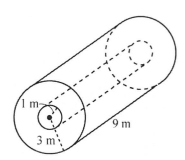

Calculate the surface area of the given figure to the nearest hundredth. _____ m²

Solution

In this figure, air can go right through the centre of this object, so all of the centre surface must be included in the calculation of the total surface area.

To find the surface area of the given figure, find the surface area of the large cylinder, subtract the area of the end pieces of the smaller cylinder, and add the area of the inside lateral surface of the small cylinder.

Large cylinder:

$$SA_{\text{large cylinder}} = A_{\text{circle bases}} + A_{\text{lateral face}}$$
$$= 2(\pi r^2) + 2(\pi rh)$$
$$= 2(3.14 \times 3^2)$$
$$\quad + 2(3.14 \times 3 \times 9)$$
$$= 2(3.14 \times 9) + 2(84.78)$$
$$= 2(28.26) + 2(84.78)$$
$$= 56.52 + 169.56$$
$$= 226.08 \text{ m}^2$$

Note that if the $\boxed{\pi}$ button on your calculator were used, the added precision would have given an answer of 226.19 m².

Small cylinder:

$A_{\text{circle bases}} = 2 \times \pi \times r^2$
$= 2 \times 3.14 \times 1^2$
$= 2 \times 3.14 \times 1$
$= 2 \times 3.14$
$= 6.28 \text{ m}^2$

Note that if the $\boxed{\pi}$ button on your calculator were used, the added precision would also have given an answer of 6.28 m^2.

$A_{\text{lateral face}} = 2\pi rh$
$= 2 \times 3.14 \times 1 \times 9$
$= 56.52 \text{ m}^2$

Note that if the $\boxed{\pi}$ button on your calculator were used, the added precision would have given an answer of 56.55 m^2.

Therefore, the surface area of the given figure is as follows:

$SA_{\text{figure}} = SA_{\text{large cylinder}} - A_{\text{small circular bases}}$
$\qquad + A_{\text{small lateral face}}$
$= 226.08 - 6.28 + 56.52$
$= 276.32 \text{ m}^2$

Note that if the $\boxed{\pi}$ button on your calculator were used, the added precision would have given an answer of 276.46 m^2.

Example

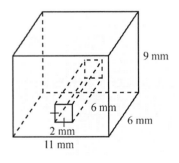

9 mm

6 mm

6 mm

2 mm

11 mm

Calculate the surface area of the given figure.

Solution

Calculate the surface area of the large prism. Then, subtract the end pieces of the smaller shape, and add the area of the rectangular insides.

Large rectangular prism:

$SA_{\text{large rectangular prism}}$
$= 2(lw) + 2(wh) + 2(lh)$
$= 2(11 \times 6) + 2(6 \times 9) + 2(11 \times 9)$
$= 2(66) + 2(54) + 2(99)$
$= 132 + 108 + 198$
$= 438 \text{ mm}^2$

Small rectangular prism:

$A_{\text{front and back}} = 2(lh)$
$= 2(2 \times 2)$
$= 2 \times 4$
$= 8 \text{ mm}^2$

$A_{\text{top and bottom}} = 2(lw)$
$= 2(2 \times 6)$
$= 2 \times 12$
$= 24 \text{ mm}^2$

$A_{\text{sides}} = 2(wh)$
$= 2(6 \times 2)$
$= 2 \times 12$
$= 24 \text{ mm}^2$

Therefore, the surface area of the given figure is as follows:

$SA_{\text{figure}} = SA_{\text{large rectangular prism}}$
$\qquad - A_{\text{front and back}}$
$\qquad + (A_{\text{top and bottom}} + A_{\text{sides}})$
$= 438 - 8 + (24 + 24)$
$= 478 \text{ mm}^2$

20M.1 Solve problems that involve SI and imperial units in surface area measurements and verify the solutions.

SOLVING PROBLEMS INVOLVING THE SURFACE AREA OF THREE-DIMENSIONAL COMPOSITE FIGURES

Surface area is the sum of the areas of the faces (sides) of a three-dimensional figure.

Three-dimensional (3-D) **composite figures** are made of two or more shapes put together. The surface area of a composite figure can be calculated using one of two methods:

- Calculate the surface area of the exposed faces of each individual prism, and then add the surface areas together.
- Calculate the complete surface area of each individual prism, and then subtract the overlapped regions from the final sum of the areas.

Many real-life problems involve the calculation of the surface area of composite figures.

Example

Jason built a model of a skateboard ramp that he and his friends would like to build in their local skate park.

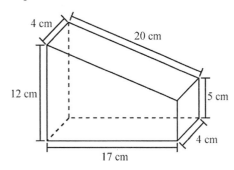

For their presentation to the city council in support of the project, Jason would like to paint every side of the model, including the bottom. He can purchase paint at a local hobby shop for $3.49 per bottle, and each bottle will cover approximately 225 cm² of wood.

How much will it cost Jason to paint the model of the ramp?

Solution

Step 1

Separate the composite 3-D object into a right triangular prism and a rectangular prism.

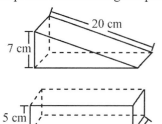

Step 2

Calculate the surface area of the right triangular prism.

$$A_{\text{front and back}} = 2\left(\frac{bh}{2}\right)$$
$$= 2\left(\frac{17 \times 7}{2}\right)$$
$$= 119 \text{ cm}^2$$

$$A_{\text{side}} = lw$$
$$= 4 \times 7$$
$$= 28 \text{ cm}^2$$

$$A_{\text{top}} = lw$$
$$= 4 \times 20$$
$$= 80 \text{ cm}^2$$

$$A_{\text{bottom}} = lw$$
$$= 4 \times 17$$
$$= 68 \text{ cm}^2$$

$$SA_{\text{triangular prism}} = 119 + 28 + 80 + 68$$
$$= 295 \text{ cm}^2$$

Step 3

Calculate the surface area of the rectangular prism.

$$A_{\text{top and bottom}} = 2(lw)$$
$$= 2(17 \times 4)$$
$$= 136 \text{ cm}^2$$

$$A_{\text{front and back}} = 2(lw)$$
$$= 2(17 \times 5)$$
$$= 170 \text{ cm}^2$$

$$A_{\text{left and right}} = 2(lw)$$
$$= 2(4 \times 5)$$
$$= 40 \text{ cm}^2$$

$$SA_{\text{rectangular prism}} = 136 + 170 + 40$$
$$= 346 \text{ cm}^2$$

Step 4

Calculate the areas of the overlapped regions. The regions that overlap are the top of the rectangular prism and the bottom of the right triangular prism. This region is rectangular in shape.

$$A_{\text{overlap}} = 2(lw)$$
$$= 2(17 \times 4)$$
$$= 2(68)$$
$$= 136 \text{ cm}^2$$

Step 5

Calculate the total surface area of the composite 3-D object.

Add the surface areas of the two prisms and subtract the area of overlap.

$$SA_{\text{composite figure}} = 295 \text{ cm}^2 + 346 \text{ cm}^2 - 136 \text{ cm}^2$$

$$SA_{\text{composite figure}} = 505 \text{ cm}^2$$

Step 6

Determine the number of bottles of paint Jason must buy.

$$\frac{505 \text{ cm}^2}{225 \text{ cm}^2 / \text{bottle}} = 2.2\overline{4} \text{ bottles}$$

Jason must buy 3 bottles of paint.

Step 7

Determine the cost of the paint.

$3.49 / \text{bottle} \times 3 \text{ bottles} = \$10.47$

It will cost Jason $10.47 to paint the model of the skateboard ramp.

20M.1 Solve problems that involve SI and imperial units in surface area measurements and verify the solutions.

EFFECT OF SCALE FACTOR ON SURFACE AREA OF PRISMS

Scale factor is a number which scales or multiplies a given quantity. It is the amount that linear measurements are multiplied by to create a new figure of the same shape but in a larger or smaller size. The new shape is in direct proportion to the original shape.

Each dimension of the original shape or object is multiplied by the scale factor to determine the size of the proportional shape or object. If the scale factor is greater than 1, the proportional shape or object will be larger than the original. If the scale factor is between 0 and 1, the proportional shape or object will be smaller than the original.

TWO-DIMENSIONAL SCALING

The dimensions of a proportional two-dimensional shape can be calculated by multiplying each corresponding dimension of the original shape by the scale factor. If the area of a shape is given, this value can be multiplied by the square of the scale factor to find the area of the proportional shape.

$$A_{\text{proportional shape}} = A_{\text{original shape}} \times \text{scale factor}^2$$

For example, the area of the original rectangle from the given table can be multiplied by the square of the scale factor to find the area of the proportional shape.

scale factor = 4

$$A_{\text{proportional shape}} = A_{\text{original shape}} \times \text{scale factor}^2$$
$$= 3 \times 4^2$$
$$= 48 \text{ yd}^2$$

TWO-DIMENSIONAL SCALING APPLIED TO SURFACE AREA OF PRISMS

The dimensions of the surface area of a three-dimensional object, such a prism, can be calculated by multiplying each corresponding dimension of the original shape by the scale factor. Each surface area is calculated, and the total surface area will be the sum of all these values. If the total surface area of an object is given, this value can be multiplied by the square of the scale factor to find the surface area of the proportional object.

$$SA_{\text{proportional object}} = SA_{\text{original object}} \times \text{scale factor}^2$$

For example, the surface area of the prism from the given table can be multiplied by the square of the scale factor to find the surface area of the proportional object.

$$\text{scale factor} = 3$$
$$SA_{\text{proportional object}} = SA_{\text{original object}} \times \text{scale factor}^2$$
$$= 22 \times 3^2$$
$$= 198 \text{ cm}^2$$

Example

Janet makes two similar rectangular prisms for a mathematics exhibition. The height of the first prism is 2 in, and the height of the second prism is 4 in. She covers all the faces of the prisms with coloured paper.

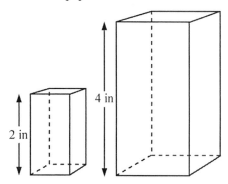

If Janet uses 10 in² of coloured paper to cover the smaller prism, how much coloured paper will she require for the larger prism? in²

Solution

Step 1
Calculate the scale factor.
Divide the height of the larger prism by the height of the smaller prism.

$$\text{scale factor} = \frac{4 \text{ in}}{2 \text{ in}} = 2$$

The height of the small prism is multiplied by 2 to get the height of the larger prism.

Step 2
Apply the scale factor to calculate the area of the larger prism.
The surface area of the smaller prism is 10. Multiply this value by the scale factor.

$$SA_2 = SA_1 \times \text{scale factor}^2$$
$$= 10 \times 2^2$$
$$= 10 \times 4$$
$$= 40 \text{ in}^2$$

Janet requires 40 in² of coloured paper to cover the larger prism.

═══════════════════════

Example

The ratio of the radii of the two cylinders shown is 1:4. The larger cylinder has a surface area of 48π cm².

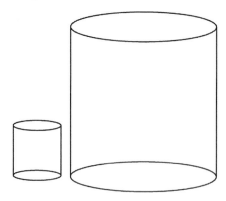

What is the surface area of the smaller cylinder?

Solution

Step 1

Calculate the scale factor.

Since the ratio of the radii is 1:4, the radius of the larger cylinder is multiplied by $\frac{1}{4}$ to get the radius of the smaller cylinder.

Step 2

Apply the scale factor to the surface area of the larger cylinder.

Let the surface area of the larger cylinder by SA_1 and the surface area of the smaller cylinder be SA_2.

The surface area of the smaller cylinder is the product of the square of the scale factor and the surface area of the larger cylinder.

$$SA_2 = SA_1 \times \text{scale factor}^2$$
$$= 48\pi \times \left(\frac{1}{4}\right)^2$$
$$= 48\pi \times \frac{1}{16}$$
$$= \frac{48\pi}{16}$$
$$= 3\pi \text{ cm}^2$$

The surface area of the smaller cylinder is 3π cm^2.

20M.1 Solve problems that involve SI and imperial units in surface area measurements and verify the solutions.

DETERMINING HOW CHANGES IN DIMENSIONS AFFECT AREA OF SHAPES

Changing the dimensions of common 2-D figures also affects the area of the shape. For any 2-D shape, a change in dimension can increase or decrease the area of the shape.

Example

The area of this rectangle is 15 units^2.

If the length of the rectangle is doubled and the width stays the same, what is the new area of the rectangle?

Solution

Step 1

Draw a diagram with the new dimensions.

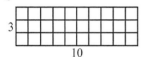

Step 2

Calculate the new area.
$$A_2 = l \times w$$
$$A_2 = 10 \times 3$$
$$A_2 = 30 \text{ units}^2$$

The area of the new rectangle is 30 units^2.

When the length doubled, the area also doubled.

Example

Samantha's flower bed is in the shape of a rectangle that is 5 m long and 3 m wide. She wants to increase the area of the flower bed by doubling its length and width.

Determine the new area of the flower bed.

Solution

Step 1

Double the length and width of the flower bed. Multiply the original length, l_1, and width, w_1, by 2.

$$l_2 = l_1 \times 2$$
$$= 5 \times 2$$
$$= 10 \text{ m}$$
$$w_2 = w_1 \times 2$$
$$= 3 \times 2$$
$$= 6 \text{ m}$$

Step 2

Determine the new area.

Use the area formula for a rectangle, and substitute 10 for l_2 and 6 for w_2.

$$A = l_2 \times w_2$$
$$= 10 \times 6$$
$$= 60$$

The new area of the flower bed is 60 m².

20M.2 Solve problems that involve SI and imperial units in volume and capacity measurements.

DERIVING VOLUME FORMULAS FOR PRISMS

Volume is the amount of space that a three-dimensional figure holds. Volume is measured in cubic units. A **cubic unit** is a cube with equal side lengths of 1 unit on all six sides.

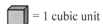 = 1 cubic unit

The volume of a prism is the number of cubic units needed to fill the space in the prism.

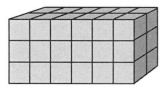

In each layer of this prism, there are 12 cubes. Since there are 3 layers of cubes, the volume is 12 + 12 + 12 = 36 cubic units.

Notice that the volume is the number of cubes in one layer multiplied by the number of layers:
12 × 3 = 36 cubic units

The volume of the prism can be found by multiplying the number of unit cubes in one layer by the number of layers in the box.

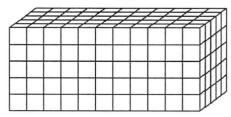

There are 11 unit cubes along the length and 5 unit cubes along the width, so 11 × 5 = 55.

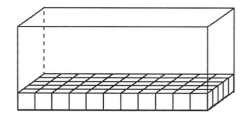

Since there are 5 layers, 55 × 5 = 275.

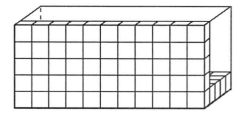

Therefore, the volume is the area of the base multiplied by the height (layers) of the prism. (11 × 5) × 5 = 275 cubic units

The formula to find the volume of a prism is $V = A_{\text{base}} \times h$, where A_{base} is the area of the base of the object and h is the distance between the two bases of the prism.

When using this formula, the base does not need to be rectangular. As long as the area of the base can be calculated, the formula can be used to find the volume.

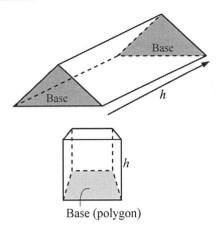

Base (polygon)

20M.2 Solve problems that involve SI and imperial units in volume and capacity measurements.

CALCULATING VOLUME OF RIGHT RECTANGULAR PRISMS

Prisms are polyhedrons with two congruent and parallel faces called bases connected by rectangular faces. *Poly* means many, and *hedra* means faces. The number of sides on the base determines the number of rectangular faces in the prism. The shape of the base determines the name of the prism and moves perpendicular ($\perp$) to the rectangular faces (sides) through space.

A cube is a special type of rectangular prism in that all the sides are the same length.

These are rectangular prisms with four rectangular faces. The bases are rectangles moving perpendicular to the rectangular faces.

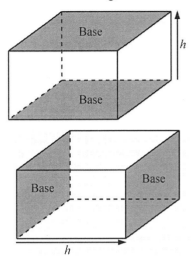

Volume is the space found inside a three-dimensional object. To calculate how much space is inside the rectangular prism, take the area of the rectangle and multiply it by how far it stretched up or across. The stretch is equal to the height of the prism. The general formula for volume is $V = A_{\text{base}} \times h$. The A_{base} is replaced with $l \times w$. Therefore, the formula for the volume of a rectangular prism is $V = (l \times w) \times h$.

To calculate the volume of a rectangular prism, substitute the known values into the volume formula and simplify. When the base is in the shape of a square, it is a special rectangular prism called a square-based prism.

Example

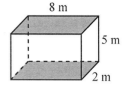

8 m

5 m

2 m

Calculate the volume of the rectangular prism.

Solution

The shape of the base is a rectangle. The height is the distance between two parallel base faces.

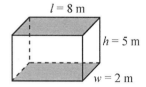

$l = 8$ m

$h = 5$ m

$w = 2$ m

$$V_{prism} = A_{base} \times h$$
$$= A_{rectangle} \times h$$
$$= (l \times w) \times h$$
$$= 8 \times 2 \times 5$$
$$= 80 \text{ m}^3$$

Example

Calculate the volume of the square-based prism:

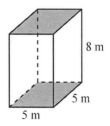

8 m

5 m

5 m

Solution

The shape of the base is a rectangle. The height is the distance between two parallel base faces.

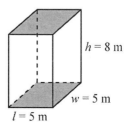

$h = 8$ m

$w = 5$ m

$l = 5$ m

$$V_{prism} = A_{base} \times h$$
$$= A_{square} \times h$$
$$= (s^2) \times h$$
$$= 5^2 \times 8$$
$$= 200 \text{ m}^3$$

Use the same process to solve volume problems in everyday situations.

Example

A juice box has dimensions of 3 cm × 2 cm × 7 cm.

How much juice can it hold in millilitres?

Solution

Step 1

Calculate the volume of the rectangular prism. The juice box is in the shape of a rectangular prism.

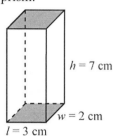

$h = 7$ cm

$w = 2$ cm

$l = 3$ cm

The dimensions are usually given as length, then width, and finally height.

Substitute these values into the volume formula.

$$V_{rectangular\ prism} = A_{base} \times h$$
$$V_{rectangular\ prism} = A_{rectangle} \times h$$
$$= (l \times w) \times h$$
$$= 3 \times 2 \times 7$$
$$= 42 \text{ cm}^3$$

Step 2

Convert the cubic centimetres into millilitres.

Recall that 1 cm^3 = 1 mL.

42 cm^3 = 42 mL

The juice box can hold 42 mL of juice.

20M.2 Solve problems that involve SI and imperial units in volume and capacity measurements.

CALCULATING THE VOLUME OF A TRIANGULAR PRISM

Prisms are polyhedrons with two congruent and parallel faces called bases connected by rectangular faces. *Poly* means many, and *hedra* means faces. The number of sides on the base determines the number of rectangular faces in the prism. The shape of the base determines the name of a prism and moves perpendicular ($\perp$) to the rectangular faces (sides) through space.

These are triangular prisms with three rectangles. The bases are triangles moving perpendicular to the rectangular faces.

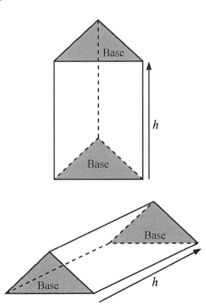

Volume is the space found inside a three-dimensional object. To calculate how much space is inside the rectangular prism, take the area of the triangle and multiply it by the distance between the two parallel congruent faces (bases). The distance is equal to the height of the prism. The general formula for volume is $V = A_{\text{base}} \times h$.

The A_{base} is replaced with $\dfrac{b \times h}{2}$. Because there are two heights in the formula, the height of the triangle is indicated as h_1 and the height of the prism is h_2.

To calculate the volume of a triangular prism, substitute the known values into the volume formula and simplify.

Example

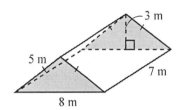

Calculate the volume of the given triangular prism.

Solution

The shape of the base is a triangle. The triangle has a base of 8 m and a height of 3 m. The height of the prism is the distance between the two triangles: 7 m.

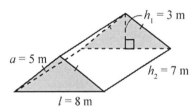

$$\begin{aligned} V_{\text{triangular prism}} &= A_{\text{base}} \times h \\ V_{\text{triangular prism}} &= A_{\text{triangle}} \times h \\ &= \frac{l \times h_1}{2} \times h_2 \\ &= \frac{8 \times 3}{2} \times 7 \\ &= \frac{24}{2} \times 7 \\ &= 12 \times 7 \\ &= 84 \text{ m}^3 \end{aligned}$$

20M.2 Solve problems that involve SI and imperial units in volume and capacity measurements.

SOLVING PROBLEMS INVOLVING THE VOLUME OF A TRIANGULAR PRISM

To solve problems involving the volume of a triangular prism, use the formula
V = area of triangular base × height of prism.

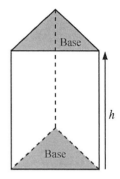

Example

A wedge of cheese has a volume of 35 cm³, and its height is 5 cm.

What is the area of the base of the wedge of cheese?

Solution

The wedge of cheese is in the shape of a triangular prism.

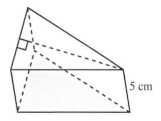

The area of the base is equal to the area of the triangle in the triangular prism.

Substitute the known values into the volume formula.

$$V_{\text{triangular prism}} = A_{\text{triangle}} \times h$$
$$35 = A_{\text{triangle}} \times 5$$
$$\frac{35}{5} = \frac{A_{\text{triangle}} \times 5}{5}$$
$$7 \text{ cm}^2 = A_{\text{triangle}}$$

The area of the triangle is 7 cm².

The wedge of cheese is in the shape of a triangular prism.

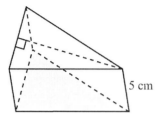

The area of the base is equal to the area of the triangle in the triangular prism.

Substitute the known values into the volume formula.

$$V_{\text{triangular prism}} = A_{\text{triangle}} \times h$$
$$35 = A_{\text{triangle}} \times 5$$
$$\frac{35}{5} = \frac{A_{\text{triangle}} \times 5}{5}$$
$$7 \text{ cm}^2 = A_{\text{triangle}}$$

The area of the triangle is 7 cm².

20M.2 Solve problems that involve SI and imperial units in volume and capacity measurements.

CALCULATING THE VOLUME OF CYLINDERS

Cylinders are three-dimensional figures with two congruent and parallel circular bases connected by a curved rectangular face. In a right cylinder, the parallel circular bases are perpendicular ($\perp$) to the curved rectangular face (side).

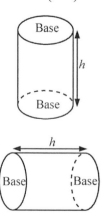

Volume is the space found inside a three-dimensional object. To calculate the volume of a right cylinder, take the area of one of the bases and multiply it by the perpendicular ($\perp$) distance to the other end of the cylinder. The perpendicular ($\perp$) distance between the parallel circular bases is equal to the height of the cylinder.

The general formula for volume is $V = A_{\text{base}} \times h$.

The general formula for the volume of a cylinder becomes $V = A_{\text{circle}} \times h$.

The A_{circle} is replaced with πr^2.

Therefore, the formula for the volume of a cylinder is $V = \pi r^2 \times h$.

To calculate the volume of a cylinder, substitute the known values into the volume formula and simplify.

Example

Calculate the volume of the given cylinder.

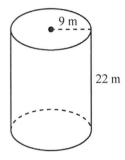

Solution

Step 1

Determine the formula to use to calculate the volume of the cylinder.

The volume of a cylinder can be calculated by multiplying the area of the base by its height. The shape of the base is a circle. The height is the measured distance between the parallel circles (bases), so the formula is as follows:

$$\begin{aligned} V_{\text{cylinder}} &= A_{\text{base}} \times h \\ &= A_{\text{circle}} \times h \\ &= \pi r^2 \times h \end{aligned}$$

Step 2

Substitute in the known values, and evaluate the equation following the order of operations.

$$\begin{aligned} V_{\text{cylinder}} &= \pi r^2 \times h \\ &= 3.14 \times 9^2 \times 22 \\ &= 3.14 \times 81 \times 22 \\ &= 5\,595.48 \text{ m}^3 \end{aligned}$$

When given a cylinder with a diameter, first calculate the **radius**.

Example

A cylindrical-shaped tank has a diameter of 8 ft and a height of 10 ft, as shown in the given diagram.

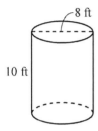

Determine the volume of the tank, to the nearest cubic foot.

Solution

Step 1

Find the radius, r, of the cylinder.

$$\begin{aligned} r &= \frac{1}{2}d \\ &= \frac{1}{2}(8) \\ &= 4 \text{ ft} \end{aligned}$$

Step 2

Determine the volume of the cylinder using the appropriate formula.

$$\begin{aligned} V_{\text{cylinder}} &= \pi r^2 h \\ &= \pi(4)^2(10) \\ &= \pi(16)(10) \\ &\approx 502.6548 \text{ ft}^3 \end{aligned}$$

The volume of the tank, to the nearest cubic foot, is 503 ft^3.

Use the same process to solve volume problems in everyday situations.

Example

A paint can has a diameter of 25 cm and is 40 cm tall.

How many millilitres of paint are there in the can if it is one-half full?

Solution

The shape of the base is a circle. The height is the measured distance between the parallel circles.

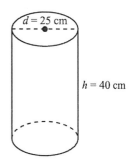

Step 1

Calculate the radius.

$$r = \frac{d}{2} = \frac{25}{2} = 12.5 \text{ cm}$$

Step 2

Calculate the volume.

$$
\begin{aligned}
V_{\text{cylinder}} &= A_{\text{circle}} \times h \\
&= \pi r^2 \times h \\
&= 3.14 \times 12.5^2 \times 40 \\
&= 3.14 \times 156.25 \times 40 \\
&= 490.625 \times 40 \\
&= 19\ 625 \text{ cm}^3
\end{aligned}
$$

Step 3

Divide the volume by 2 because the can is only one-half full.

$$19\ 625 \div 2 = 9\ 812.5 \text{ cm}^3$$

Step 4

Convert centimetres cubed into millilitres.

$$9\ 812.5 \text{ cm}^3 = 9\ 812.5 \text{ mL}$$

The can, which is one-half full, contains 9812.5 mL of paint.

20M.2 Solve problems that involve SI and imperial units in volume and capacity measurements.

SOLVING PROBLEMS INVOLVING THE VOLUME OF A CYLINDER

To solve problems that involve the volume of a cylinder, use the formula $V = \pi r^2 h$, where r is the radius of the circular base, and h is the height.

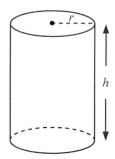

You can use your knowledge about calculating the volume of a cylinder to solve a wide variety of real-world problems. Whenever you have a problem you need to solve, you should use the following problem-solving process:

1. Read the question carefully, and determine what is being asked.
2. Make a plan. Decide which operations you need to use and in which order.
3. Solve the problem. Carry out the plan that you made.
4. Decide if your answer is reasonable.

The following strategies can help you better understand a problem and assist you in solving it:

- Look for keywords.
- Decide what information is important.
- Pay close attention to the numbers given in the problem.
- Draw a picture or diagram of the problem.
- Make predictions about what your answer will look like. Will the number be big or small?
- Think about the operation you are using. For example, if you are multiplying, you know that your answer will be larger than the numbers you are multiplying.
- Compare your answer with your predictions to see if your answer is reasonable.
- Estimate or round values to see if your answer is reasonable.

Example

Joshua bought 6 280 cm³ of wax to make candles to sell at his store. He wants each candle to be 25 cm tall with a diameter of 8 cm.

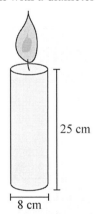

25 cm

8 cm

How many candles can Joshua make if he uses all the wax?

Solution

Step 1

Determine what is being asked.

The question is asking for the number of candles that can be made with 6 280 cm³ of wax. Each candle will have a height of 25 cm and a diameter of 8 cm.

Step 2

Make a plan.

Each candle is in the shape of a cylinder.

Calculate the volume of one candle by using the formula for the volume of a cylinder, $V = \pi r^2 h$, and the dimensions of the candle.

To determine how many candles Joshua can make, divide the amount of wax by the volume of one candle.

Step 3

Solve the problem.

1. Calculate the volume of one candle. The diameter should be 8 cm, so the radius will be 4 cm.
$$V = \pi(4)^2(25)$$
$$V = \pi(16)(25)$$
$$V \approx (3.14)(400)$$
$$V \approx 1\ 256$$

2. Determine the number of candles that Joshua can make by using division.
$$6\ 280 \div 1\ 256 = 5$$

Step 4

Decide if your answer is reasonable.

Use estimation to check your answer. Round 3.14 to 3, leave the radius as the whole number 4, and leave the height as 25.

$$V \approx (3)(4)^2(25)$$
$$V \approx (3)(16)(25)$$
$$V \approx 1\ 200$$

Determine how much wax would be needed to make 5 candles.

$$1\ 200 \times 5 = 6\ 000$$

This is close to the total amount of wax, so the answer is reasonable.

Joshua can make 5 candles.

20M.2 Solve problems that involve SI and imperial units in volume and capacity measurements.

DERIVING THE VOLUME FORMULA FOR A CYLINDER

Volume measures how much space an object occupies. Volume is measured in cubic units, or units^3.

Cylinders are three-dimensional figures with two congruent and parallel circular bases connected by a curved rectangular face. In a right cylinder, the parallel circular bases are perpendicular ($\perp$) to the curved rectangular face (side).

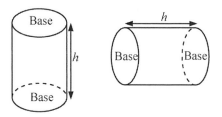

To derive the volume formula for a cylinder, start with the base, which is a circle. This is a two-dimensional shape. To calculate its area, use the formula for the area of a circle, $A = \pi r^2$.

Now, put another circle with the exact same dimensions on top of it. This is a three-dimensional object because it has height. To calculate how much space it takes up (volume), multiply the original area by 2. The formula becomes $\pi r^2 \times 2$.

If two more circles with the exact same dimensions are added, the area of the circle is multiplied by 4. The equation becomes $V = \pi r^2 \times 4$.

Therefore, the volume formula for a cylinder is the area of the base multiplied by the height of the object, or $V_{\text{cylinder}} = \pi r^2 \times h$.

20M.2 Solve problems that involve SI and imperial units in volume and capacity measurements.

RELATING THE VOLUME OF A RECTANGULAR PRISM TO THE VOLUME OF A PYRAMID

The volume of an object is how much three dimensional space it occupies. Three-dimensional (3-D) shapes have three dimensions. Because of the three dimensions volume is presented in cubic units such as cm^3.

A rectangular prism is a 3-D figure with bases or ends that have the same size and rectangular shape and the opposite sides are parallel to one another. In general, the volume of a prism can be determined by multiplying the area of the base by the height. Therefore, the volume of a rectangular prism can be determined by multiplying the area of the base, which is a rectangle, by the height, h. Since the area of a rectangle is calculated by applying the formula $A = l \times w$, the volume, V, of a rectangular prism can be determined by applying the formula $V = (l \times w) \times h$ or $V = lwh$.

A cube is a prism.

Example

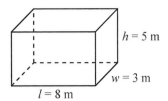

Calculate the volume of the rectangular prism.

Solution

Step 1

Substitute the known values into the volume formula for a rectangular prism.

$V_{\text{rectangular prism}} = lwh$
$= 8 \times 3 \times 5$

Step 2

Evaluate $8 \times 3 \times 5$

$V_{\text{rectangular prism}} = 8 \times 3 \times 5$
$= 120$

The volume of the rectangular prism is 120m^3.

Example

Make a rectangular prism (box) with an open top and bottom from a sheet of construction paper. Tape the sides of the rectangular prism together so that it remains rigid.

Make a pyramid with an open base from a piece of construction paper such that its base and height are identical in measure to that of the rectangular prism. Tape the sides of the pyramid together so that it remains rigid.

Fill the entire pyramid with rice, and empty it into the rectangular prism. Repeat this until the rectangular prism is completely filled with rice.

Note: It should take about 3 pyramids of rice to fill the prism.

The volumes of rectangular prisms and pyramids have a special relationship.

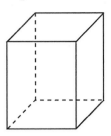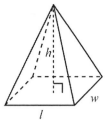

In the pyramid diagram, notice the height forms a right angle with the base of the pyramid.

If you compare a rectangular prism and a pyramid of the same base and height in terms of their respective volumes, you will find that the volume of the rectangular prism is 3 times the volume of the pyramid.

Therefore, the formula for the volume of a pyramid is $V_{\text{pyramid}} = \frac{1}{3}lwh$ or $V_{\text{pyramid}} = \frac{lwh}{3}$.

Example

A pyramid has a base measuring 15 m by 12 m and a height of 9 m.

Determine the volume of the pyramid.

Solution

Step 1

Substitute the known values into the volume formula for a pyramid.

$V_{\text{pyramid}} = \frac{(lw)h}{3}$
$= \frac{(15 \times 12) \times 9}{3}$

Step 2

Solve for the volume.

Follow the order of operations when solving equations.

$V_{\text{pyramid}} = \frac{1\ 620}{3}$
$= 540 \text{ m}^3$

Volume is always calculated in cubic units or units^3. The volume of the pyramid is 540 m^3.

Step 1

Substitute the known values into the volume formula for a pyramid.

$$V_{\text{pyramid}} = \frac{(lw)h}{3}$$
$$= \frac{(15 \times 12) \times 9}{3}$$

Step 2

Solve for the volume.

Follow the order of operations when solving equations.

$$V_{\text{pyramid}} = \frac{1\ 620}{3}$$
$$= 540 \text{ m}^3$$

Volume is always calculated in cubic units or units^3. The volume of the pyramid is 540 m^3.

Step 1

Substitute the known values into the volume formula for a pyramid.

$$V_{\text{pyramid}} = \frac{(lw)h}{3}$$
$$= \frac{(15 \times 12) \times 9}{3}$$

Step 2

Solve for the volume.

Follow the order of operations when solving equations.

$$V_{\text{pyramid}} = \frac{1\ 620}{3}$$
$$= 540 \text{ m}^3$$

Volume is always calculated in cubic units or units^3. The volume of the pyramid is 540 m^3.

Step 1

Substitute the known values into the volume formula for a pyramid.

$$V_{\text{pyramid}} = \frac{(lw)h}{3}$$
$$= \frac{(15 \times 12) \times 9}{3}$$

Step 2

Solve for the volume.

Follow the order of operations when solving equations.

$$V_{\text{pyramid}} = \frac{1\ 620}{3}$$
$$= 540 \text{ m}^3$$

Volume is always calculated in cubic units or units^3. The volume of the pyramid is 540 m^3.

What is the volume of a rectangular prism with the same base and height as the pyramid?

Solution

Step 1

Determine the volume of one of the shapes.

The volume of the pyramid is 540 m^3.

Step 2

Since the pyramid and the prism have the same base and height, it will take 3 pyramids to equal the volume of the rectangular prism. Multiply the volume of the pyramid by 3.

$540 \times 3 = 1\ 620$

The volume of the rectangular prism is 1 620 m^3.

20M.2 Solve problems that involve SI and imperial units in volume and capacity measurements.

DERIVING THE VOLUME FORMULA FOR A PYRAMID

Volume measures how much space an object occupies. Volume is measured in cubic units, or units^3.

A *pyramid* is a polyhedron with a base in the shape of a polygon and the same number of triangular faces as there are sides in the base. The triangular faces meet at the vertex of the pyramid.

An important relationship exists between a rectangular prism and a pyramid that each have identical bases and heights. The math involved in proving this relationship is quite complex. However, a rather simple activity will illustrate the concept.

Example

Make a rectangular prism (box) with an open top and bottom from a sheet of construction paper. Tape the sides of the rectangular prism together so that it remains rigid, and set the rectangular prism on a table so that the tabletop acts as the base of the prism.

Make a pyramid with an open base from a piece of construction paper so that its base and height have identical measures to those of the rectangular prism. Tape the sides of the pyramid together so that it remains rigid.

Fill the entire pyramid with rice, and empty it into the rectangular prism. Repeat this until the rectangular prism is completely filled with rice.

It should take about three pyramids of rice to fill the prism.

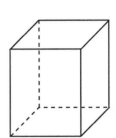 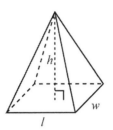

Notice that the height of the pyramid forms a right angle with its base.

If you compare a rectangular prism with a pyramid of the same base and height in terms of their respective volumes, you will find that the volume of the rectangular prism is three times the volume of the pyramid.

Therefore, the formula for the volume of a pyramid can be expressed as $V_{\text{pyramid}} = \frac{1}{3}lwh$ or

$V_{\text{pyramid}} = \frac{lwh}{3}$.

20M.2 Solve problems that involve SI and imperial units in volume and capacity measurements.

CALCULATING THE VOLUME OF A PYRAMID

The general formula for the volume of a pyramid is $V_{\text{pyramid}} = \frac{1}{3}A_{\text{base}}h$, where A_{base} is the area of the base and h is the height. The volume of any pyramid is $\frac{1}{3}$ the volume of a prism with the same base and height.

The formula for the volume of a pyramid with a rectangular base is $V_{\text{pyramid}} = \frac{1}{3}lwh$ or

$V_{\text{pyramid}} = \frac{lwh}{3}$.

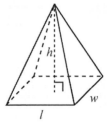

Example

A pyramid has a base measuring 15 m by 12 m and a height of 9 m.

Determine the volume of the pyramid.

Solution

Step 1

Substitute the known values into the volume formula for a pyramid.

$$V_{\text{pyramid}} = \frac{(lw)h}{3}$$
$$= \frac{(15 \times 12) \times 9}{3}$$

Step 2

Solve for the volume.

Follow the order of operations when solving equations.

$$V_{\text{pyramid}} = \frac{1\ 620}{3}$$
$$= 540\ \text{m}^3$$

Volume is always calculated in cubic units or units^3. The volume of the pyramid is $540\ \text{m}^3$.

Step 1

Substitute the known values into the volume formula for a pyramid.

$$V_{\text{pyramid}} = \frac{(lw)h}{3}$$
$$= \frac{(15 \times 12) \times 9}{3}$$

Step 2

Solve for the volume.

Follow the order of operations when solving equations.

$$V_{\text{pyramid}} = \frac{1\ 620}{3}$$
$$= 540\ \text{m}^3$$

Volume is always calculated in cubic units or units^3. The volume of the pyramid is $540\ \text{m}^3$.

Step 1

Substitute the known values into the volume formula for a pyramid.

$$V_{\text{pyramid}} = \frac{(lw)h}{3}$$
$$= \frac{(15 \times 12) \times 9}{3}$$

Step 2

Solve for the volume.

Follow the order of operations when solving equations.

$$V_{\text{pyramid}} = \frac{1\ 620}{3}$$
$$= 540\ \text{m}^3$$

Volume is always calculated in cubic units or units^3. The volume of the pyramid is $540\ \text{m}^3$.

Step 1

Substitute the known values into the volume formula for a pyramid.

$$V_{\text{pyramid}} = \frac{(lw)h}{3}$$
$$= \frac{(15 \times 12) \times 9}{3}$$

Step 2

Solve for the volume.

Follow the order of operations when solving equations.

$$V_{\text{pyramid}} = \frac{1\ 620}{3}$$
$$= 540\ \text{m}^3$$

Volume is always calculated in cubic units or units^3. The volume of the pyramid is $540\ \text{m}^3$.

Example

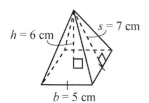

$h = 6$ cm $s = 7$ cm $b = 5$ cm

Calculate the volume of the given square pyramid.

Solution

Pyramids have one-third the volume of rectangular prisms with the same dimensions. Therefore, the formula for the volume of a square pyramid can be expressed as the volume formula for a rectangular prism divided by 3.

$$V_{\text{square pyramid}} = \frac{A_{\text{base}} \times h}{3}$$
$$= \frac{b^2 \times h}{3}$$
$$= \frac{5^2 \times 6}{3}$$
$$= \frac{25 \times 6}{3}$$
$$= \frac{150}{3}$$
$$= 50$$

The volume of the given square pyramid is $50\ \text{cm}^3$.

20M.2 Solve problems that involve SI and imperial units in volume and capacity measurements.

SOLVING PROBLEMS INVOLVING VOLUME OF PYRAMIDS

Problems involving the volume of pyramids can be solved once the formulas have been determined.

To solve problems involving the volume of pyramids, use the formula $V_{pyramid} = \frac{1}{3}A_{base}h$, where A_{base} is the area of the base and h is the height.

Rectangular Pyramids	
$a_{rectangle} = lw$ $V = \frac{1}{3}lwh$ **OR** $V = \frac{lwh}{3}$	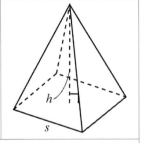
Square Pyramids	
$a_{square} = s^2$ $V = \frac{1}{3}(s^2)h$ **OR** $V = \frac{s^2 h}{3}$	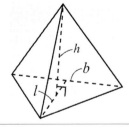
Triangular Pyramids	
$a_{triangle} = \frac{1}{2}bh$ $V = c\frac{1}{3}h_{pyramid}\left(\frac{1}{2}bh_{triangle}\right)$ **OR** $V = \frac{bh_{triangle}h_{pyramid}}{6}$	

Example

For a class project, Yani plans to build two different models of pyramids. One of the models will be a square-based pyramid, and the other model will be a rectangular-based pyramid. The height of the square-based pyramid will be 60 cm, and each side length of the base will be 28 cm. The height of the rectangular-based pyramid will be 62 cm, and the base will be 25 cm by 30 cm.

Determine which pyramid will have a greater volume, and calculate how much greater the volume will be.

Solution

The volume, V, of a pyramid can be determined by applying the formula $V = \frac{1}{3}(A_{base} \times h)$, where A_{base} is the area of the base and h is the height of the pyramid.

Step 1
Determine the area of the base of the square-based pyramid.
The area, A, of the base of the square-based pyramid can be determined by applying the formula $A = s^2$, where s is the side length of the base.
Substitute 28 for s.
$A = s^2$
$A = 28^2$
$A = 784$ cm^2

Step 2
Determine the volume of the square-based pyramid.

Apply the formula $V = \frac{1}{3}(A_{base} \times h)$.

Substitute 784 for A_{base} and 60 for h.

$V = \frac{1}{3}(A_{base} \times h)$

$V = \frac{1}{3}(784 \times 60)$

$V = \frac{1}{3} \times 47\ 040$

$V = 15\ 680$ cm^3

Step 3

Determine the area of the base of the rectangular-based pyramid.

The area, A, of the base of the rectangular-based pyramid can be determined by applying the formula $A = lw$, where l is the length of the base and w is the width of the base.

Substitute 30 for l and 25 for w.

$A = lw$
$A = 30 \times 25$
$A = 750 \text{ cm}^2$

Step 4

Determine the volume of the rectangular-based pyramid.

Apply the formula $V = \frac{1}{3}\left(A_{\text{base}} \times h\right)$.

Substitute 750 for A_{base} and 62 for h.

$V = \frac{1}{3}\left(A_{\text{base}} \times h\right)$

$V = \frac{1}{3}(750 \times 62)$

$V = \frac{1}{3} \times 46\ 500$

$V = 15\ 500 \text{ cm}^3$

Step 5

Determine which pyramid has the greater volume by subtracting one volume from the other.

$15\ 680 - 15\ 500 = 180 \text{ cm}^3$

The volume of the square-based pyramid will be 180 cm^3 greater than the volume of the rectangular-based pyramid.

20M.2 Solve problems that involve SI and imperial units in volume and capacity measurements.

DERIVING THE VOLUME FORMULA FOR A CONE

Volume measures how much space an object occupies. Volume is measured in cubic units, or units^3.

A *cone* is a solid with a circular base, a curved face, and one vertex.

The volume of a cone has a special relationship to the volume of a cylinder. If you compare the volume of a cone with the volume of a cylinder that has the same base and height as the cone, you will find that the volume of the cylinder is three times the volume of the cone.

The base of a cylinder and the base of a cone are both circular.

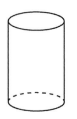

Therefore, you can derive the formula for the volume of a cone from the formula for the volume of a cylinder.

$V_{\text{cone}} = \frac{1}{3}V_{\text{cylinder}}$

$V_{\text{cone}} = \frac{1}{3}\left(A_{\text{base}} \times h\right)$

$V_{\text{cone}} = \frac{1}{3}\left(\pi r^2 \times h\right)$

$V_{\text{cone}} = \frac{\pi r^2 h}{3}$

Example

Use a sheet of construction paper to make a cylinder with an open top and bottom. Tape the cylinder together so that it remains rigid.

Roll another piece of construction paper into a cone so that its tip touches the bottom of the cylinder.

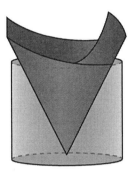

Tape the cone together so that it remains rigid. Trim the edge of the cone so that it is the same height as the cylinder.

Fill the cone to the top with rice, and empty it into the cylinder. Repeat this process until the cylinder is filled with rice. It should take about three cones of rice to fill the cylinder.

20M.2 Solve problems that involve SI and imperial units in volume and capacity measurements.

CALCULATING THE VOLUME OF A CONE

The volume of a cone can be found using the formula $V_{cone} = \dfrac{A_{base}h}{3}$, where A_{base} is the area of the base and h is the height. The equation can also be expressed as $V_{cone} = \dfrac{\pi r^2 h}{3}$.

Base (circle)

Example

Determine the volume of a cone, rounded to the nearest tenth of a centimetre, with a base radius of 6 cm and height of 4 cm.

Solution

Step 1

Substitute the known values into the volume formula for a cone.

$$V_{cone} = \frac{\pi r^2 h}{3}$$
$$= \frac{\pi (6)^2 (4)}{3}$$

Step 2

Solve for the missing variable.

Follow the order of operations when solving questions.

$$V_{cone} = \frac{3.14(36)(4)}{3}$$
$$= \frac{452.16}{3}$$
$$= 150.72$$

Volume is always calculated in cubic units or units^3. Rounded to the tenths position, the volume of the cone is 150.7 cm^3.

Example

A cone has a base radius of 11.5 cm and height of 7.4 cm.

To the nearest tenth of a centimetre, determine the volume of the cone.

Solution

Step 1

Substitute the known values into the volume formula for a cone.

$$V_{cone} = \frac{(\pi r^2)h}{3}$$

$$= \frac{(3.14 \times 11.5^2)(7.4)}{3}$$

Step 2

Solve for the missing variable.

Follow the order of operations when solving equations.

$$V_{cone} = \frac{(3.14 \times 132.25)(7.4)}{3}$$

$$= \frac{3\ 072.961}{3}$$

$$\approx 1\ 024.3$$

Volume is always calculated in cubic units or units^3. Rounded to the tenths position, the volume of the cone is 1 024.3 cm^3.

20M.2 Solve problems that involve SI and imperial units in volume and capacity measurements.

SOLVING PROBLEMS INVOLVING THE VOLUME OF A CONE

To solve problems involving the volume of a cone, use the formula $V_{cone} = \frac{\pi r^2 h}{3}$, in which r is the radius of the circular base and h is the height.

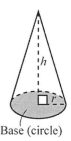

Base (circle)

Example

A snow cone has a diameter of 5.5 cm and a height of 13 cm.

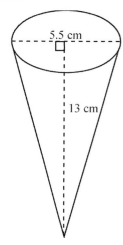

How much ice is needed to fill the snow cone to the brim?

Solution

Step 1

Determine the radius of the cone.

$$\frac{5.5 \text{ cm}}{2} = 2.75 \text{ cm}$$

Step 2

Calculate the volume of the cone.

The volume of a cone is one-third the volume of a cylinder with the same base and height.

$$V = \frac{\pi r^2 h}{3}$$

Use the volume formula for a cone, substitute in the values for radius and height, and evaluate.

$$V = \frac{\pi r^2 h}{3}$$

$$= \frac{\pi (2.75)^2 (13)}{3}$$

$$\approx 102.9526 \text{ cm}^3$$

To the nearest whole cubic centimetre, the amount of ice needed to fill the snow cone to the brim is 103 cm^3.

20M.2 Solve problems that involve SI and imperial units in volume and capacity measurements.

DERIVING THE VOLUME FORMULA FOR A SPHERE

Volume measures how much space an object occupies. Volume is measured in cubic units, or units^3.

A **sphere** is a three-dimensional ball in which every point on its curved face is the same distance from its centre. The **radius** is the distance between a point on the curved face of a sphere and the centre.
The volume of a sphere is two-thirds the volume of a cylinder with the same dimensions.

Consider a sphere with the same radius as the radius of the base of the cylinder.

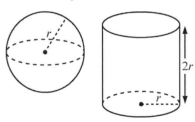

Since the height of the cylinder is equal to the diameter of the sphere ($h = 2r$), the formula for the volume of a sphere can now be derived from the formula for the volume of a cylinder.

$$V_{\text{cylinder}} = (A_{\text{base}})(\text{height})$$
$$V_{\text{cylinder}} = (\pi r^2)h$$
$$V_{\text{sphere}} = \frac{2}{3}(A_{\text{base}})(\text{height})$$
$$V_{\text{sphere}} = \frac{2}{3}(\pi r^2)(2r)$$
$$V_{\text{sphere}} = \frac{2(2\pi r^3)}{3}$$
$$V_{\text{sphere}} = \frac{4\pi r^3}{3}$$

20M.2 Solve problems that involve SI and imperial units in volume and capacity measurements.

CALCULATING THE VOLUME OF A SPHERE

The volume of a **sphere** is two-thirds the volume of a cylinder with the same dimensions.

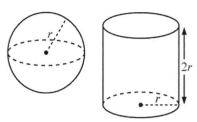

That is, the radius of the sphere is the same as the radius of the base of the cylinder and the height of the cylinder is equal to the diameter of the sphere.

Since the height of the cylinder is equal to the diameter of the sphere, $h = 2r$. The formula for the volume of a sphere can now be derived from the formula for the volume of a cylinder:

$$V_{\text{cylinder}} = (A_{\text{base}})(\text{height})$$
$$= (\pi r^2)h$$
$$V_{\text{sphere}} = \frac{2}{3}\left(A_{\text{base}}\right)\left(\text{height}\right)$$
$$V_{\text{sphere}} = \frac{2}{3}\left(\pi r^2\right)\left(2r\right)$$
$$V_{\text{sphere}} = \frac{2 \times 2\pi r^3}{3}$$
$$V_{\text{sphere}} = \frac{4\pi r^3}{3}$$

Example

Calculate the volume of the given sphere rounded to the nearest tenth of a cm^3.

$$V_{sphere} = \frac{4\pi r^3}{3}$$
$$= \frac{4 \times 3.14 \times 7^3}{3}$$
$$= \frac{4 \times 3.14 \times 343}{3}$$
$$= \frac{4\ 308.08}{3}$$
$$= 1\ 436.02\bar{6}$$
$$= 1\ 436.0 \text{ cm}^3$$

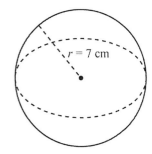

$r = 7$ cm

Calculate the volume of the given sphere to the nearest cm^3.

$$V_{sphere} = \frac{4\pi r^3}{3}$$
$$= \frac{4 \times 3.14 \times 4^3}{3}$$
$$= \frac{4 \times 3.14 \times 64}{3}$$
$$= \frac{803.84}{3}$$
$$= 267.94\bar{6}$$
$$= 268 \text{ cm}^3$$

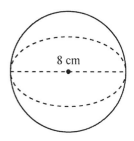

8 cm

Often, the size of a ball is specified by its circumference instead of its radius or diameter. The following illustrates one way to find the volume of the ball, if only the circumference is known.

Example

The circumference of a baseball is 22 cm.

Determine the volume of the baseball rounded to the nearest tenth of a cubic centimetre(cm^3).

Solution

Determine the radius of the baseball rounded to the nearest hundredth of cm.

$$C = \pi d$$
$$22 = 3.14d$$
$$\frac{22}{3.14} = \frac{3.14d}{3.14}$$
$$7.006\ 369\ 43 = d$$
$$d = 7.006\ 369\ 43 \text{ cm}$$
$$r = \frac{d}{2} = \frac{7.006\ 369\ 43}{2}$$
$$= 3.503\ 1847 \text{ cm}$$
$$= 3.50 \text{ cm}$$

Now, substitute the known values into the volume formula, and solve.

$$V_{sphere} = \frac{4\pi r^3}{3}$$
$$= \frac{4 \times 3.14 \times 3.50^3}{3}$$
$$= \frac{4 \times 3.14 \times 42.875}{3}$$
$$= \frac{538.51}{3}$$
$$= 179.50$$
$$= 179.5 \text{ cm}^3$$

The volume of the baseball is 179.5 cm^3.

20M.2 Solve problems that involve SI and imperial units in volume and capacity measurements.

SOLVING PROBLEMS INVOLVING THE VOLUME OF A SPHERE

To solve problems involving the volume of a sphere, use the formula $V_{\text{sphere}} = \dfrac{4\pi r^3}{3}$, in which r is the radius.

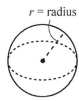

r = radius

Example

A necklace is made up of 24 spherical silver beads. Each bead has a radius of 0.5 cm.

What is the total volume of silver in the necklace?

Solution

Step 1

Determine the volume of each bead.

Use 3.14 as the approximate value of π.

$$V_{\text{sphere}} = \frac{4\pi r^3}{3}$$
$$\approx \frac{4 \times 3.14 \times 0.5^3}{3}$$
$$\approx \frac{4 \times 3.14 \times 0.125}{3}$$
$$\approx \frac{1.57}{3}$$
$$\approx 0.52\bar{3} \text{ cm}^3$$

Each bead contains approximately $0.52\bar{3}$ cm^3 of silver.

Step 2

Determine the total volume of silver in the entire necklace.

Multiply the volume of silver in one bead by the number of beads in the necklace.

$$V_{\text{silver}} \approx 0.52\bar{3} \text{ cm}^3 \times 24$$
$$\approx 12.56 \text{ cm}^3$$

The necklace contains 12.56 cm^3 of silver.

20M.2 Solve problems that involve SI and imperial units in volume and capacity measurements.

CALCULATING THE VOLUME OF A 3-D COMPOSITE FIGURE

Finding the volume of 3-D composite figures is much easier than finding the surface area.

For figures with no missing parts, find the volume of each part and add their values together.

Example

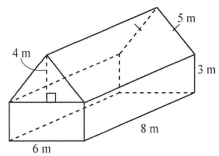

Find the volume of the given composite figure.

Solution

$$V_{\text{composite figure}} = V_{\text{rectangular prism}} + V_{\text{triangular prism}}$$

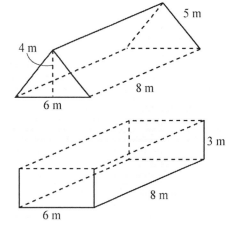

For the rectangular prism

$l = 8$ m

$w = 6$ m.

$h = 3$ m

$V_{\text{rectangular prism}} = lwh$

$= 8 \times 6 \times 3$

$= 144 \text{ m}^3$

For the triangular prism

$b = 6$ m

$h = 4$ m

$l = 8$ m

$V_{\text{triangular prism}} = \dfrac{bhl}{2}$

$= \dfrac{6 \times 4 \times 8}{2}$

$= \dfrac{192}{2}$

$= 96 \text{ m}^3$

$V_{\text{composite figure}} = V_{\text{rectangular prism}} + V_{\text{triangular prism}}$

$= 144 + 96$

$= 240 \text{ m}^3$

For figures with pieces missing, find the volume of each part and subtract their values.

Example

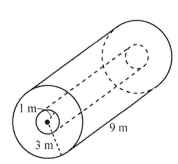

Find the volume of the given figure to the nearest hundredth.

Solution

To find the volume of a figure that has one or more pieces missing, find the volume of the figure and then subtract the volume of the missing piece(s).

Therefore, to find the volume of the given figure, subtract the volume of the small cylinder on the inside from the volume of the large cylinder.

$V_{\text{large cylinder}} = \pi r^2 h$

$= 3.14 \times 3^2 \times 9$

$= 3.14 \times 9 \times 9$

$= 254.34 \text{ m}^3$

Note that if the $\boxed{\pi}$ button on your calculator were used, the added precision would have given an answer of 254.47 m³.

$V_{\text{small cylinder}} = \pi r^2 h$

$= 3.14 \times 1^2 \times 9$

$= 3.14 \times 1 \times 9$

$= 28.26 \text{ m}^3$

Note that if the $\boxed{\pi}$ button on your calculator were used, the added precision would have given an answer of 28.27 m³.

$V_{\text{figure}} = V_{\text{large cylinder}} - V_{\text{small cylinder}}$

$= 254.34 - 28.26$

$= 226.08 \text{ m}^3$

Note that if the $\boxed{\pi}$ button on your calculator were used, the added precision would have given an answer of 226.20 m³.

20M.2 Solve problems that involve SI and imperial units in volume and capacity measurements.

DETERMINING HOW CHANGES IN DIMENSIONS AFFECT THE VOLUME OF SOLIDS

Changing the dimensions of any three-dimensional geometric shape affects the volume of the shape. There must be a change in dimension to increase or decrease the volume of a shape.

Example

Jude has a fish tank in the shape of a rectangular prism that is 7 cm long, 7 cm wide, and 15 cm high.

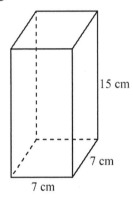

He buys a bigger fish tank with the same shape but 5 cm longer, the same width, and 6 cm higher than the original fish tank.

How much additional water is needed to fill the new fish tank?

Solution

Step 1

Calculate the volume of the first fish tank, V_1.

Substitute $l = 7$, $w = 7$, and $h = 15$ into the volume formula for a rectangular prism and solve.

$$\begin{aligned} V_1 &= l \times w \times h \\ &= 7 \times 7 \times 15 \\ &= 735 \text{ cm}^3 \end{aligned}$$

Step 2

Calculate the dimensions of the second fish tank.

$$\begin{aligned} l_2 &= 7 + 5 \\ &= 12 \\ w_2 &= w_1 \\ &= 7 \\ h_2 &= 15 + 6 \\ &= 21 \end{aligned}$$

Step 3

Calculate the volume of the new fish tank, V_2.

Substitute $l_2 = 12$, $w_2 = 7$, and $h_2 = 21$ into the volume formula for a rectangular prism and solve.

$$\begin{aligned} V_2 &= l_2 \times w_2 \times h_2 \\ &= 12 \times 7 \times 21 \\ &= 1\ 764 \text{ cm}^3 \end{aligned}$$

Step 4

Calculate the additional amount of water needed to fill the second fish tank.

$$\begin{aligned} V_2 - V_1 &= 1\ 764 - 735 \\ &= 1\ 029 \text{ cm}^3 \end{aligned}$$

Jude needs $1\ 029$ cm^3 of additional water to fill the second fish tank.

Example

For a class project, George is building a model of an Egyptian pyramid. The height of the model square pyramid is 25 in, and each side length of the square base is 16 in. He wants to increase the volume of his model pyramid. To avoid damaging his model, he found that he can either double the height of the square pyramid or add 6 in to each side length of the square base.

What change in dimension should George make to his model in order to increase the volume the most?

Solution

Calculate the volume for each possible change in dimension, and compare.

Step 1

Calculate the volume when the height is doubled.

The height of the new pyramid is $2(25) = 50$ in. Use the volume formula for a pyramid to find the new volume.

$$V_1 = \frac{A_{\text{base}} \times h}{3}$$
$$= \frac{(16)(16)(50)}{3}$$
$$= \frac{12\ 800}{3}$$
$$\approx 4\ 266.7 \text{ in}^3$$

Step 2

Calculate the volume when 6 in are added to each side length of the square base.

Each new side length of the square base is $16 + 6 = 22$ in.

Use the volume formula for a pyramid to find the new volume.

$$V_2 = \frac{A_{\text{base}} \times h}{3}$$
$$= \frac{(22)(22)(25)}{3}$$
$$= \frac{12\ 100}{3}$$
$$\approx 4\ 033.3 \text{ in}^3$$

Therefore, George should double the height of his square pyramid to increase its volume the most.

1. A box that is in the shape of a cube has side lengths of 35 cm. What is the total surface area of the box?

   A. 1 225 cm²   **B.** 2 450 cm²

   C. 2 675 cm²   **D.** 7 350 cm²

Use the following information to answer the next question.

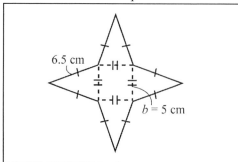

Written Response

2. Construct a 3-D shape using the given net.

Use the following information to answer the next question.

A can of tuna has a radius of 3.5 cm. The wrapper on the outside of the can does not overlap, and when peeled off, the area of the wrapper is 109.9 cm².

3. What is the height of the can of tuna, to the nearest whole number?

   A. 5 cm   **B.** 5.5 cm

   C. 6 cm   **D.** 6.5 cm

Use the following information to answer the next question.

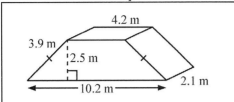

4. What is the surface area of the given trapezoidal prism?

A. 118.62 m²   **B.** 104.04 m²

C. 82.62 m²   **D.** 74.43 m²

Use the following information to answer the next question.

A pyramid is given.

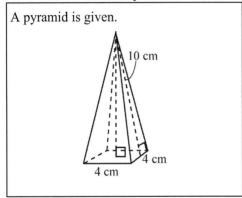

| Written Response |

5. Calculate the surface area of this pyramid.

Use the following information to answer the next question.

This composite object is built with 3 cm cubes.

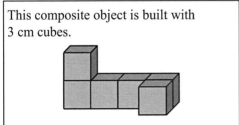

6. What is the surface area of the given object?

A. 324 cm²   **B.** 279 cm²

C. 234 cm²   **D.** 216 cm²

Use the following information to answer the next question.

A flower vase is in the shape of a rectangular prism.

16 cm

9 cm

4 cm

7. What is the surface area of the exterior of the vase?

A. 421 cm²   **B.** 452 cm²

C. 489 cm²   **D.** 517 cm²

Use the following information to answer the next question.

A wedge of cheese is in the shape of a triangular prism. The dimensions are shown in the given figure.

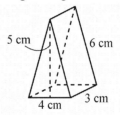

Tom would like to wrap the wedge of cheese in tinfoil.

| Numerical Response |

8. Tom will need _____ cm² of tinfoil to wrap the wedge of cheese.

Use the following information to answer the next question.

A diagram of a liquid oxygen storage tank is given. It is a compound shape made up of a cylinder with a half of a sphere on one end and a conical shape on the other end. Measurements are given in metres (m).

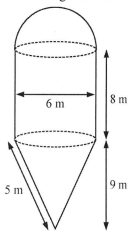

The special material that covers the structure costs $325/m², and an additional 5 % of extra material is needed to allow for cutting and waste.

Numerical Response

9. To the nearest thousand, what is the total cost of the material needed to cover the storage tank? $_____

Use the following information to answer the next question.

The given right circular cone has a surface area of 198 cm² and a radius of 3 cm.

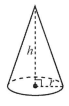

10. What is the height of the cone, rounded to the nearest tenth?

    A. 13.0 cm   B. 17.8 cm

    C. 18.0 cm   D. 18.3 cm

Use the following information to answer the next question.

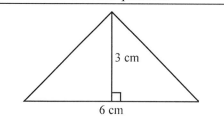

The triangle shown has a height of 3 cm and a length of 6 cm.

11. If the height of the triangle is decreased by 1 cm and the base is increased by 3 cm, what is the area of the new triangle?

    A. 6 cm²   B. 9 cm²

    C. 13 cm²   D. 18 cm²

Use the following information to answer the next question.

An outside light fixture is in the shape of an inverted square-based pyramid. The light fixture has a circular hole in the top where a light bulb is to be inserted. The slant height of the light fixture is 32 cm, and the diameter of the circular hole is 16 cm.

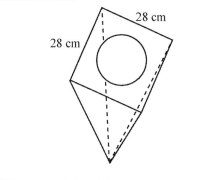

12. To the nearest whole number, the surface area of the light fixture is

    A. 1 772 cm²   B. 1 943 cm²

    C. 2 186 cm²   D. 2 375 cm²

Use the following information to answer the next question.

The surface area of a sphere is 394.24 cm².

Numerical Response

13. Rounded to the nearest tenth, the diameter of the sphere is _____ cm.

Use the following information to answer the next question.

A right rectangular prism with the given dimensions is shown.

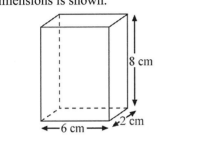

8 cm

6 cm   2 cm

Numerical Response

14. To the nearest cubic centimetre, the maximum volume of the right rectangular pyramid that would fit snugly inside the illustrated rectangular right prism is _____ cm³.

Use the following information to answer the next question.

The given cylinder has a diameter of 14 cm and a height of 14 cm.

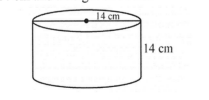

14 cm

14 cm

15. What is the volume of the cylinder?
    A. 2 154 cm³   **B.** 4 308 cm³
    C. 6 426 cm³   **D.** 8 616 cm³

Numerical Response

16. The formula for the volume of a sphere is $V = \dfrac{4}{3}\pi r^3$. If the volume of a ball is 36π cm³, then the radius of the sphere is _____ cm.

Use the following information to answer the next question.

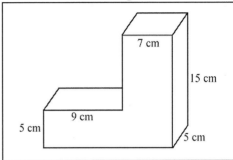

7 cm

15 cm

5 cm

9 cm

5 cm

17. What is the volume of the given figure?
    A. 225 cm³   **B.** 300 cm³
    C. 525 cm³   **D.** 750 cm³

Use the following information to answer the next question.

The given diagram illustrates a two-man tent. This tent is in the shape of a triangular prism.

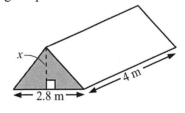

x

2.8 m

4 m

18. If the volume of the tent shown is 8.96 m³, what is the area of the front, or shaded section, of the tent?
    A. 1.6 m²   **B.** 2.24 m²
    C. 3.2 m²   **D.** 4.48 m²

A conical container with a diameter of 1.4 m and a height of 3.7 m is used to transport rocks.

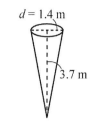

$d = 1.4$ m

3.7 m

19. If the rocks are sold at a rate of $22.00/\text{m}^3$ and 3.14 is used as the value of π, what will be the cost to the nearest cent to fill the container completely?

    A. $39.52   **B.** $41.75

    C. $44.38   **D.** $46.93

Sharon wants to fill two identical flower pots with dirt. The flower pots have an attached base, but the pots themselves are spherical in shape with a radius of 40 cm. Through an opening at the top, Sharon will fill each flower pot 90% full of dirt.

Numerical Response

20. If Sharon uses 3.14 as the value of π and rounds her answer to the nearest whole number, how much dirt will she require to fill the two flower pots? _____ cm^3

21. What is the volume of a pyramid with a base of 15 m by 12 m that is 14 m high?

    A. 840 m^3

    B. 1 470 m^3

    C. 2 520 m^3

    D. 2 856 m^3

Greg is building a sandcastle and uses a pail in the shape of a cylinder with the given dimensions to gather the sand.

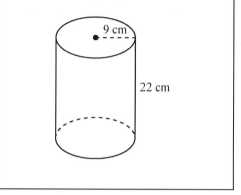

9 cm

22 cm

Numerical Response

22. If Greg fills the pail with sand 6 times, the amount of sand he uses to build his castle is _____ cm^3.

Kelly's math teacher asked her to measure a particular triangular prism and then calculate its volume.
Kelly made these measurements:

- Height of triangular base: 6 cm
- Length of triangular base: 9 cm
- Height of triangular prism: 12 cm

23. What is the volume of the triangular prism Kelly measured?

    A. 648 cm^3 **B.** 324 cm^3

    C. 192 cm^3 **D.** 90 cm^3

Use the following information to answer the next question.

At a gardening store, two different types of a particular style of flower pot are available. Each type is in the shape of an inverted pyramid, as illustrated in the given diagrams.

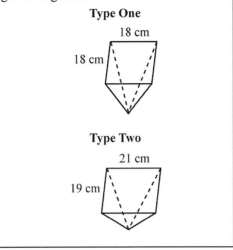

Type One

18 cm

18 cm

Type Two

21 cm

19 cm

24. If the depth (height) of the type-one flower pot is 20 cm and the depth (height) of the type-two flower pot is 16 cm, which of the following statements about the volumes of the two flower pots is **true**?

A. The volume of a type-two flower pot is 24 cm³ more than the volume of a type-one flower pot.

B. The volume of a type-two flower pot is 75 cm³ more than the volume of a type-one flower pot.

C. The volume of a type-one flower pot is 32 cm³ more than the volume of a type-two flower pot.

D. The volume of a type-one flower pot is 96 cm³ more than the volume of a type-two flower pot.

Use the following information to answer the next question.

A triangular prism is shown.

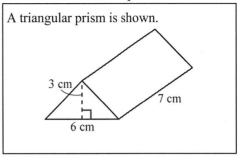

3 cm

7 cm

6 cm

Written Response

25. What is the volume of the given triangular prism?

ANSWERS AND SOLUTIONS
MEASUREMENT

1. D	6. C	11. B	16. 3	21. A
2. WR	7. B	12. D	17. D	22. 33572.88
3. A	8. 68	13. 11.2	18. B	23. B
4. C	9. 119000	14. 32	19. B	24. C
5. WR	10. B	15. A	20. 482304	25. WR

1. D

Step 1

Since all the side lengths of a cube are equal, multiply 35 by 35 to determine the area of one of the faces (surfaces) of the cube. $35 \times 35 = 1225$ cm^2

Step 2

Since all six faces (surfaces) are congruent, multiply the area of one face (surface) by 6.

1 225 × 6 = 7350 cm^2

The total surface area of the box is 7 350 cm^2.

2. WR

Imagine that you are gluing the edges of the net together.

When all the edges meet up, the following shape is formed:

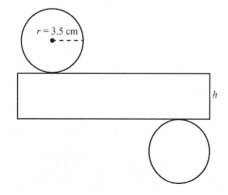

This shape is a square pyramid.

3. A

Step 1
Draw the net of the shape.

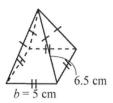

Step 2
Calculate the diameter of the circle.
$d = 2r = 2 \times 3.5 = 7$ cm

Step 3
Calculate the circumference of the circle, since the width of the rectangle is equal to the circumference of the circle. Use 3.14 as π.
$$C = \pi d$$
$$= 3.14 \times 7$$
$$= 21.98 \text{ cm}$$

Step 4
Determine the height of the tuna can using the area formula for a rectangle.
Substitute in the known values and simplify the equation.
$$A_{rectangle} = h \times w$$
$$109.9 = h \times 21.98$$
$$\frac{109.9}{21.98} = \frac{21.98h}{21.98}$$
$$5 = h$$

The height of the tuna can is approximately 5 cm.

4. C

Step 1
Draw the net of the shape.

A trapezoidal prism is made up of four rectangular faces (both sides, bottom, and top in the diagram) that join the two trapezoidal bases (front and back).

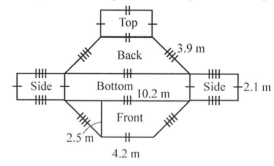

Step 2

Calculate the area of each face.

Solve for the area of each face by applying the appropriate formula.

$A_{bottom} = lw$
$= (10.2)(2.1)$
$= 21.42 \text{ m}^2$

$A_{front\ and\ back} = 2\left[\dfrac{h}{2}(b_1 + b_2)\right]$
$= h(b_1 + b_2)$
$= 2.5(4.2 + 10.2)$
$= 2.5(14.4)$
$= 36 \text{ m}^2$

$A_{2\ sides} = 2lw$
$= 2(3.9)(2.1)$
$= 16.38 \text{ m}^2$

$A_{top} = lw$
$= (4.2)(2.1)$
$= 8.82 \text{ m}^2$

Step 3

Add the areas of the faces.

$SA_{trapezoidal\ prism}$
$= A_{bottom} + A_{front\ and\ back} + A_{2\ sides} + A_{top}$
$= 21.42 + 36 + 16.38 + 8.82$
$= 82.62 \text{ m}^2$

The surface area of the trapezoidal prism is 82.62 m^2.

5. WR

The formula used to calculate the surface area of a square-based pyramid is $SA = b^2 + 2(bs)$. Substitute 4 for b and 10 for s, and then simplify.

$SA_{square\ pyramid}$
$= b^2 + 2(bs)$
$= (4)^2 + 2(4 \times 10)$
$= 16 + 2(40)$
$= 16 + 80$
$= 96 \text{ cm}^2$

6. C

Step 1

Count the number of exposed faces of the composite object.

The front and back each have 5 exposed faces.

Each side has 3 exposed faces.

The top and bottom each have 5 exposed faces.

On the 6 cubes, there are 26 exposed faces.

Step 2

Calculate the area of one face of a cube.

$A = s^2$
$= 3^2$
$= 9 \text{ cm}^2$

The area of one face of a cube is 9 cm².

Step 3

Calculate the total surface area of the composite object.

$SA = A_{one\ face} \times$ number of exposed faces
$= 9 \times 26$
$= 234 \text{ cm}^2$

The total surface area of the composite object is 234 cm².

7. B

Step 1

Calculate the areas of the faces.

Looking at the diagram, it can be seen that the faces of the front and back are the same size. The faces of the sides (left and right) are also the same size

The top and bottom have the same size, but the top will be open, so its area will not contribute to the surface area of the exterior of the vase.

Calculate the area of each face. For the pairs of matching faces, calculate the area of one face, and then multiply by 2 in order to find the areas of both faces.

$A_{front\ and\ back} = 2(lw)$
$A_{front\ and\ back} = 2(16 \times 4)$
$A_{front\ and\ back} = 2(64)$
$A_{front\ and\ back} = 128 \text{ cm}^2$

$A_{sides} = 2(lw)$
$A_{sides} = 2(16 \times 9)$
$A_{sides} = 2(144)$
$A_{sides} = 288 \text{ cm}^2$

$A_{top} = lw$
$A_{top} = 4 \times 9$
$A_{top} = 36 \text{ cm}^2$

Step 2

Calculate the surface area.

Add the areas of the faces.

$SA_{prism} = A_{front\ and\ back} + A_{sides} + A_{top}$
$= 128 + 288 + 36$
$= 452 \text{ cm}^2$

The surface area of the flower vase is 452 cm².

8. 68

Step 1

Draw the net of the shape.

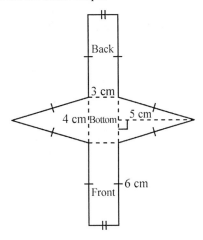

Step 2

Calculate the area of the faces.

Calculate the area of the front and back faces.

$A_{\text{front and back}} = 2(l \times w)$

$A_{\text{front and back}} = 2(3 \times 6)$

$A_{\text{front and back}} = 2(18)$

$A_{\text{front and back}} = 36$

Calculate the area of the bottom face.

$A_{\text{bottom}} = l \times w$

$A_{\text{bottom}} = 3 \times 4$

$A_{\text{bottom}} = 12$

Calculate the area of the triangular faces.

$A_{\text{triangle}} = 2\left(\dfrac{bh}{2}\right)$

$A_{\text{triangle}} = 2\left(\dfrac{4 \times 5}{2}\right)$

$A_{\text{triangle}} = 20$

Step 3

Calculate the total surface area of the triangular prism.

$SA_{\text{cheese}} = A_{\text{front and back}} + A_{\text{bottom}} + A_{\text{triangle}}$

$SA_{\text{cheese}} = 36 + 12 + 20$

$SA_{\text{cheese}} = 68\,\text{cm}^2$

Tom will need 68 cm^2 of tinfoil to wrap the cheese.

9. 119000

Step 1

Determine the radius of the shapes.

$r = \dfrac{d}{2}$

$\quad = \dfrac{6}{2}$

$\quad = 3$

Step 2

Determine the total surface area of the composite shape.

$SA_T = \dfrac{1}{2}\left(4\pi r^2\right) + 2\pi rh + \pi rs$

$\quad = \dfrac{1}{2}\left(4\pi(3^2)\right) + 2\pi(3)(8) + \pi(9)(5)$

$\quad = 18\pi + 48\pi + 45\pi$

$\quad = 111\pi$

Step 3

Add the 5 % of extra material.

$111\pi \times 1.05 = 116.55\pi$

Step 4

Determine the total cost of the material.

$116.55\pi \times 325 = 118\ 999.60$

The cost of the material, to the nearest thousand, is $119 000.

10. B

Step 1

Determine the length of the lateral face of the cone. Substitute 198 for SA_{cone} and 3 for r into the surface area of a cone formula, $SA_{\text{cone}} = \pi r^2 + \pi rs$. Then, isolate s.

$SA_{\text{cone}} = \pi r^2 + \pi rs$

$198 = \pi(3)^2 + \pi(3)s$

$198 - 9\pi = \pi(3)s$

$\dfrac{198 - 9\pi}{3\pi} = s$

Step 2

Substitute 3.14 for π, and solve for s.

$s = \dfrac{198 - 9\pi}{3\pi}$

$\quad \cong \dfrac{198 - 9(3.14)}{3(3.14)}$

$\quad \cong \dfrac{198 - 28.26}{9.42}$

$\quad \cong \dfrac{169.74}{9.42}$

$\quad \cong 18.0191\ldots$

Step 3

Calculate the height of the cone.

Since the cone is a right circular cone, use the Pythagorean theorem to find the height.

$r^2 + h^2 = s^2$

$(3)^2 + h^2 \cong (18.0191)^2$

$h^2 \cong (18.0191)^2 - (3)^2$

$h^2 \cong 324.6882 - 9$

$h^2 \cong 315.6882$

$h \cong \sqrt{315.6882}$

$h \cong 17.7676\ldots$

$h \cong 17.8\ \text{cm}$

11. B

Step 1

Make the required changes to the dimensions of the given triangle.

$h = 3 - 1$
$ = 2$ cm
$b = 6 + 3$
$ = 9$ cm

Step 2

Calculate the area of the new triangle.

$A = \dfrac{1}{2}bh$

$ = \dfrac{1}{2}(9)(2)$

$ = 9$ cm^2

12. D

The surface area, SA, of a pyramid can be determined by applying the formula $SA = A_{base} + A_{lateral\ faces}$, where A_{base} is the area of the base and $A_{lateral\ faces}$ is the area of the lateral faces.

Step 1

Determine the area of the base (top) of the light fixture.

If the base of the light fixture did not have a circular hole cut into it, the area of the base would be $28 \times 28 = 784$ cm^2.

However, since there is a circular hole in the base, the actual area of the base is 784 cm^2 minus the area of the circular hole.

The formula $A = \pi r^2$ can be used to determine the area of the circular hole. Substitute $16 \div 2 = 8$ for r, and then solve for A.

$A = \pi(8)^2$
$A = 64\pi$
$A \approx 201.06$ cm^2

Thus, the area of the base is approximately 784 cm$^2 - 201.06$ cm$^2 = 582.94$ cm^2.

Step 2

Determine the area of the lateral faces of the light fixture.

Each of the four lateral faces in the light fixture is triangular in shape. The area, A, of each triangle can be determined by applying the formula $A = \dfrac{1}{2}bh$, where b is the length of the base of the triangle and h is the height.

Since the lateral faces are congruent, the total area of the lateral faces can be determined by using the formula $A = 4 \times \left(\dfrac{1}{2}bh\right)$.

Substitute 28 for b and 32 for h, and then solve for A.

$A = 4 \times \left(\dfrac{1}{2} \times 28 \times 32\right)$
$A = 4 \times 448$
$A = 1\ 792$ cm^2

Step 3

Determine the surface area of the light fixture.
Apply the surface area formula for a pyramid.

$SA = A_{base} + A_{lateral\ faces}$

Substitute 582.94 cm^2 for A_{base} and 1 792 cm^2 for $A_{lateral\ faces}$.

$SA = 582.94$ cm$^2 + 1\ 792$ cm^2
$SA = 2\ 374.94$ cm^2

To the nearest whole number, the surface area of the light fixture is 2 375 cm^2.

13. 11.2

Step 1

Rearrange the formula for the surface area of a sphere, $SA_{sphere} = 4\pi r^2$, to solve for r.

$SA_{sphere} = 4\pi r^2$

$\dfrac{SA_{sphere}}{4\pi} = r^2$

$\sqrt{\dfrac{SA_{sphere}}{4\pi}} = r$

Step 2

Substitute 3.14 for an approximation of π and 394.24 for SA_{sphere} and evaluate.

$r = \sqrt{\dfrac{SA_{sphere}}{4\pi}}$

$ \cong \sqrt{\dfrac{394.24}{4 \times 3.14}}$

$ \cong \sqrt{\dfrac{394.24}{12.56}}$

$ \cong \sqrt{31.388\ 535}$

$ \cong 5.6025$ cm

Step 3

Determine the diameter.

$d = r \times 2$
$\cong 5.6025 \times 2$
$\cong 11.2050$ cm
$d \cong 11.2$

14. 32

The volume of a right pyramid is $\frac{1}{3}$ the volume of a right prism with the same length, width, and height. Determine the maximum volume of the pyramid.

$V_{\text{pyramid}} = \frac{1}{3} V_{\text{prism}}$

$= \frac{1}{3} \left(A_{\text{base}} \times h \right)$

$= \frac{1}{3} (lw) \times h$

Substitute 6 for l, 2 for w, and 8 for h.

$V_{\text{pyramid}} = \frac{1}{3} (6 \times 2 \times 8)$

$= \frac{1}{3} (96)$

$= 32$ cm^3

The maximum volume of the pyramid that would fit snugly inside the prism is 32 cm^3.

15. A

Step 1

Calculate the radius of the circular base.

$\text{radius} = \dfrac{\text{diameter}}{2}$

$= \dfrac{14}{2}$

$= 7$

Step 2

Calculate the volume of the cylinder using the formula $V = A_{\text{base}} \times h$. Let $\pi = 3.14$.

$V = A_{\text{base}} \times h$

$= \pi r^2 \times h$

$= 3.14 \times 7^2 \times 14$

$= 3.14 \times 49 \times 14$

$= 2\ 154.04$

Rounded to the nearest whole number, the volume of the cylinder is 2 154 cm^3.

16. 3

The formula for the volume of a sphere is

$V = \frac{4}{3} \pi r^3$.

To find the radius of the ball, substitute $V = 36\pi$ into the formula.

$36\pi = \frac{4}{3} \pi r^3$

Divide both sides by π.

$36 = \frac{4}{3} r^3$

Multiply both sides by 3.

$108 = 4r^3$

Divide both sides by 4.

$r^3 = 27$
$r = 3$

17. D

$V =$ Volume of left rectangular prism+ Volume of right rectangular prism

Left prism
$V =$ area of the base $\times$ height of object
$V = (l \times w) \times$ height
$V = (9 \times 5) \times 5$
$V = 45 \times 5$
$V = 225$ cm^3

Right prism
$V =$ area of the base $\times$ height of object
$V = (l \times w) \times$ height
$V = (7 \times 5) \times 15$
$V = 35 \times 15$
$V = 525$ cm^3

$V =$ Volume of left rectangular prism $+$ Volume of right rectangular prism
$V = 225$ cm$^3 + 525$ cm$^3 = 750$ cm^3

18. B

In order to determine the volume of the tent, which is in the shape of a triangular prism, it is necessary to consider one of the triangular faces as the base of the tent.

Step 1

Let x represent the height of one of the triangular faces, and determine an expression for the area of the base of the tent by applying the formula for the area of a triangle.

Substitute 2.8 for b and x for h in the formula $A = \dfrac{bh}{2}$, and then simplify.

$A = \dfrac{bh}{2}$

$A = \dfrac{2.8 \times x}{2}$

$A = 1.4x$ m

Step 2

Solve for x by applying the formula for the volume of a triangular prism.

Substitute $1.4x$ for A_{base}, 4 (the given height) for h, and 8.96 (the given volume) for V in the formula $V = A_{\text{base}} \times h$. Solve for x.

$V = A_{\text{base}} \times h$

$8.96 = (1.4x)(4)$

$8.96 = 5.6x$

1.6 m $= x$

The value of x, the height of the triangular face, is 1.6 m.

Step 3

Determine the area of the front of the tent by applying the formula for the area of a triangle.

Substitute 2.8 for b and 1.6 for h in the formula $A = \dfrac{bh}{2}$, and solve for A.

$A = \dfrac{bh}{2}$

$A = \dfrac{2.8 \times 1.6}{2}$

$A = \dfrac{4.48}{2}$

$A = 2.24$ m^2

The area of the front of the tent is 2.24 m^2.

19. **B**

Step 1

Determine the radius of the cone.

$r = \dfrac{d}{2}$

$r = \dfrac{1.4}{2}$

$r = 0.7$

Step 2

Calculate the volume of the cone.

$V_{\text{cone}} = \dfrac{\pi r^2 h}{3}$

$V_{\text{cone}} \approx \dfrac{(3.14)(0.7)^2(3.7)}{3}$

$V_{\text{cone}} \approx \dfrac{(3.14)(0.49)(3.7)}{3}$

$V_{\text{cone}} \approx \dfrac{5.692\,82}{3}$

$V_{\text{cone}} \approx 1.8976$ m^3

Step 3

Determine the cost of the rocks.

Multiply the volume of the cone by the rate that the rocks are being sold.

cost $= V_{\text{cone}} \times 22.00$

cost $\approx 1.8976 \times 22.00$

cost $\approx \$41.75$

Therefore, the cost of the rocks to fill the conical container will be \$41.75.

20. **482304**

Step 1

Determine the volume of one flower pot by applying the formula for the volume of a sphere, $V = \dfrac{4}{3}\pi r^3$ or $V = \dfrac{4\pi r^3}{3}$.

Substitute 3.14 for π and 40 for r in the formula $V = \dfrac{4}{3}\pi r^3$, and solve for V.

$V \approx \dfrac{4 \times 3.14 \times 40^3}{3}$

$V \approx \dfrac{4 \times 3.14 \times 64\,000}{3}$

$V \approx \dfrac{803\,840}{3}$

$V \approx 267\,946.67$

The volume of one flower pot is approximately $267\,946.67$ cm^3.

Step 2

Determine the total volume of the two flower pots.

$267\,946.67 \times 2 \approx 535\,893.34$

The total volume of the two flower pots is approximately $535\,893.34$ cm^3.

Step 3
Determine the amount of dirt required to fill the two flower pots.
Since each flower pot is to be filled 90% full of dirt, the amount of dirt required to fill the two flower pots can be determined as follows:
90% × 535 893.34
≈ 0.90 × 535 893.34
≈ 482 304.006
To the nearest whole number, Sharon will require 482 304 cm^3 of dirt to fill the two flower pots.

21. **A**

Step 1
Substitute the given values into the volume formula for a pyramid.
$$V = \frac{lwh}{3}$$
$$= \frac{(15)(12)(14)}{3}$$

Step 2
Calculate the volume of the pyramid.
$$V = \frac{2\ 520}{3}$$
$$= 840\ m^3$$

22. **33572.88**

Step 1
Calculate the volume of the cylinder.
The shape of the base is a circle. The height is the measured distance between the parallel circles (bases).

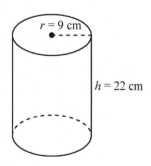

$r = 9$ cm

$h = 22$ cm

Substitute 3.14 for π, 9 for r, and 22 for h.
$$V_{cylinder} = A_{base} \times h$$
$$= A_{circle} \times h$$
$$= \pi r^2 \times h$$
$$= 3.14 \times 9^2 \times 22$$
$$= 3.14 \times 81 \times 22$$
$$= 5\ 595.48\ cm^3$$

Step 2
Multiply the volume of the cylinder by 6.
$6 \times 5\ 595.48 = 33\ 572.88$ cm^3
Greg's sandcastle contains 33 572.88 cm^3 of sand.

23. **B**

Determine the volume of the triangular prism by using the formula for volume.
V = area of base × height of prism
$$V = \left(\frac{base \times height}{2}\right) \times h$$

Substitute the numbers for the length of the base (9 cm), the height of the base (6 cm), and the height of the prism (12 cm) into the formula.
$$V = \left(\frac{9 \times 6}{2}\right) \times 12$$
$$V = 27 \times 12 = 324\ cm^3$$
The volume of the prism Kelly measured is 324 cm^3.

24. **C**

The volume, V, of each flower pot can be determined by applying the formula $V = \frac{1}{3}(A_{base} \times h)$, in which A_{base} is the area of the base and h is the height of the flower pot.

Step 1
Determine the volume of a type-one flower pot.
The area of the top (base), A_{base}, of a type-one flower pot is $18 \times 18 = 324$ cm^2, and the height, h, of a type-one flower pot is given as $20cm$. The volume of a type-one flower pot can now be determined by applying the formula $V = \frac{1}{3}(A_{base} \times h)$.

Substitute 324 for A_{base} and 20 for h, and then solve for V.
$$V = \frac{1}{3}(324 \times 20)$$
$$V = \frac{1}{3} \times 6\ 480$$
$$V = 2\ 160$$
The volume of a type-one flower pot is 2 160 cm^3.

Step 2

Determine the volume of a type-two flower pot.
The area of the top (base), A_{base}, of a type-two flower pot is $21 \times 19 = 399$ cm^2, and the height of a type-two flower pot is given as 16 cm. The volume of a type-two flower pot can now be determined by applying the formula $V = \frac{1}{3}(A_{base} \times h)$.

Substitute 399 for A_{base} and 16 for h, and then solve for V.

$$V = \frac{1}{3}(399 \times 16)$$

$$V = \frac{1}{3} \times 6\ 384$$

$$V = 2\ 128$$

The volume of a type-two flower pot is 2 128 cm^3.

Step 3

Determine the correct statement from the given alternatives.

The volume of a type-one flower pot is

$2\ 160 - 2\ 128 = 32$ cm^3 more than the volume of a type-two flower pot.

25. **WR**

You can find the volume of the triangular prism by using one of two methods.

Method 1

Find the area of the rectangular prism with the same dimensions, and divide by 2.

$$V = \frac{lwh}{2}$$

$$V = \frac{6 \times 7 \times 3}{2}$$

$$V = \frac{126}{2}$$

$$V = 63 \text{ cm}^3$$

Method 2

Find the area of the triangular base, and multiply that area by the height of the prism.

$$V = Bh$$

$$V = \frac{6 \times 3}{2} \times 7$$

$$V = \frac{18}{2} \times 7$$

$$V = 9 \times 7$$

$$V = 63 \text{ cm}^3$$

UNIT TEST — MEASUREMENT

Use the following information to answer the next question.

One type of concrete block has a length of 40 cm, a width of 20 cm, and a height of 15 cm.

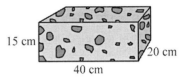

15 cm   20 cm
40 cm

The other type of concrete block has a length of 35 cm, a width of 20 cm, and a height of 20 cm.

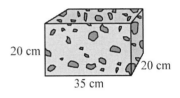

20 cm   20 cm
35 cm

1. What is the difference between the total surface areas of the two types of concrete blocks?

   A. 190 cm^2 **B.** 195 cm^2

   C. 200 cm^2 **D.** 205 cm^2

Use the following information to answer the next question.

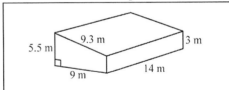

5.5 m   9.3 m   3 m
9 m   14 m

2. What is the surface area of the given trapezoidal prism?

   A. 455.9 m^2 **B.** 451.7 m^2

   C. 447.5 m^2 **D.** 413.4 m^2

Use the following information to answer the next question.

A triangular prism is given.

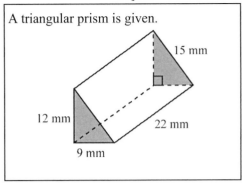

15 mm
12 mm   22 mm
9 mm

Written Response

3. Determine the surface area of the given triangular prism.

Use the following information to answer the next question.

The front wheel of a steam roller is 2 m high and 8 m across.

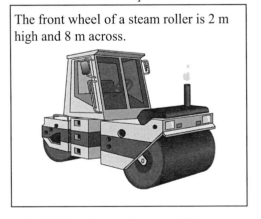

4. What is the entire surface area of the steam roller's front wheel?

   A. 50.25 m^2

   B. 56.52 m^2

   C. 62.74 m^2

   D. 69.36 m^2

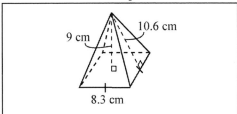

9 cm   10.6 cm

8.3 cm

Written Response

5.   Find the surface area of the given shape to
the tenths place.

The cylinder has a height of 10 cm and a
radius of 2 cm. The rectangular prism has
a height of 9 cm, a width of 3 cm, and a
length of 14 cm.

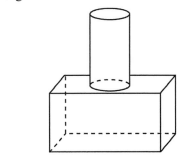

6.   Using $\pi = 3.14$, what is the surface area of
this object to the nearest whole number?

   A. 240 cm^2 **B.** 311 cm^2

   C. 516 cm^2 **D.** 541 cm^2

Jason is having a birthday party, and his
parents bought him a birthday cake.
An overhead view of the birthday cake
with its dimensions are shown in the given
diagram.

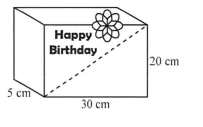

Happy Birthday

20 cm

5 cm

30 cm

7.   What is the surface area of Jason's
birthday cake?

   A. 1 700 cm^2 **B.** 1 800 cm^2

   C. 1 900 cm^2 **D.** 2 000 cm^2

Leigh Ann would like to replace the lining
of her tent. In order to determine how
much lining she will need, she draws a
sketch of the tent, which is in the shape of
a triangular prism.

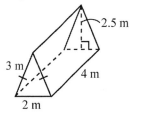

2.5 m

3 m

4 m

2 m

Numerical Response

8.   How much lining will Leigh Ann need to
cover the outside of the tent? _____
m^2

Use the following information to answer the next question.

A cylindrical juice container is constructed with a radius of 6.5 cm and a surface area of 1 225 cm^2.

Numerical Response

9. Expressed to the nearest tenth, the height of the juice container is _____ cm.

Use the following information to answer the next question.

An image of a right circular cone is given.

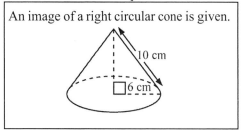

10 cm

□6 cm

10. Rounded to the nearest hundredth, what is the total surface area of this cone?
  A. 301.44 cm^2 **B.** 263.81 cm^2
  C. 122.46 cm^2 **D.** 103.62 cm^2

Use the following information to answer the next question.

A Christmas tree ornament is in the shape of an enclosed rectangular-based pyramid, as shown.

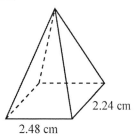

2.24 cm

2.48 cm

Each face with a 2.48 cm base has a slant height of 3.96 cm, and each face with a 2.24 cm base has a slant height of 4 cm.

11. To the nearest whole number, the surface area of the Christmas tree ornament is
  A. 44 cm^2 **B.** 43 cm^2
  C. 24 cm^2 **D.** 23 cm^2

12. The radius of a sphere is 8 cm. Rounded to the nearest whole number, what is the surface area of the sphere?
  A. 810 cm^2 **B.** 804 cm^2
  C. 797 cm^2 **D.** 793 cm^2

Use the following information to answer the next question.

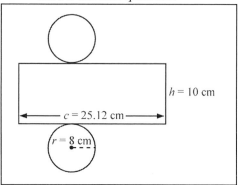

$h = 10$ cm

$c = 25.12$ cm

$r = 8$ cm

Written Response

13. Construct a 3-D shape using the net.

Use the following information to answer the next question.

A sheet-metal company builds a variety of storage tanks and bins for the farming industry. Over the next month, the manufacturing team needs to build 11 grain silos and 6 fuel tanks to fill their orders. Sketches of a silo and a fuel tank are shown.

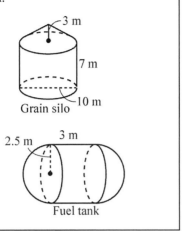

Grain silo

Fuel tank

Numerical Response

14. Rounded to the nearest 100 m^2, what is the total amount of metal needed to fill the orders if the total amount includes an extra 30% added for waste? _____ m^2

Use the following information to answer the next question.

Sarah is making a wooden box to hold her knitting materials. The box will be 45 cm by 26 cm by 20 cm.

Written Response

15. What is the volume of Sarah's knitting box?

Use the following information to answer the next question.

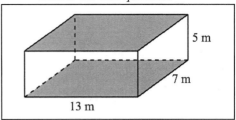

Written Response

16. Calculate the volume of the rectangular prism.

Use the following information to answer the next question.

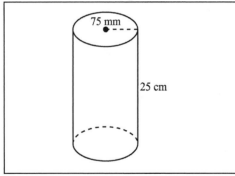

Written Response

17. Calculate the volume of the cylinder.

18. What is the volume of a ball that has a diameter of 24 cm? Use $\pi = 3.14$.

A. 1 848.12 cm^3 **B.** 3 240.28 cm^3

C. 7 234.56 cm^3 **D.** 9 472.84 cm^3

Use the following information to answer the next question.

A cylinder prism is stacked on top of a rectangular prism to form the composite figure illustrated in the diagram.

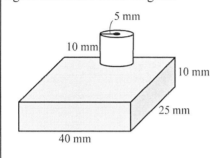

Use $\pi = 3.14$ for all necessary calculations.

Numerical Response

19. The volume of the composite figure, to the nearest whole number, is _____ mm^3.

Use the following information to answer the next question.

The given diagram illustrates one of the ramps in a skateboard park.

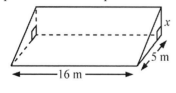

20. If the volume of the ramp shown is 136 m^3, then the value of x to the nearest tenth is

A. 3.4 m   **B.** 3.8 m

C. 4.2 m   **D.** 4.5 m

Use the following information to answer the next question.

The top section of a model rocket is made up of two geometric shapes: a cylinder and a cone.

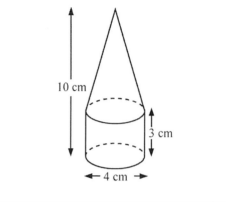

21. If the cone at the top of the model rocket is filled with sand to help stabilize its flight, how much sand could it hold, rounded to the nearest tenth of a cubic centimetre?

A. 27.6 cm^3 **B.** 28.5 cm^3

C. 29.3 cm^3 **D.** 30.1 cm^3

Use the following information to answer the next question.

Grain is piled in a grain bin in the shape of a cone. The pile has a base radius of 20 m and a height of 5.5 m.

Numerical Response

22. What is the volume of grain, to the nearest hundred cubic metres? _____ m^3

23. A pyramid has a base measuring 20 cm by 30 cm and a height of 36 cm. What is the volume of the pyramid?

A. 21 600 cm^3 **B.** 7 200 cm^3

C. 600 cm^3 **D.** 28.7 cm^3

Use the following information to answer the next question.

In order to play a particular game, the sum of the volumes of these two playground balls must be approximately 26.2 dm³.

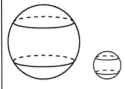

Numerical Response

24. If the radius of the larger ball is 1.7 dm, then, rounded to the nearest tenth of a cubic decimetre, the volume of the smaller ball (where $\pi = 3.14$) must be _____ dm³.

Use the following information to answer the next question.

An insulated container has an inner holding tank that has a diameter of 10 cm and a height of 20 cm. The outer wall is 2 cm larger on either side and on the bottom.

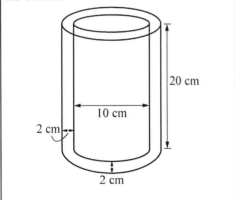

25. Rounded to the nearest unit, what is the volume of the space between the inner holding tank and the outer wall?

A. 1 570 cm³

B. 1 815 cm³

C. 2 123 cm³

D. 3 385 cm³

Use the following information to answer the next question.

Ariel built a model of a square-based Egyptian pyramid for a school science fair project.

Numerical Response

26. If the height of the pyramid is 36 cm and the volume of the pyramid is 21 168 cm³, then the side length of the base of the pyramid is _____ cm.

ANSWERS AND SOLUTIONS — UNIT TEST

1. C	7. A	13. WR	19. 10785	25. B
2. B	8. 29	14. 6600	20. A	26. 42
3. WR	9. 23.5	15. WR	21. C	
4. B	10. A	16. WR	22. 2300	
5. WR	11. C	17. WR	23. B	
6. C	12. B	18. C	24. 5.6	

1. C

Calculate the areas of the three different-sized surfaces on each block. Double each of the areas, since the surfaces come in pairs (top—bottom; front —back; side—opposite side). Add the three products.

Step 1

First block:

$2 \times (20 \times 40) = 1\ 600\ cm^2$

$2 \times (15 \times 40) = 1\ 200\ cm^2$

$2 \times (15 \times 20) = 600\ cm^2$

$1\ 600 + 1\ 200 + 600 = 3\ 400\ cm^2$

Step 2

Second block:

$2 \times (20 \times 35) = 1\ 400\ cm^2$

$2 \times (20 \times 35) = 1\ 400\ cm^2$

$2 \times (20 \times 20) = 800\ cm^2$

$1\ 400 + 1\ 400 + 800 = 3\ 600\ cm^2$

Step 3

Subtract the two surface areas to determine the difference. $3\ 600 - 3\ 400 = 200\ cm^2$

The difference between the two surface areas is $200\ cm^2$.

2. B

Step 1

Draw the net of the shape.

A right trapezoidal prism is made up of four rectangular faces (front, bottom, back, and top in the diagram) that join the two trapezoidal bases (sides).

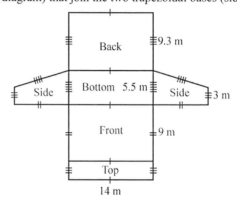

Step 2

Calculate the area of each face.

Solve for the area of each face by applying the appropriate formula.

$A_{sides} = h(b_1 + b_2)$
$\quad\quad = 9(3 + 5.5)$
$\quad\quad = 9(8.5)$
$\quad\quad = 76.5\ m^2$

$A_{front} = lw$
$\quad\quad = (14)(3)$
$\quad\quad = 42\ m^2$

$A_{bottom} = lw$
$\quad\quad\quad = (14)(9)$
$\quad\quad\quad = 126\ m^2$

$A_{back} = lw$
$\quad\quad\ = (14)(5.5)$
$\quad\quad\ = 77\ m^2$

$A_{top} = lw$
$\quad\quad = (14)(9.3)$
$\quad\quad = 130.2\ m^2$

Step 3

Add the areas of the faces.

$SA_{\text{trapezoidal prism}}$
$= A_{\text{sides}} + A_{\text{front}} + A_{\text{bottom}} + A_{\text{back}} + A_{\text{top}}$
$= 76.5 + 42 + 126 + 77 + 130.2$
$= 451.7 \text{ m}^2$

The surface area of the trapezoidal prism is 451.7 m^2.

3. WR

Step 1

Determine the areas of the three rectangular faces using the formula $A = l \times w$.

Although each rectangular face has the same length, they each have a different width. One rectangular face has a width of 9 mm and a length of 22 mm. Another rectangular face has a width of 12 mm and a length of 22 mm. The final rectangular face has a width of 15 mm and a length of 22 mm.

Substitute the appropriate lengths and widths into the formula.

• $A = 9 \text{ mm} \times 22 \text{ mm} = 198 \text{ mm}^2$

• $A = 12 \text{ mm} \times 22 \text{ mm} = 264 \text{ mm}^2$

• $A = 15 \text{ mm} \times 22 \text{ mm} = 330 \text{ mm}^2$

Determine the combined area of the three rectangular faces.

$198 \text{ mm}^2 + 264 \text{ mm}^2 + 330 \text{ mm}^2 = 792 \text{ mm}^2$

Step 2

Determine the area of the triangular base using the formula $A = \dfrac{b \times h}{2}$.

Substitute the length of the triangular base (9 mm) and the height of the triangle (12 mm) into the formula.

$A = \dfrac{9 \text{ mm} \times 12 \text{ mm}}{2} = \dfrac{108 \text{ mm}^2}{2}$

$A = 54 \text{ mm}^2$

Since there are two congruent triangular bases, multiply the area by 2.

$54 \text{ mm}^2 \times 2 = 108 \text{ mm}^2$

Step 3

Determine the surface area.

Add the combined area of the three rectangular faces and the two triangular bases.

$SA = 792 \text{ mm}^2 + 108 \text{ mm}^2$

$SA = 900 \text{ mm}^2$

The surface area of the triangular prism is 900 mm^2.

4. B

Step 1

Draw the net.

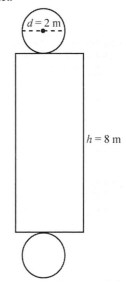

Step 2

Calculate the radius.

$r = \dfrac{d}{2} = \dfrac{2}{2} = 1 \text{ m}$

Step 3

Calculate the surface area of the front wheel.

Determine the areas of all the faces that make up the front wheel.

$A_{\text{circles}} = 2(\pi \times r^2)$
$\qquad = 2(3.14 \times 1^2)$
$\qquad = 2(3.14)$
$\qquad = 6.28$

$A_{\text{rectangle}} = h \times \pi d$
$\qquad = 8 \times 3.14 \times 2$
$\qquad = 50.24$

Add up all the areas.

$SA_{\text{cylinder}} = A_{\text{circles}} + A_{\text{rectangle}}$
$\qquad = 6.28 + 50.24$
$\qquad = 56.52 \text{ m}^2$

The surface area of the steam roller's front wheel is 56.52 m^2.

5. WR

The formula used to calculate the surface area of a square-based pyramid is $SA = b^2 + 2(bs)$.

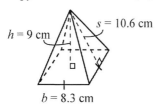

$s = 10.6$ cm
$h = 9$ cm
$b = 8.3$ cm

Substitute 8.3 for b and 10.6 for s, and then simplify.

$$SA_{\text{square prism}} = b^2 + 2(bs)$$
$$= (8.3)^2 + 2(8.3 \times 10.6)$$
$$= (8.3 \times 8.3) + 2(8.3 \times 10.6)$$
$$= (68.89) + 2(87.98)$$
$$= 68.89 + 175.96$$
$$= 244.85$$
$$\approx 244.9 \text{cm}^2$$

6. C

Step 1

Calculate the surface area of the rectangular prism.

$$SA = 2lw + 2lh + 2wh$$
$$= 2(14 \times 3) + 2(14 \times 9) + 2(3 \times 9)$$
$$= 2(42) + 2(126) + 2(27)$$
$$= 84 + 252 + 54$$
$$= 390 \text{ cm}^2$$

The surface area of the rectangular prism is 390 cm².

Step 2

Calculate the surface area of the cylinder.

$$SA = 2\pi r^2 + 2\pi rh$$
$$= 2(3.14)(2^2) + 2(2)(3.14)(10)$$
$$= 2(3.14)(4) + 2(2)(3.14)(10)$$
$$= 25.12 + 125.60$$
$$= 150.72\backslash \text{ cm}^2$$

The surface area of the cylinder is 150.72 cm².

Step 3

Calculate the area of overlap.

The area of overlap occurs at the point at which both objects connect. The area of overlap is two times the area of the circular base of the cylinder. The area of overlap is subtracted from the total surface area of the composite object because it is not an exposed surface but hidden within the object.

$$A = 2\pi r^2$$
$$= 2(3.14)(2^2)$$
$$= 2(3.14)(4)$$
$$= 25.12 \text{ cm}^2$$

The area of overlap is 25.12 cm².

Step 4

Calculate the surface area of the object.

Add the surface area of the cylinder to the surface area of the rectangular prism, and subtract the area of overlap.

$$SA_{\text{composite object}}$$
$$= SA_{\text{cylinder}} + SA_{\text{rectangular prism}} - A_{\text{overlap}}$$
$$= 390 + 150.72 - 25.12$$
$$= 515.60 \text{ cm}^2$$

The surface area of the composite 3-D object to the nearest whole number is 516 cm².

7. A

Step 1

Calculate the area of each face.

In the diagram, the following faces are the same size: the top and the bottom, the front and the back, and the two sides.

Therefore, the area of each of these pairs of faces can be found by calculating the area of one face and multiplying by 2.

$$A_{\text{front and back}} = 2(lw)$$
$$= 2(30 \times 5)$$
$$= 2(150)$$
$$= 300 \text{ cm}^2$$

$$A_{\text{sides}} = 2(lw)$$
$$= 2(5 \times 20)$$
$$= 2(100)$$
$$= 200 \text{ cm}^2$$

$$A_{\text{top and bottom}} = 2(lw)$$
$$= 2(30 \times 20)$$
$$= 2(600)$$
$$= 1\ 200 \text{ cm}^2$$

Step 2

Calculate the total surface area.

Add the areas of the faces.

$$SA_{\text{rectangular prism}}$$
$$= A_{\text{top and bottom}} + A_{\text{sides}} + A_{\text{front and back}}$$
$$= 1\ 200 + 200 + 300$$
$$= 1\ 700 \text{ cm}^2$$

The surface area of Jason's cake is 1 700 cm².

8. 29

The lining must cover the total surface area of the tent, excluding the bottom rectangular face.

Step 1

Draw the net of the triangular prism.

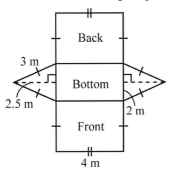

Step 2

Calculate the area of the faces of the tent.

The front and back rectangular faces of the net are the same size. The two triangular sides are the same size as well.

Find the area for one of each face shape and multiply by 2.

$$A_{\text{front and back}} = 2(l \times w)$$
$$= 2(4 \times 3)$$
$$= 2(12)$$
$$= 24$$

$$A_{\text{triangles}} = 2\left(\frac{bh}{2}\right)$$
$$= (2)\left(\frac{2 \times 2.5}{2}\right)$$
$$= 2(2.5)$$
$$= 5$$

Step 3

Calculate the total surface area.

$$SA_{\text{tent}} = A_{\text{front and back}} + A_{\text{triangles}}$$
$$= 24 + 5$$
$$= 29 \text{ m}^2$$

The amount of lining needed to cover the outside of the tent is 29 m².

9. 23.5

Substitute 6.5 for r, 3.14 for π, and 1 225 for SA in the formula $SA = 2\pi r^2 + 2\pi rh$. Solve for h.

$$1\ 225 \approx 2(3.14)(6.5)^2 + 2(3.14)(6.5)h$$
$$1\ 225 \approx 265.33 + 40.82h$$
$$959.67 \approx 40.82h$$
$$h \approx 23.5$$

The height of the cylindrical juice container is about 23.5 cm.

10. A

Determine the total surface area of a cone by adding the areas of the circular base and lateral face. Use 3.14 as an approximation to π.

$$SA_{\text{cone}} = A_{\text{base}} + A_{\text{lateral face}}$$
$$= \pi r^2 + r\pi s$$
$$= \pi(6)^2 + (6 \times \pi \times 10)$$
$$= (3.14 \times 36)$$
$$\quad + (6 \times 3.14 \times 10)$$
$$= 113.04 + 188.4$$
$$= 301.44$$
$$SA_{\text{cone}} = 301.44 \text{ cm}^2$$

The total surface area of the cone is 301.44 cm².

11. C

The surface area, SA, of a pyramid can be determined by applying the formula $SA = A_{\text{base}} + A_{\text{lateral faces}}$, where A_{base} is the area of the base and $A_{\text{lateral faces}}$ is the area of the lateral faces.

Step 1

Determine the area of the base of the Christmas tree ornament.

Since the base of the ornament is in the shape of a rectangle, the area, A, of the base can be determined by applying the formula $A = lw$, where l is the length and w is the width of the rectangle.

$A = lw$

Substitute 2.48 for l and 2.24 for w, and then solve for A.

$$A = 2.48 \times 2.24$$
$$A = 5.5552 \text{ cm}^2$$

Step 2

Determine the area of the lateral faces of the Christmas tree ornament.

Two of the lateral faces are triangular in shape, have bases that are 2.48 cm long, and have slant heights of 3.96 cm.

The other two lateral faces are triangular in shape, have bases that are 2.24 cm long, and have slant heights of 4 cm.

The area of each triangle can be determined by applying the formula $A = \frac{1}{2}bh$, where b is the length of the base and h is the slant height.

If A_1 is the area of the two lateral faces that have 2.48 cm bases and A_2 is the area of the two lateral faces that have 2.24 cm bases, then the area, A, of the lateral faces of the Christmas tree ornament can be determined as follows:

$A = A_1 + A_2$

$A = 2\left(\frac{1}{2}bh\right) + 2\left(\frac{1}{2}bh\right)$

$A = \left(\begin{array}{c} 2\left(\frac{1}{2} \times 2.48 \times 3.96\right) \\ + 2\left(\frac{1}{2} \times 2.24 \times 4\right) \end{array} \right)$

$A = 2(4.9104) + 2(4.48)$

$A = 9.8208 + 8.96$

$A = 18.7808 \text{ cm}^2$

Step 3

Determine the surface area of the Christmas tree ornament.

Apply the formula $SA = A_{\text{base}} + A_{\text{lateral faces}}$.

Substitute 5.5552 for A_{base} and 18.7808 for $A_{\text{lateral faces}}$.

$SA = 5.5552 + 18.7808$

$SA = 24.336$

To the nearest whole number, the surface area of the Christmas tree ornament is 24 cm^2.

12. B

Determine the surface area of the sphere by using the formula $SA_{\text{sphere}} = 4\pi r^2$.

Substitute 3.14 for π and 8 for r.

$SA_{\text{sphere}} = 4\pi r^2$

$SA_{\text{sphere}} \approx 4 \times 3.14 \times (8)^2$

$SA_{\text{sphere}} \approx 4 \times 3.14 \times 64$

$SA_{\text{sphere}} \approx 803.84$

$SA_{\text{sphere}} \approx 804 \text{ cm}^2$

13. WR

A cylinder is made up of one rectangular face that goes around two circle bases. Since the radius of each circle base is 8 cm, the diameter of each circle base will be 16 cm.

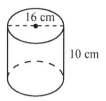

14. 6600

Step 1

Determine the slant height, s, of the conical top of the grain silo by applying the Pythagorean theorem.

$a^2 + b^2 = s^2$

$3^2 + 5^2 = s^2$

$9 + 25 = s^2$

$\sqrt{34} = s$

$5.83 \approx s$

Step 2

Determine the surface area of the grain silo.

$SA_{\text{grain silo}} = SA_{\text{cylinder(no top)}} + SA_{\text{cone(no bottom)}}$

$= \left[2\pi r^2 + 2\pi rh - \pi r^2 \right] + \left[\pi r^2 + \pi rs - \pi r^2 \right]$

$= \left[\pi r^2 + 2\pi rh \right] + \left[\pi rs \right]$

Substitute 5 for r, 7 for h, and 5.83 for s.

$SA_{\text{grain silo}} \approx \left[\pi(5^2) + 2\pi(5)(7) \right] + \left[\pi(5)(5.83) \right]$

$\approx \left[25\pi + 70\pi \right] + \left[29.15\pi \right]$

$\approx 124.15\pi$

$\approx 390.0 \text{ m}^2$

Step 3

Determine the surface area of the fuel tank.

$SA_{\text{fuel tank}} = SA_{\text{2 half-spheres}} + SA_{\text{cylinder(no bases)}}$

$= \left[4\pi r^2 \right] + \left[2\pi r^2 + 2\pi rh - 2\pi r^2 \right]$

$= 4\pi r^2 + 2\pi rh$

Substitute 2.5 for r and 3 for h.

$SA_{\text{fuel tank}} = 4\pi(2.5)^2 + 2\pi(2.5)(3)$

$= 25\pi + 15\pi$

$= 40\pi$

$\approx 125.7 \text{ m}^2$

Step 4

Determine the total surface area of 11 grain silos and 6 fuel tanks.

$SA_{\text{11 grain silos,6 fuel tanks}}$

$\approx 11(390.0) + 6(125.7)$

$4\ 290.0 + 754.2$

$5\ 044.2 \text{ m}^2$

Step 5

Determine the total amount of metal required, including the extra 30% added for waste.

$A_{\text{metal}} \approx 5\ 044.2 + 30\%$ of $5\ 044.2$

$A_{\text{metal}} \approx 5\ 044.2 + 0.30(5\ 044.2)$

$A_{\text{metal}} \approx 5\ 044.2 + 1\ 513.26$

$A_{\text{metal}} \approx 6\ 557.5$

$A_{\text{metal}} \approx 6\ 600\ \text{m}^2$

Rounded to the nearest $100\ \text{m}^2$, the total amount of metal needed is $6\ 600\ \text{m}^2$.

15. WR

Step 1

Substitute the known values into the volume formula for a prism.

$V_{\text{rectangular prism}} = lwh$
$\phantom{V_{\text{rectangular prism}}} = 45 \times 26 \times 20$

Step 2

Solve for the volume.

$V_{\text{prism}} = 45 \times 26 \times 20$
$\phantom{V_{\text{prism}}} = 23\ 400\ \text{cm}^3$

16. WR

The shape of the base is a rectangle. The height is the distance between two parallel base faces.

$V_{\text{rectangular base}} = A_{\text{base}} \times h$
$V_{\text{rectangular base}} = A_{\text{rectangle}} \times h$
$\phantom{V_{\text{rectangular base}}} = (l \times w) \times h$
$\phantom{V_{\text{rectangular base}}} = 13 \times 7 \times 5$
$\phantom{V_{\text{rectangular base}}} = 455\ \text{m}^3$

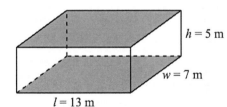

$h = 5\ \text{m}$

$w = 7\ \text{m}$

$l = 13\ \text{m}$

17. WR

Step 1

Convert millimetres to centimetres.

$1\ \text{mm} = 0.1\ \text{cm}$
$75\ \text{mm} = 7.5\ \text{cm}$

Step 2

Calculate the volume.

The shape of the base is a circle. The height is the measured distance between the parallel circles.

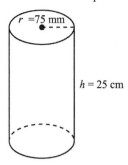

$r = 75\ \text{mm}$

$h = 25\ \text{cm}$

Substitute the known values into the formula and solve following order of operations.

$V = A_{\text{base}} \times h$
$V = A_{\text{circle}} \times h$
$ = \pi r^2 \times h$
$ = 3.14 \times 7.5^2 \times 25$
$ = 3.14 \times 56.25 \times 25$
$ = 4\ 415.63\ \text{cm}^3$

18. C

Step 1

Find the radius of the ball.

The radius of the ball is half the diameter.

$r = \dfrac{d}{2} = \dfrac{24}{2} = 12\ \text{cm}$

Step 2

Use the radius of the ball to calculate the volume of the ball.

$V_{\text{sphere}} = \dfrac{4\pi r^3}{3}$

$\phantom{V_{\text{sphere}}} = \dfrac{4 \times 3.14 \times 12^3}{3}$

$\phantom{V_{\text{sphere}}} = \dfrac{4 \times 3.14 \times 1\ 728}{3}$

$\phantom{V_{\text{sphere}}} = \dfrac{21\ 703.68}{3}$

$\phantom{V_{\text{sphere}}} = 7\ 234.56\ \text{cm}^3$

The volume of the ball is $7\ 234.56\ \text{cm}^3$.

19. 10785

Step 1

Calculate the volume of the rectangular prism using the formula

$V = $ area of the base $\times$ height of object
$V = (l \times w) \times$ height
$V = (40 \times 25) \times 10$
$V = 1\ 000 \times 10$
$V = 10\ 000\ \text{mm}^3$

Step 2

Calculate the volume of the cylinder using the formula

V = area of the base × height of object

$V = \pi r^2 \times$ height

$V = (3.14)(5)^2 \times 10$

$V = (3.14)(25) \times 10$

$V = 78.5 \times 10$

$V = 785 \text{ mm}^3$

Step 3

Find the total volume of the composite figure using the formula

Volume = rectangular prism + cylinder prism.

$V = 10\ 000 + 785 = 10\ 785$

The total volume of the composite figure is 10 785 mm³

20. **A**

The skateboard ramp is in the shape of a triangular prism. In order to determine its volume, it is necessary to consider one of the triangular faces as the base of the ramp.

Step 1

Determine an expression for the area of the base of the ramp by applying the formula for the area of a triangle, $A = \dfrac{bh}{2}$.

Substitute 5 for b and x for h, and then simplify as follows:

$A = \dfrac{bh}{2}$

$A = \dfrac{5 \times x}{2}$

$A = 2.5x$

Step 2

Solve for x by applying the formula for the volume of a triangular prism, $V = A_{\text{base}} \times h$.

Substitute $2.5x$ for A_{base}, 16 for h, and 136 for V, and then solve for x as follows:

$V = A_{\text{base}} \times h$

$136 = (2.5x)(16)$

$136 = 40x$

$3.4 = x$

The value of x is 3.4 m.

21. **C**

Step 1

Determine the radius of the cone's circular base.

$r = \dfrac{d}{2}$

$= \dfrac{4}{2}$

$= 2 \text{ cm}$

Step 2

Determine the height of the cone.

$h_{\text{cone}} = h_{\text{rocket}} - h_{\text{cylinder}}$

$= 10 - 3$

$= 7 \text{ cm}$

Step 3

Calculate the volume of the cone. Use 3.14 as an approximation to π.

$V_{\text{cone}} = \dfrac{\pi r^2 h}{3}$

$\cong \dfrac{(3.14)(2)^2(7)}{3}$

$\cong \dfrac{(3.14)(4)(7)}{3}$

$\cong \dfrac{87.92}{3}$

$\cong 29.3 \text{ cm}^3$

The cone at the top of the model rocket could be filled with 29.3 cm³ of sand.

22. **2300**

Step 1

Substitute the known values into the formula

$V_{\text{cone}} = \dfrac{(\pi r^2)h}{3}$.

$V_{\text{cone}} \approx \dfrac{(3.14 \times 20^2)(5.5)}{3}$

Step 2

Solve for the unknown variable.

$V_{\text{cone}} \approx \dfrac{(3.14 \times 400)(5.5)}{3}$

$V_{\text{cone}} \approx \dfrac{6\ 908}{3}$

$V_{\text{cone}} \approx 2\ 302.66$

Rounded to the nearest hundred cubic meters, the volume of grain is 2 300 m³.

23. **B**

Step 1

Substitute the given values in the volume formula for a pyramid.

$V = \dfrac{lwh}{3}$

$= \dfrac{(20)(30)(36)}{3}$

Step 2

Calculate the volume of the pyramid.

$V = \dfrac{21\ 600}{3}$

$= 7\ 200 \text{ cm}^3$

24. 5.6

Step 1

Determine the volume of the larger playground ball (V_1) by applying the formula for the volume of a sphere.

Substitute 3.14 for π and 1.7 for r in the formula $V = \frac{4}{3}\pi r^3$, and then solve for V_1.

$$V_1 = \frac{4}{3}\pi r^3$$

$$V_1 = \frac{4 \times 3.14 \times 1.7^3}{3}$$

$$V_1 = \frac{4 \times 3.14 \times 4.913}{3}$$

$$V_1 \approx 20.6$$

Step 2

Determine the volume of the smaller playground ball (V_2).

Since the sum of the volumes of the larger playground ball (V_1) and the smaller playground ball (V_2) is 26.2 dm^3, V_2 can be determined by subtracting V_1 from the sum of $V_1 + V_2$.

$$V_1 + V_2 \approx 26.2$$

$$20.6 + V_2 \approx 26.2$$

$$V_2 \approx 26.2 - 20.6$$

$$V_2 \approx 5.6$$

The volume of the smaller playground ball is approximately 5.6 dm^3.

25. B

Step 1

Calculate the volume of the inner holding tank.

The holding tank is in the shape of a cylinder, so substitute the given values into the volume formula for a cylinder and simplify.

$$\begin{aligned} V_{\text{cylinder}} &= A_{\text{base}} \times h \\ &= A_{\text{circle}} \times h \\ &= \pi r^2 \times h \\ &= 3.14 \times 5^2 \times 20 \\ &= 3.14 \times 25 \times 20 \\ &= 78.5 \times 20 \\ &= 1\ 570 \text{ cm}^3 \end{aligned}$$

Step 2

Calculate the dimensions of the outer wall of the insulated container.

The dimensions of the outer wall of the insulated container are 2 cm larger on either side and on the bottom than the inner walls. That means 4 cm must be added to the diameter and 2 cm to the height.

$$d = 10 + 4 = 14 \text{ cm}$$
$$h = 20 + 2 = 22 \text{ cm}$$

Step 3

Calculate the volume of the outer wall of the insulated container.

The outer wall is in the shape of a cylinder, so substitute the given values into the volume formula for a cylinder and simplify.

$$\begin{aligned} V_{\text{cylinder}} &= A_{\text{base}} \times h \\ &= A_{\text{circle}} \times h \\ &= \pi r^2 \times h \\ &= 3.14 \times 7^2 \times 22 \\ &= 3.14 \times 49 \times 22 \\ &= 153.86 \times 22 \\ &= 3\ 384.92 \text{ cm}^3 \end{aligned}$$

Step 4

Calculate the air space in between the outer wall and the holding tank of the insulated container.

Subtract the volume of the holding tank from the volume of the outer wall.

$$\begin{aligned} V_{\text{air space}} &= V_{\text{outer wall}} - V_{\text{holding tank}} \\ &= 3\ 384.92 - 1\ 570 \\ &= 1\ 814.92 \text{ cm}^3 \end{aligned}$$

Rounded to the nearest unit, the volume of the air space is 1 815 cm^3.

26. 42

The volume, V, of a pyramid can be determined by applying the formula $V = \frac{1}{3}(A_{\text{base}} \times h)$,

where A_{base} is the area of the base and h is the height of the pyramid.

Step 1

Determine an expression for the area of the base of the pyramid.

If x represents the side length of the base of the pyramid, then the area of the base of the pyramid would be represented by the expression $x \times x$, or x^2.

Step 2

Determine the value of x.

Apply the formula $V = \frac{1}{3}\left(A_{\text{base}} \times h\right)$. Substitute 21 168 for V, x^2 for A_{base}, and 36 for h. Then, solve for x.

$$21\ 168 = \frac{1}{3}\left(x^2 \times 36\right)$$
$$21\ 168 = \frac{1}{3}\left(36x^2\right)$$
$$21\ 168 = 12x^2$$
$$\frac{21\ 168}{12} = x^2$$
$$1\ 764 = x^2$$
$$\sqrt{1\ 764} = x$$
$$42 = x$$

The side length of the base of the pyramid is 42 cm.

Geometry

GEOMETRY

Table of Correlations

	Outcome	Practice Questions	Unit Test Questions	Practice Test
20G	Geometry			
20G.1	Solve problems that involve two and three right triangles.	1, 2, 3, 4, 5, 6	1, 2, 3, 4, 5, 6	27, 28, 29
20G.2	Solve problems that involve scale.	7, 8, 9	7, 8, 9	30, 31, 32
20G.3	Model and draw 3-D objects and their views.	10, 11, 12, 13, 14	10, 11, 12	33, 34, 35
20G.4	Draw and describe exploded views, component parts and scale diagrams of simple 3-D objects.			

20G.1 Solve problems that involve two and three right triangles.

USING THE PYTHAGOREAN THEOREM TO FIND THE MISSING SIDE OF A TRIANGLE

The Pythagorean theorem relates the three sides of a right-angled triangle. When two of the lengths on a right-angled triangle are known, the Pythagorean theorem can be used to find the third side.

The Pythagorean theorem is $a^2 + b^2 = c^2$, where a and b are the shorter sides of a triangle, and c is the longest side. The longest side, also called the hypotenuse, is always opposite the right angle.

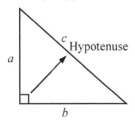

When the missing side of the triangle is the long side, use addition to find the length. The equation $a^2 + b^2 = c^2$ can be used to find the missing long side. If the missing side of the triangle is one of the two shorter sides, the missing side will be shorter than the long side, so the equation $c^2 - a^2 = b^2$ can be used to find the missing side.

Use the following steps to find the missing side of a triangle using the Pythagorean theorem:

1. Identify the values of a, b, and c.
2. Decide whether to add or subtract.
3. Substitute the values into the formula.
4. Solve the equation to find the unknown side.

Example

A triangle is given.

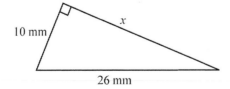

Find the missing side of the triangle.

Solution

Step 1

Identify the values for a, b, and c.

The longest side of the triangle is the 26 mm, so $c = 26$. The unknown side, x, and the 10 mm side are the a- and b-values.

Step 2

Decide whether to add or subtract.

The missing side is one of the short sides of the triangle, so use the formula that includes subtraction $(c^2 - a^2 = b^2)$.

Step 3

Substitute the values into the formula.

$$c^2 - a^2 = b^2$$
$$26^2 - 10^2 = x^2$$

Step 4

Solve the equation to find the unknown side. Take the square root of both sides of the equation in the last step to find the value of x.

$$26^2 - 10^2 = x^2$$
$$676 - 100 = x^2$$
$$576 = x^2$$
$$576 = x^2$$
$$\sqrt{576} = \sqrt{x^2}$$
$$24 = x$$

The missing side is 24 mm long.

20G.1 Solve problems that involve two and three right triangles.

USING THE PYTHAGOREAN THEOREM TO SOLVE PROBLEMS

The Pythagorean theorem can be used to solve many different types of problems. Usually, drawing a diagram to illustrate the problem is the first step in solving the question. A diagram can help identify where the right-angle triangle is and where the hypotenuse and legs of the triangle are.

Example
Trevor wants to put shingles on the roof of his carport. He knows the carport is 4 m wide and 4.5 m high at its tallest point. He also knows that it is 3 m from the ground to where the roof starts. He needs to know the slant height of the roof of the carport so that he can find the area of the roof. He draws a diagram to show this.

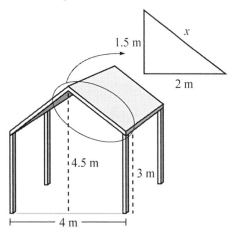

He finds that the right-angle triangle that is formed has a width of 2 m because it is half the width of the carport, and the height of the triangle is 1.5 m because 4.5 − 3 = 1.5. These are the legs of the triangle. The unknown length is the hypotenuse. The unknown length can be calculated as follows:

$$a^2 + b^2 = c^2$$
$$2^2 + 1.5^2 = c^2$$
$$6.25 = c^2$$
$$\sqrt{6.25} = \sqrt{c^2}$$
$$2.5 = c$$

The slant height of the roof of the carport is 2.5 m.

Use the following steps to solve a problem using the Pythagorean theorem:

1. Draw a diagram to illustrate the problem.
2. Substitute the known values into the equation $a^2 + b^2 = c^2$.
3. Simplify the equation, and square root both sides to find the missing side.

Example
Carolyn is making a triangular garden in her back yard. The right-angled corner of her garden has sides that are 2 m and 3 m long.

Rounded to the tenths place, how long is the other side of the triangular garden?

Solution

Step 1
Draw and label a figure that illustrates the problem.
Label the sides making the right angle as *a* and *b*. The other side (the side not making the right angle) will be side *c* because it is opposite the right angle.

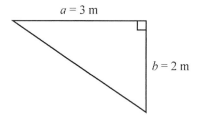

Step 2
Substitute the known values into the Pythagorean theorem, and solve for the unknown.
Simplify by following the order of operations.

$$a^2 + b^2 = c^2$$
$$3^2 + 2^2 = c^2$$
$$9 + 4 = c^2$$
$$13 = c^2$$
$$\sqrt{13} = \sqrt{c^2}$$
$$3.605\,551\,275 = c$$

The other side of the garden is 3.6 m.

Geometry   94   Castle Rock Research

20G.1 Solve problems that involve two and three right triangles.

SOLVING PROBLEMS USING THE SINE RATIO

The sine ratio can be used to solve problems involving the measures of sides and angles in real-life applications. When solving these types of problems, the following definitions are helpful to remember:

- The **angle of elevation** is upward from the horizontal.
- The **angle of depression** is downward from the horizontal.

Example

A 12 m ladder is leaning against a building. The angle formed between the ladder and the ground is 40°.

Rounded to the nearest tenth, how far is the top of the ladder from the ground?

Solution

Step 1

Draw a diagram that represents the information given in the problem.

Use variables to indicate the measure of the sides you are trying to find.

The length of the ladder is represented by the hypotenuse of the triangle.

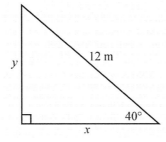

Step 2

Identify the ratio to use in order to solve for y.

Start from the given angle, which is 40°.

Side y is the opposite side since it is across from the given angle, and the side measuring 12 m is the hypotenuse.

The trigonometric ratio that compares the length of the opposite side to the length of the hypotenuse is sine.

$$\sin \theta = \frac{\text{opposite}}{\text{hypotenuse}}$$

Step 3

Substitute the known values from the triangle into the sine ratio.

$$\sin 40° = \frac{y}{12}$$

Step 4

Find the decimal equivalent to sin 40°.

Type in $\boxed{4}\ \boxed{0}$, and then press $\boxed{\sin}$ or type in $\boxed{\text{SIN}}\ \boxed{4}\ \boxed{0}\ \boxed{\text{ENTER}}$.

The screen will show 0.642 787 6097.

The decimal equivalent, to 3 decimal places, for sin40° is 0.643.

Step 5

Write the equivalent ratios.

Substitute 0.643 for sin 40°, and place it over 1.

$$\frac{0.643}{1} = \frac{y}{12}$$

Step 6

Use cross products to solve for y.

$$0.643 \times 12 = y \times 1$$
$$7.716 = y$$

The value of y can also be determined by using your calculator and typing $\boxed{4}\ \boxed{0}\ \boxed{\sin}\ \boxed{\times}\ \boxed{1}$ $\boxed{2}\ \boxed{=}$ or typing $\boxed{\sin}\ \boxed{(}\ \boxed{4}\ \boxed{0}\ \boxed{)}\ \boxed{\times}\ \boxed{1}\ \boxed{2}$ $\boxed{\text{ENTER}}$, depending on your calculator.

Rounded to the nearest tenth, the top of the ladder is 7.7 m above the ground.

Example

To the nearest degree, find the angle of elevation of a ramp that is 15 m long if the top end of the ramp is 2 m above the ground.

Solution

Step 1

Draw a diagram that represents the information given in the problem.

Use a variable to indicate the measure of the angle you are trying to find.

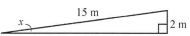

Step 2

Identify the ratio to use in order to solve for x. Start from angle x.

The side measuring 2 m is the opposite side, since it is across angle x. The side measuring 15 m is the hypotenuse. The trigonometric ratio that compares the length of the opposite side to the length of the hypotenuse is sine.

$$\sin \theta = \frac{\text{opposite}}{\text{hypotenuse}}$$

Step 3

Substitute the known values from the triangle into the sine ratio.

$$\sin x = \frac{2}{15}$$

Step 4

Calculate the measure of angle x by using the $\sin^{-1}$ button on the calculator.

Type in $\boxed{2}$ $\boxed{\div}$ $\boxed{1}$ $\boxed{5}$ $\boxed{=}$

The screen will show $0.1\bar{3}$.

Then, type in $\boxed{0}$ $\boxed{.}$ $\boxed{1}$ $\boxed{3}$ $\boxed{3}$ $\boxed{\text{SHIFT}}$ $\boxed{\sin^{-1}}$

or type in $\boxed{\text{2ND}}$ $\boxed{\sin^{-1}}$ $\boxed{.}$ $\boxed{1}$ $\boxed{3}$ $\boxed{3}$

$\boxed{\text{ENTER}}$, depending on your calculator.

The screen will show 7.642 985 44.

To the nearest degree, the angle of elevation of the ramp is 8°.

20G.1 Solve problems that involve two and three right triangles.

SOLVING PROBLEMS USING THE COSINE RATIO

The cosine ratio can be used to solve problems involving the measures of sides and angles in real-life applications. When solving these types of problems, the following definitions are helpful to remember:

- The **angle of elevation** is upward from the horizontal.
- The **angle of depression** is downward from the horizontal.

Example

Rounded to the nearest tenth, how far is the base of the ladder from the building?

Solution

Step 1

Draw a diagram that represents the information given in the problem.

Use variables to indicate the measure of the sides you are trying to find.

The length of the ladder is represented by the hypotenuse of the triangle.

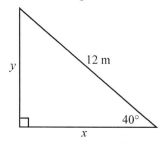

Step 2

Identify the ratio to use in order to solve for x.

Start from the given angle, which is 40°.

Side x is the adjacent side since it it next to the given angle, and the side measuring 12 m is the hypotenuse.

The trigonometric ratio that compares the length of the adjacent side to the length of the hypotenuse is cosine.

$$\cos \theta = \frac{\text{adjacent}}{\text{hypotenuse}}$$

Step 3

Substitute the known values from the triangle into the cosine ratio.

$$\cos 40° = \frac{x}{12}$$

Step 4

Find the decimal equivalent of cos 40°.

Type in $\boxed{4}\,\boxed{0}$, and then press $\boxed{\cos}$ or type in $\boxed{\text{COS}}\,\boxed{4}\,\boxed{0}\,\boxed{\text{ENTER}}$, depending on your calculator.

The screen will show 0.766 044 4431.

The decimal equivalent, to three decimal places, for cos 40° is 0.766.

Step 5

Write the equivalent ratios.

Substitute 0.766 for cos 40°, and place it over 1.

$$\frac{0.766}{1} = \frac{x}{12}$$

Step 6

Use cross products to solve for x.

$$0.766 \times 12 = x \times 1$$
$$9.192 = x$$

Note: The value of x can be determined in one step by using your calculator and typing $\boxed{4}\,\boxed{0}$ $\boxed{\cos}\,\boxed{\times}\,\boxed{12}\,\boxed{=}$ or typing $\boxed{\text{COS}}\,\boxed{(}\,\boxed{4}\,\boxed{0}\,\boxed{)}\,\boxed{\times}\,\boxed{12}\,\boxed{\text{ENTER}}$, depending on your calculator.

The base of the ladder is 9.2 m from the building.

20G.1 Solve problems that involve two and three right triangles.

Solving Problems Using the Tangent Ratio

The tangent ratio can be used to solve problems involving the measures of sides and angles in real-life applications. When solving these types of problems, the following definitions are helpful to remember:

- The **angle of elevation** is upward from the horizontal.
- The **angle of depression** is downward from the horizontal.

Example

A helicopter is involved in an air rescue mission of a sinking sailboat. The pilot determines that the angle of depression from the helicopter to the sailboat is 15°. The helicopter is flying at an altitude of 800 m.

What is the horizontal distance from the helicopter to the sailboat, to the nearest tenth of a metre?

Solution

Step 1

Draw a diagram that represents the information given in the problem.

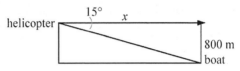

Step 2

Identify the ratio to use in order to solve for x. Start from the given angle which is 15°.

The side measuring 800 m is the opposite side since it is across from the given angle. The side labelled x is the adjacent side since it is next to the given angle and is not the hypotenuse.

The trigonometric ratio that compares the length of the opposite side to the length of the adjacent is tangent.

$$\tan \theta = \frac{\text{opposite}}{\text{adjacent}}$$

Step 3

Substitute the known values from the triangle into the tangent ratio.

$$\tan 15° = \frac{800}{x}$$

Step 4

Find the decimal equivalent to tan 15°.

Type in $\boxed{1}\,\boxed{5}$, and then press $\boxed{\tan}$ or $\boxed{\text{TAN}}\,\boxed{1}\,\boxed{5}\,\boxed{\text{ENTER}}$, depending on your calculator.

The screen will show 0.267 949 1924.

The decimal equivalent, to 3 decimal places, for tan 15° is 0.268.

Step 5

Write the equivalent ratios.

Substitute 0.268 for tan 15° and place it over 1.

$$\frac{0.268}{1} = \frac{800}{x}$$

Step 6

Use cross products to solve for x.

$0.268 \times x = 800 \times 1$

$0.268x = 800$

Divide both sides by 0.268.

$$\frac{0.268x}{0.268} = \frac{800}{0.268}$$

$x = 2\ 985.074\ 627$

Rounded to the nearest tenth of a metre, the horizontal distance from the helicopter to the sailboat is 2 985.1 m.

20G.1 Solve problems that involve two and three right triangles.

SOLVING PROBLEMS BY APPLYING THE PRIMARY TRIGONOMETRIC RATIOS AND THE PYTHAGOREAN THEOREM

The primary trigonometric ratios and the Pythagorean theorem can be used to solve problems involving the measures of sides and angles in real-life applications. When solving these types of problems, recall these key definitions:

- The **angle of elevation** is up from the horizontal.
- The **angle of depression** is down from the horizontal.

Example

A cat watches a bird in a tree. The cat is sitting 7.1 m from the base of the tree. The bird is at an angle of elevation of 40° from the cat.

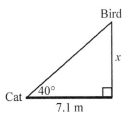

How high up in the tree is the bird?

$\tan 40° = \dfrac{x}{7.1}$

$x = 7.1 \tan 40°$

$x \approx 6.0$ m

The bird is 6.0 m from the ground.

Example

Lexi is standing in her yard. She sees a cat sitting directly west of her. Directly east of her is a dog. Lexi's eye level is 1.48 m high. To look directly at where the cat is sitting, she looks down at an angle of depression of 30°. To the dog, the angle of depression is 25°.

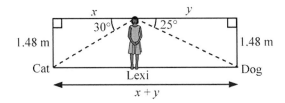

How far apart are the cat and dog?

Notice that $x + y$ at eye level will be the same as $x + y$ on the ground.

The distance between the cat and dog = $x + y$.

$\tan 30° = \dfrac{1.48}{x}$

$x = \dfrac{1.48}{\tan 30°}$

$\tan 25° = \dfrac{1.48}{y}$

$y = \dfrac{1.48}{\tan 25°}$

distance = $x + y$

$ = \dfrac{1.48}{\tan 30°} + \dfrac{1.48}{\tan 25°}$

$ \approx 5.74$ m

The cat and the dog are 5.74 m apart.

20G.1 Solve problems that involve two and three right triangles.

CALCULATING UNKNOWN VALUES USING TWO RIGHT TRIANGLES

Many trigonometry questions require more than one calculation in order to determine the desired information. In some cases, the order of these calculations is not important, while in others, the order is crucial to determine the unknown values.

Some general problem-solving steps are as follows:

1. Read the problem carefully. Determine which measures are given and which measure needs to be calculated.
2. If a diagram is not given, draw a sketch to represent the situation presented in the problem.
3. Examine the diagram to decide which primary trigonometric ratio to apply.
4. Make substitutions into the appropriate formula, and use correct algebraic steps to solve for the unknown value. Avoid or minimize rounding until the last step.
5. Check your calculations.
6. Write a concluding statement.

Some of these problem-solving suggestions are used in the following problems.

Example

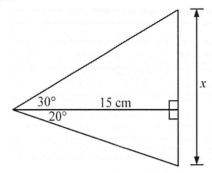

Calculate the value of *x*, to the nearest hundredth, in the given diagram.

Solution

In order to determine the entire length of *x*, the question must be broken down into two separate calculations. First, label (assign variables to) the first lengths that can be calculated.

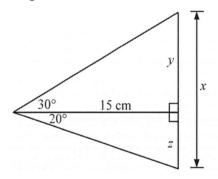

The value of *x* is equal to the sum of *y* and *z*.
$x = y + z$

It does not matter which length, *y* or *z*, is calculated first.

Use the tangent ratio to calculate the measure of *y* and *z*.

$$\tan 30° = \frac{y}{15}$$
$$y = 15(\tan 30°)$$
$$y \approx 8.66 \text{ cm}$$
$$\tan 20° = \frac{z}{15}$$
$$z = 15(\tan 20°)$$
$$z \approx 5.46 \text{ cm}$$

In order to avoid rounding errors, the expressions for y and z can be substituted into the equation $x = y + z$. Rounding will only need to be done at the end of the question.

$x = y + z$
$x = 15(\tan 30°) + 15(\tan 20°)$
$x \approx 14.12$ cm

In the following problem, the use of two primary trigonometric ratios is applied.

Example

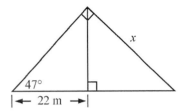

Calculate the value of x to the nearest tenth of a metre.

Solution

Step 1

Label the measures of the unknown angles. These can be determined by applying the fact that the sum of angles in a triangle total 180°.

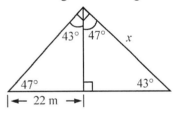

Step 2

Calculate the measure of another unknown side so that the value of x can be determined.

Label the two unknown sides y and z as shown.

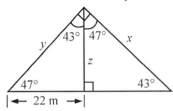

The value of x can be calculated once the measure of either y or z are known. The measure of z will be calculated in this example.

Use the tangent ratio to calculate the length of z.

$\tan 47° = \dfrac{z}{22}$
$z = 22(\tan 47°)$
$z \approx 23.6$ m

Step 3

Find the measure of x using the exact value of z or the expression for z.

$\sin 43° = \dfrac{z}{x}$
$x(\sin 43°) = z$
$x = \dfrac{z}{\sin 43°}$
$x = \dfrac{22(\tan 47°)}{\sin 43°}$
$x \approx 34.6$ m

The length of side x is about 34.6 m.

20G.2 Solve problems that involve scale.

INTERPRETING SCALE DRAWINGS

A **scale drawing**, such as a blueprint or a map, is made when the actual dimensions of an object are either too small or too big to draw clearly.

To interpret a scale drawing, refer to the scale that has been provided with the image. The scale used in a scale drawing is a **ratio** that compares two units of measurement: one unit is used to measure the actual dimensions of an object, and the other unit is used to measure the dimensions of the drawing that represents the object. For example, the scale on a map might be given as 1 inch:10 miles. This means that 1 inch on the map is being used to represent 10 miles in real life.

The information provided in a scale drawing can be used to calculate the measurement of objects that have been represented in the drawing. To use a scale drawing in this way, set up a **proportion** between the ratios that compare the relationship between the units used to measure the actual object and the units used to measure its representation, and then solve for the unknown measurement.

Example

An interior designer wants to show the possible furniture placement in a room to a client. The designer makes a scale drawing.

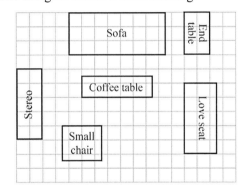

The scale is 1 square:14 inches.

What is the actual length of the sofa in feet and inches?

Solution

Step 1

Set up the proportion.

Write an equation using x to represent the actual length of the sofa.

$$\frac{7.5 \text{ squares}}{1 \text{ square}} = \frac{x \text{ inches}}{14 \text{ inches}}$$

Step 2

Solve for the value of x.

Apply the cross-product strategy to solve.

$$1x = 14 \text{ in} \times 7.5$$
$$x = 14 \text{ in} \times 7.5$$
$$x = 105 \text{ inches}$$

The real sofa is 105 inches in length.

Step 3

Determine the number of feet.

Use the scale of 12 inches = 1 foot.

Write an equation using proportions and solve.

$$\frac{x \text{ ft}}{1 \text{ ft}} = \frac{105 \text{ in}}{12 \text{ in}}$$
$$x = \frac{1 \times 105}{12}$$
$$x = 8.75 \text{ ft}$$

The actual measure of the sofa is 8.75 feet. The measure needs to be in feet and inches.

Step 4

Change 0.75 feet into inches.

Write an equation using proportions and solve.

$$\frac{0.75 \text{ ft}}{1 \text{ ft}} = \frac{x \text{ in}}{12 \text{ in}}$$
$$0.75 \times 12 = 1x$$
$$9 \text{ in} = x$$

The actual measurement of the sofa is 8.75 feet = 8 feet 9 inches.

20G.2 Solve problems that involve scale.

ENLARGEMENTS OF TWO-DIMENSIONAL SHAPES

Scale drawings are used when objects are too large or too small to be drawn on a piece of paper.

The **scale factor** between the original shape and the new image is a number that indicates how much larger or smaller the shape was made. The scale factor can be calculated using the formula

$$\text{scale factor} = \frac{\text{image length}}{\text{original length}}.$$

If the scale factor is greater than 1, the image will be an **enlargement** of the original shape. In other words, the new image will be larger than the original figure.

Knowing the scale factor makes it possible to draw the image of a diagram. To draw a scale diagram, use the following steps:

1. Draw and label the original figure.
2. Use the scale factor formula to determine the length of each side in the image diagram.
3. Draw and label the image diagram. Use the prime symbol (′) to indicate that this is the image.
4. Join each original point to its corresponding point on the image, and label the scale factor on the diagram.

Example

Isosceles triangle *ABC* has two legs measuring 2 cm and a base measuring 1.3 cm. Using a scale factor of 2.5, draw the image of the triangle.

Solution

Step 1

Draw and label the original figure.

Step 2

Use the scale factor formula to determine the length of each side in the image diagram.

Two legs of the original triangle measure 2 cm.

$$\text{scale factor} = \frac{\text{image length}}{\text{original length}}$$

$$2.5 = \frac{A'C'}{2}$$

$$2(2.5) = 2\left(\frac{A'C'}{2}\right)$$

$$5 = A'C'$$

The base of the original triangle measures 1.3 cm.

$$\text{scale factor} = \frac{\text{image length}}{\text{original length}}$$

$$2.5 = \frac{B'C'}{1.3}$$

$$1.3(2.5) = 1.3\left(\frac{B'C'}{1.3}\right)$$

$$3.25 = B'C'$$

The image triangle has two legs measuring 5 cm and a base measuring 3.25 cm.

Step 3

Draw and label the image diagram. Use the prime symbol (′) to indicate that this is the image.

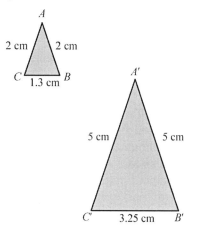

Step 4

Join each original point to its corresponding point on the image, and label the scale factor on the diagram.

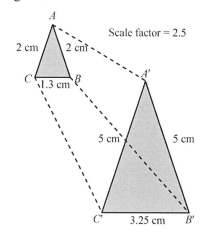

20G.2 Solve problems that involve scale.

REDUCTIONS OF TWO-DIMENSIONAL SHAPES

Scale drawings are used when objects are too large or too small to be drawn on a piece of paper.

The **scale factor** between the original shape and the new image is a number that indicates how much larger or smaller than the original shape the image was made. The scale factor can be calculated using the formula scale factor $= \dfrac{\text{image length}}{\text{original length}}$.

If the scale factor is less than 1, the image will be a **reduction** of the original shape. In other words, the new image will be smaller than the original figure.

Knowing the scale factor makes it possible to draw the image of a diagram. To draw a scale diagram, follow these steps:

1. Draw and label the original figure.
2. Use the scale factor formula to determine the length of each side of the image diagram.
3. Draw and label the image diagram. Use the prime symbol (′) to indicate that this is the image.
4. Join each original point to its corresponding point on the image, and label the scale factor on the diagram.

Example

The rectangle *ABCD* has a length measuring 12 cm and a width measuring 9 cm.

Using a scale factor of $\dfrac{1}{3}$, draw the image of the rectangle.

Solution

Step 1

Draw and label the original figure.

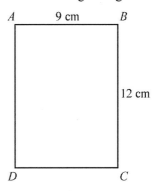

Step 2

Use the scale factor formula to determine the length of each side in the image diagram.

The length of the original rectangle is 12 cm.

$$\text{scale factor} = \frac{\text{image length}}{\text{original length}}$$
$$\frac{1}{3} = \frac{B'C'}{12}$$
$$12\left(\frac{1}{3}\right) = 12\left(\frac{B'C'}{12}\right)$$
$$4 = B'C'$$

The width of the original rectangle is 9 cm.

$$\text{scale factor} = \frac{\text{image width}}{\text{original width}}$$
$$\frac{1}{3} = \frac{A'B'}{9}$$
$$9\left(\frac{1}{3}\right) = 9\left(\frac{A'B'}{9}\right)$$
$$3 = A'B'$$

The image rectangle has a length of 4 cm and a width of 3 cm.

Step 3

Draw and label the image diagram. Use the prime symbol (') to indicate that this is the image.

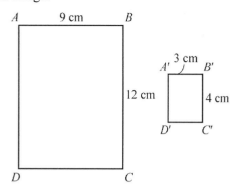

Step 4

Join each original point to its corresponding point on the image, and label the scale factor on the diagram.

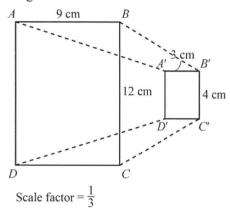

Scale factor = $\frac{1}{3}$

20G.3 Model and draw 3-D objects and their views.

SKETCHING PLAN AND ELEVATION VIEWS FROM 3-D OBJECTS

Three-dimensional objects have three dimensions: length, width, and height. Three-dimensional objects can be drawn in two-dimensions from a plan view or elevation view. **Plan view** is drawing the object as seen from the top or bottom.

Elevation view is drawing the object from the front, rear, or side view.

Example

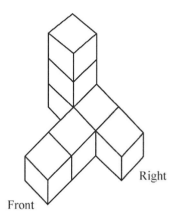

For this three-dimensional diagram, draw the two-dimensional diagram from a top plan view and from the front and right elevation views.

Solution

Step 1

Draw the plan view.

Identify the tiles that are on the top of the drawing.

To make it clear, shade the tiles that are on the top.

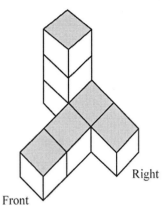

Front
Right

Step 2

Draw the shaded tiles in two-dimensions.

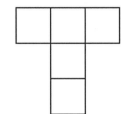

Step 3

Draw the front elevation view.

Identify the tiles you would see if standing in front of the object.

To make it clear, shade the tiles that are seen from the front.

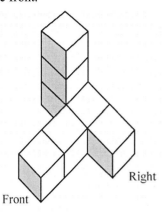

Front
Right

Step 4

Draw the shaded tiles in two-dimensions.

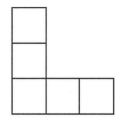

Step 5

Draw the right side elevation view.

Identify the tiles you would see if standing on the right side of the object.

To make it clear, shade the tiles that are seen from the right.

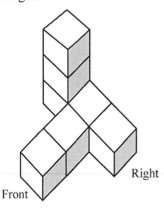

Front
Right

Step 6
Draw the shaded tiles in two-dimensions.

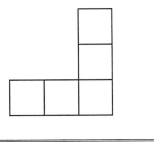

20G.3 Model and draw 3-D objects and their views.

SKETCHING 3-D OBJECTS GIVEN PLAN AND ELEVATION VIEWS

Three-dimensional objects have three dimensions: length, width, and height. Three-dimensional objects can be drawn when given the plan view and elevation view. **Plan view** is drawing the object as seen from the top or bottom of the object.
Elevation view is drawing the object from the front, rear, or side view.

Example

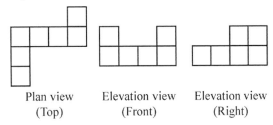

Plan view   Elevation view   Elevation view
(Top)   (Front)   (Right)

Given these views, draw a three-dimensional diagram.

Solution

Step 1
Determine the heights of each view.
Use the plan view to label the front of each square with the height of the blocks indicated by the front view.
Use the plan view to label the right side of each square with the height as indicated by the right side view.

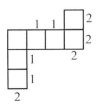

Step 2
Draw the three-dimensional figure.
Cross-reference the number from the front view and the right side view for each block in the plan view. If the two numbers are the same, that is the height of the block in that square of the plan view.

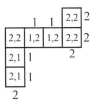

If the two numbers are different, the height of the block in that square (on the plan view) is the smaller number.

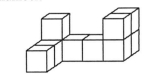

20G.3 Model and draw 3-D objects and their views.

SKETCHING DIFFERENT VIEWS OF THREE-DIMENSIONAL OBJECTS

There may be times when it is necessary to draw different views of a three-dimensional object.

You can sketch two-dimensional (2-D) views of three-dimensional (3-D) objects that are built with connecting cubes. For example, this is an image of a 3-D figure built out of connecting cubes.

Look at the figure from the front, the side, and the top. You can sketch these different views on dotted paper. Each square on the dotted paper represents the face of one of the connecting cubes.

- From the front, you see three cubes, one above the other. Draw three squares, one above the other on the dotted paper.
- From the side, you also see three cubes, one above the other. Draw another three squares, one above the other on the dotted paper.
- From the top, you see only one cube because the three cubes are directly below each other. Draw one square on the dotted paper.

The two-dimensional representations, or sketches, of the three different views will look like this:

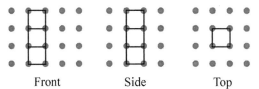

| Front | Side | Top |

Example

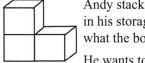

Andy stacked three identical boxes in his storage shed. This figure is what the boxes looked like.

He wants to draw 2-D views of the squares from the front, the side, and the top.

In order to sketch the 2-D views accurately from the given 3-D figure, you need to examine what the boxes look like from the front, the side, and the top.

Front View

When you look at the boxes directly from the front, you see two boxes on the bottom and one box above the box on the left. The second sketch is what you will draw.

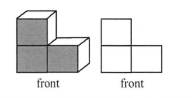

front   front

Side View

When you look at the boxes directly from the side, you see two boxes, one above the other. The second sketch is what you will draw.

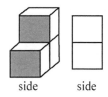

side   side

This view does not show the second box on the bottom.

Top View

When you look at the boxes directly from the top, you see two boxes side by side. The second sketch is what you will draw.

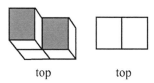

top   top

This view does not show the two layers of boxes.

The 2-D views of the three boxes Andy stacked will look like this.

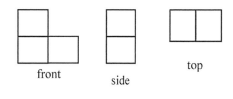

front   side   top

20G.4 Draw and describe exploded views, component parts and scale diagrams of simple 3-D objects.

IDENTIFYING THE CORRESPONDING PARTS OF TWO SIMILAR SHAPES

Two shapes are considered to be similar if they have the same corresponding angles. If the corresponding angles of the two shapes are the same, then one shape will be an enlargement of the other shape.

Example
Two shapes are given.

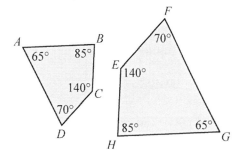

Each of the shapes have four angles measuring 65°, 85°, 140°, and 70°, respectively. Match the equal angles to find the corresponding vertices.

- $\angle A = \angle G$
- $\angle B = \angle H$
- $\angle C = \angle E$
- $\angle D = \angle F$

The corresponding vertices can be used to find the corresponding sides. For example, if $\angle A = \angle G$ and $\angle B = \angle H$, then $\overline{AB}$ corresponds to $\overline{GH}$.

- $\overline{AB}$ corresponds to $\overline{GH}$.
- $\overline{BC}$ corresponds to $\overline{HE}$.
- $\overline{CD}$ corresponds to $\overline{EF}$.
- $\overline{DA}$ corresponds to $\overline{FG}$.

To identify the corresponding parts of two similar shapes, follow these steps:

1. Identify the vertices that are corresponding by identifying the equal angles.
2. Use the vertices to identify the corresponding sides.

Example
Triangle *ACD* is similar to triangle *ABE*.

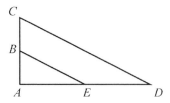

These can be drawn separately to make it easier to identify the corresponding parts.

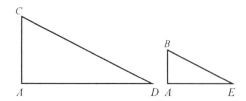

Identify the lengths and angles from $\triangle ACD$ that correspond to $\triangle ABE$.

Solution

Step 1
Identify the vertices that are corresponding by identifying the equal angles.
The angle measures are not marked, but the question stated that the triangles are similar, which means the angles must be the same. Decide which angles look the same in order to identify the corresponding angles.

- Angle *A* is shared by both shapes, so $\angle A = \angle A$.
- Angle *B* is approximately the same size as angle *C*, so $\angle B = \angle C$.
- Angle *E* is approximately the same size as angle *D*, so $\angle E = \angle D$.

Step 2
Use the vertices to identify the corresponding sides.

- $\overline{AB}$ corresponds to $\overline{AC}$.
- $\overline{AE}$ corresponds to $\overline{AD}$.
- $\overline{BE}$ corresponds to $\overline{CD}$.

Use the following information to answer the next question.

Michael is sitting in a movie theatre at a certain point, *M*, as shown in the given diagram. With a clinometer, he measures the angle of elevation to the top of the screen as 38°. With a tape measure, he measures a distance of 28 ft from his seat to the bottom of the screen.

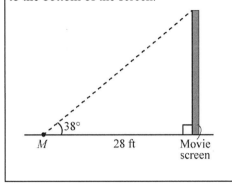

1. Rounded to the nearest foot, what is the height of the movie screen?
   A. 45 ft   B. 35 ft
   C. 22 ft   D. 17 ft

Use the following information to answer the next question.

A guy wire is to be attached halfway up a tower that is 48 m tall. The guy wire will make an angle of 58° with the ground. In order to secure the wire, an extra metre of wire is required at each end.

2. Expressed to the nearest tenth, what is the total length of wire required?
   A. 22.4 m   B. 30.3 m
   C. 40.4 m   D. 58.6 m

Use the following information to answer the next question.

A circular water pipe has a diameter of 40 centimetres (cm).

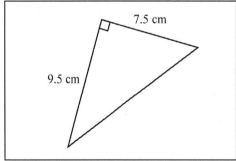

Numerical Response

3. If the width of the water surface in the pipe is 26 cm, what is the maximum depth of the water in the pipe to the nearest tenth of a centimetre? _____ cm

Use the following information to answer the next question.

Written Response

4. Solve for the missing side of the right triangle to the nearest tenth of a centimetre.

Use the following information to answer the next question.

Olivia looks out the window of her apartment building and sees a sports car parked down the street at an angle of depression of 18°. A little farther down the street, she sees a police car parked at an angle of depression of 15°.
Her apartment window is 35 m above street level.

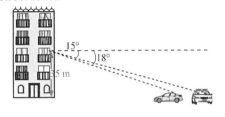

Numerical Response

5. To the nearest tenth of a metre, how far apart are the sports car and the police car? _____ m

Use the following information to answer the next question.

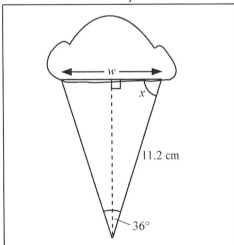

6. Rounded to the nearest tenth of a centimetre, the width, *w*, of the ice-cream cone's opening is
   A. 3.5 cm   B. 5.4 cm
   C. 6.9 cm   D. 10.7 cm

Use the following information to answer the next question.

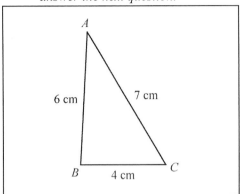

7. If triangle *ABC* is enlarged to make triangle *XYZ*, such that the shortest side measures 6 cm, then the longest side of triangle *XYZ* will measure
   A. 14.5 cm   B. 10.5 cm
   C. 9 cm   D. 8 cm

Use the following information to answer the next question.

Mark wants to make a map of his backyard. He measures his backyard in feet (ft) and draws a scale diagram.

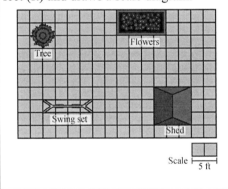

Numerical Response

8. What is the actual length of the shortest distance between the swing set and the shed? _____ ft

Use the following information to answer the next question.

A rectangle with a length of 4 ft and a width of 1.8 ft is enlarged by a scale factor of 5.

9. Which of the following rectangles is the scale image of the original rectangle after it has been enlarged?

A.
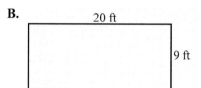
4 ft
2 ft

B.
20 ft
9 ft

C.
34 ft
19 ft

D.
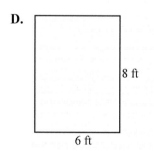
8 ft
6 ft

Use the following information to answer the next question.

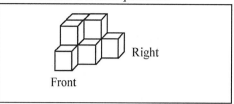
Right
Front

10. Which of the following sets of diagrams represents the top, front, right, and left perspectives of the object in the given diagram?

A.   Top   Front   Right   Left

B.   Top   Front   Right   Left
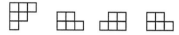

C.   Top   Front   Right   Left
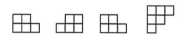

D.   Top   Front   Right   Left

Use the following information to answer the next question.

Jacob built an object out of connecting cubes.

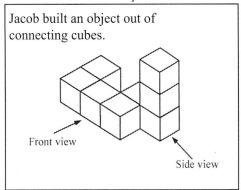

Front view

Side view

11. What is the top view of the given object?

A.

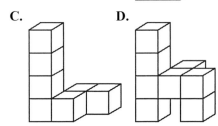

B.

C.

D.

Use the following information to answer the next question.

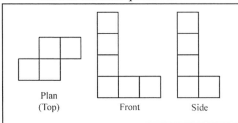

Plan (Top) Front Side

12. Which of the following diagrams shows the three-dimensional view of the object?

A. **B.**

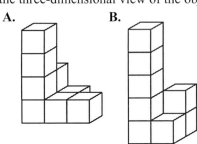

C. **D.**

Use the following information to answer the next question.

Mike made this structure out of building blocks.

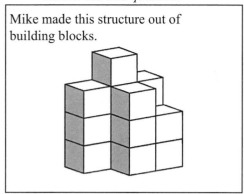

13. Which of the following sets of views is correct for this structure?

A.

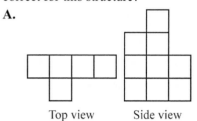

Top view   Side view

B.

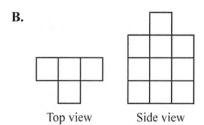

Top view   Side view

C.

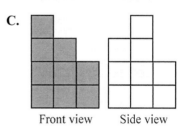

Front view   Side view

D.

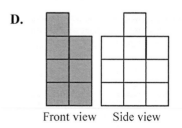

Front view   Side view

Use the following information to answer the next question.

The given diagrams represent the top, front, and side views of a group of geometric blocks.

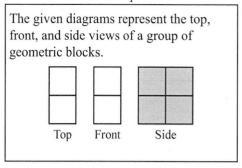

Top   Front   Side

14. Which of the following groups of blocks is **best** represented by the given diagrams?

A.   **B.**

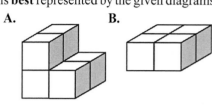

C.   **D.**

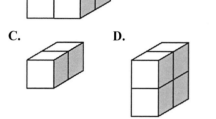

ANSWERS AND SOLUTIONS
GEOMETRY

1. C	5. 22.9	9. B	13. D
2. B	6. C	10. B	14. D
3. 35.2	7. B	11. D	
4. WR	8. 12.5	12. C	

1. C

Step 1

Draw a diagram representing the situation. Label the triangle with a variable for the unknown measurement.

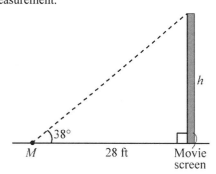

Step 2

Apply the appropriate trigonometric ratio to solve for the unknown height.

$$\tan \theta = \frac{\text{opposite}}{\text{hypotenuse}}$$
$$\tan 38° = \frac{h}{28}$$
$$28 \times \tan 38° = h$$
$$21.88 \text{ ft} \approx h$$

Therefore, the height of the movie screen is approximately 22 ft.

2. B

Step 1

Draw a diagram to represent the given information. Let x represent the length of wire from the ground to the tower.

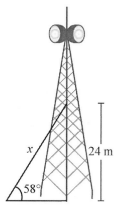

Step 2

Identify which trigonometric ratio to use to solve for x.

The 24 m side, which is half the height of the tower, is opposite the 58° angle. The length of wire from the ground to the tower, x, is the hypotenuse. Since the opposite side and the hypotenuse are involved, the sine ratio should be used.

$$\sin \theta = \frac{O}{H}$$

Step 3

Substitute the variables into the equation, and solve for x.

$$\sin 58° = \frac{24}{x}$$
$$x \sin 58° = 24$$
$$x = \frac{24}{\sin 58°}$$
$$x \approx 28.3$$

Since an extra metre of wire is required at each end, the total length of wire required is
28.3 m + 2 m = 30.3 m.

3. **35.2**

Step 1

Find the height of water above the diameter line using the Pythagorean theorem.

$h^2 = 20^2 - 13^2$

$h^2 = 400 - 169$

$h^2 = 231$

$h = \sqrt{231}$

$h = 15.198\ldots$

Step 2

Find the total depth, including the height of the diameter line.

$d = h + 20$

$d = 15.198\ldots + 20$

$d = 35.198\ldots$

The depth of the water in the pipe, to the nearest tenth of a centimetre, is 35.2 cm.

4. **WR**

Step 1

Substitute the known values into the Pythagorean theorem.

Label one side a, the second side b and the third side c. Substitute the given values into the equation.

$a^2 + b^2 = c^2$

$9.5^2 + 7.5^2 = c^2$

Step 2

Solve for the missing side.

Follow order of operations. Calculate the exponents.

$9.5^2 + 7.5^2 = c^2$

$90.25 + 56.25 = c^2$

$146.5 = c^2$

Take the square root of both sides to solve for c.

$\sqrt{146.5} = \sqrt{c^2}$

$12.103\ 718\ 44 = c$

$c = 12.1$

The missing side is 12.1 cm long.

5. **22.9**

Step 1

Determine the sports car's horizontal distance, x_1, from the apartment building.

$$\tan \theta = \frac{\text{opposite}}{\text{adjacent}}$$

$$\tan 18° = \frac{35}{x_1}$$

$$(\tan 18°)x_1 = 35$$

$$(0.3249\ldots)x_1 \approx 35$$

$$x_1 \approx \frac{35}{0.3249}$$

$$x_1 \approx 107.7 \text{ m}$$

Step 2

Determine the police car's horizontal distance, x_2, from the apartment building.

$$\tan \theta = \frac{\text{opposite}}{\text{adjacent}}$$

$$\tan 15° = \frac{35}{x_2}$$

$$(\tan 15°)x_2 = 35$$

$$(0.2679\ldots)x_2 \approx 35$$

$$x_2 \approx \frac{35}{0.2679}$$

$$x_2 \approx 130.6 \text{ m}$$

Step 3

Subtract the sports car's horizontal distance from the police car's horizontal distance.

$x_2 - x_1 = 130.6 - 107.7$

$\qquad\quad = 22.9 \text{ m}$

The sports car and the police car are 22.9 m apart.

6. **C**

Step 1

Determine the angle that will be used to solve for w. Since the cone is made up of two right triangles, the line passing through 36° will bisect that angle as well as the width of the ice-cream cone's opening. Thus, the angle in the triangle is 18°.

Step 2

Label the opposite side with the letter y.

Note: $w = 2y$

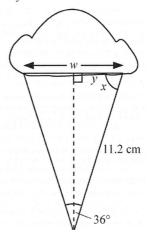

Step 3

Identify the ratio to use to solve for y.

The required angle is $18°$.

Identify the sides you have to work with.

The side measuring 11.2 cm is the hypotenuse.
The side labelled y is the opposite side.
The trigonometric ratio that uses the opposite side and the hypotenuse is sine.

$$\sin \theta = \frac{\text{opposite}}{\text{hypotenuse}}$$

Step 4

Substitute the known values from the triangle into the sine ratio.

$$\sin 18° = \frac{y}{11.2}$$

Step 5

Use cross products to solve for y.

$$\frac{\sin 18°}{1} = \frac{y}{11.2}$$
$$\sin 18°(11.2) = y(1)$$
$$3.46 = y$$

Step 6

Solve for w.

Since $w = 2y$,
$w = 2(3.46) = 6.92$

Step 7

Round answer to the nearest tenth of a centimetre.
$6.92 \rightarrow 6.9$

The opening of the ice-cream cone is 6.9 cm wide.

7. **B**

The shortest side of triangle ABC is 4 cm. Since triangle XYZ is simply an enlargement of triangle ABC, the two triangles are similar. Therefore, the shortest side of triangle ABC corresponds to the shortest side of triangle XYZ.

$$\text{Enlarged triangle} = \frac{\text{shortest side of } \triangle XYZ}{\text{shortest side of } \triangle ABC}$$

$$= \frac{6 \text{ cm}}{4 \text{ cm}} = \frac{3}{2} = 1.5$$

Therefore, the length of the longest side of triangle XYZ is $1.5 \times$ the length of the longest side of triangle ABC.
$= 1.5 \times 7$ cm
$= 10.5$ cm

8. **12.5**

Step 1

Count the number of units on the map between the swing set and the shed.

The shed is 5 units away from the swing set.

Step 2

Use the scale to find the actual distance.
The scale tells that 2 units on the map are equivalent to 5 ft.
Divide 5 units by 2 units.
$5 \div 2 = 2.5$
Multiply 2.5 by 5.
$2.5 \times 5 = 12.5$
The shortest distance between the swing set and the shed is 12.5 ft.

9. **B**

Step 1

Draw and label the original figure.

4 ft

1.8 ft

Step 2

Apply the scale factor to determine the length of the new rectangle.

$$\text{scale factor} = \frac{\text{image length}}{\text{original length}}$$

$$5 = \frac{\text{image length}}{4}$$
$$4(5) = \text{image length}$$
$$20 \text{ ft} = \text{image length}$$

Step 3

Apply the scale factor to determine the width of the new rectangle.

$$\text{scale factor} = \frac{\text{image width}}{\text{original width}}$$

$$5 = \frac{\text{image width}}{1.8}$$
$$1.8(5) = \text{image width}$$
$$9 \text{ ft} = \text{image width}$$

Step 4

Draw and label the original figure with the image figure.

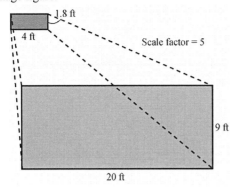

Scale factor = 5

The enlarged rectangle has a length of 20 ft and a width of 9 ft.

10. **B**

Step 1

Draw the plan view. Identify the tiles that are on the top of the drawing.

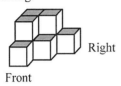

Step 2

Draw the two-dimensional view of the top.

Top

Step 3

Draw the front view. Identify the tiles that are at the front of the drawing.

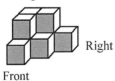

Step 4

Draw the two-dimensional view of the front.

Front

Step 5

Draw the right side view. Identify the tiles that are on the right side of the drawing.

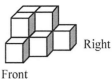

Step 6

Draw the two-dimensional view of the right side.

Right

Step 7

Draw the left side view.

This side is hidden, but from the right, the first block is 1 high, the second block is 2 high, and the third block is 2 high.

Draw the two-dimensional view of the left side.

Left

11. **D**

When you look at the object from the top, you can see six blocks. These six blocks are shaded in the given image. The top view does not show the layers of blocks.

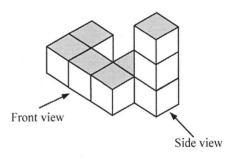

The left-most column is two blocks deep, and the second column contains only one block near the front. The third column contains two blocks. Finally, the last column is only one block, near the back of the shape. The top view looks like the given diagram.

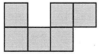

12. C

Step 1

Determine the height of the front and right view. Label each of the front squares with the height of the blocks as indicated by the front view. Label each of the right side views with the height of the blocks as indicated by the right side view.

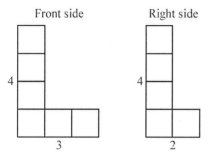

Front side   Right side

4   4

3   2

Step 2

Draw the three-dimensional view.

Cross-reference the number from the front view and the right side view. If the two numbers are the same, that is the height of the object in that square of the plan view.

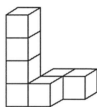

13. D

Step 1

Draw the front view.

Identify the tiles that are on the front of the drawing.

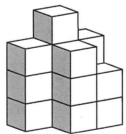

Step 2

Draw the two-dimensional view of the front.

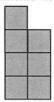

Front view

Step 3

Draw the side view.

Identify the tiles that are on the side of the drawing.

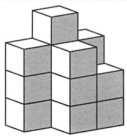

Step 4

Draw the two-dimensional view of the side.

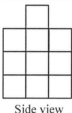

Side view

14. D

Determine the height of each view.

Step 1

Label the front square with the height of the blocks indicated by the front view.

2

Label each of the right side views with the height of the blocks as indicated by the right side view.

2

2

2

Step 2

Draw the three-dimensional view.

Cross-reference the number from the front view and the right side view. If the two numbers are the same, that is the height of the object in that square of the plan view.

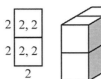

UNIT TEST — GEOMETRY

Numerical Response

1. A boy flying a kit decides to anchor the kite to the ground. If the string of the kite is 150 m long and makes an angle of 60° with the ground, then approximately how high is the kite above the ground (to the nearest tenth of a metre)? _____ m

Use the following information to answer the next question.

> John is at the top of a vertical cliff, 25 m directly above sea level. He spots a sailboat out on the sea at an angle of depression of 25° from the top of the cliff.

2. The distance of the sailboat from the base of the cliff is approximately
   A. 11.7 m   B. 27.6 m
   C. 53.6 m   D. 59.2 m

Use the following information to answer the next question.

> From the crow's-nest of a ship, a sailor spots a lifeboat at an angle of depression of 25.5°. The crow's-nest is located 15.8 m above ocean level.

Numerical Response

3. Expressed to the nearest tenth, the distance from the crow's-nest to the lifeboat is _____ m.

Use the following information to answer the next question.

> Mikhail builds a shelter. A cross section of the shelter has the shape and dimensions shown in the diagram. The value of θ is equal to the measure of $\angle BDC$.
>
>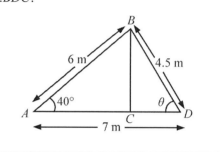

4. The value of θ is approximately
   A. 57.7°   B. 48.6°
   C. 41.4°   D. 32.3°

Use the following information to answer the next question.

> In order to hang a circular mirror, a triangular bracket is glued onto the back of it, as shown. Each edge of the triangular bracket is 24 centimetres (cm).
>
>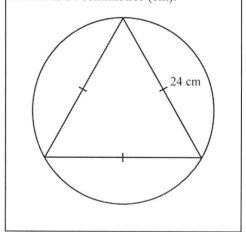

Numerical Response

5. To the nearest square centimetre, what is the area of the bracket? _____ cm^2

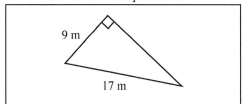

Written Response

6. Use the Pythagorean theorem to solve for the missing side of the triangle, rounded to the nearest tenth of a metre.

Dave and Vance wanted to make a scale drawing of their bedroom. They decided on a scale that would work and used grid paper to make the drawing, as shown.

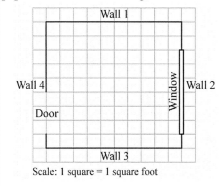

Scale: 1 square = 1 square foot

7. Based on the given scale drawing, the length measurement of the window in the boys' room is

   A. 6 in
   B. 6 ft
   C. 6 cm
   D. 6 m

The given diagram shows circle C, with centre (−3, 2), and circle D, with centre (1, 2).

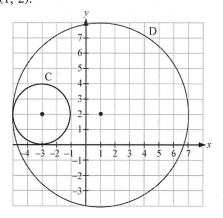

8. What is the scale factor used to transform circle C into circle D?

   A. $\frac{1}{6}$
   B. $\frac{1}{3}$
   C. 3
   D. 6

Numerical Response

9. A tomato plant is 75 cm tall in real life. What is the height of the tomato plant in a diagram that has a scale factor of 1:25? _____ cm

Use the following information to answer the next question.

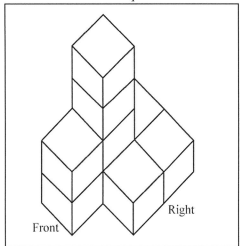

Right

Front

Written Response

10. Draw the two-dimensional plan of the given three-dimensional diagram. Include the plan view (top) and the elevation views (front and right side).

Use the following information to answer the next question.

The given diagram shows an object that is made out of blocks, as seen from the front.

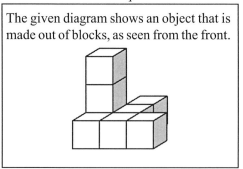

11. Which of the following diagrams shows a view of the given object?

A.

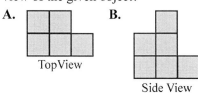

TopView

B.

Side View

C.

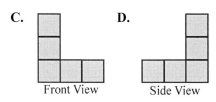

Front View

D.

Side View

Use the following information to answer the next question.

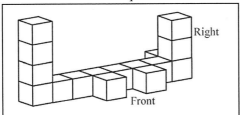

12. Which of the following diagrams shows the front view of the given object?

A.

B.

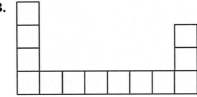

C.

D.

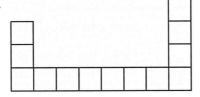

ANSWERS AND SOLUTIONS — UNIT TEST

1. 129.9	4. A	7. B	10. WR
2. C	5. 249	8. C	11. C
3. 36.7	6. WR	9. 3	12. B

1. 129.9

Begin with a sketch for clarity.

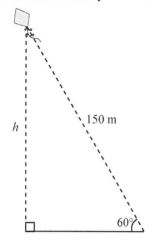

Recall,

$$\sin \theta = \frac{\text{opposite}}{\text{hypotenuse}}$$

$$\sin 60° = \frac{h}{150}$$
$$150 \times \sin 60° = h$$
$$129.9 \text{ m} \approx h$$

2. C

Step 1

Draw a diagram to represent the given information.

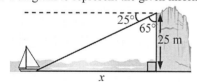

Since the angle of depression is measured relative to the horizontal, it is on the outside of the triangle. The angle between the cliff wall and the line of sight to the sailboat is $90° - 25° = 65°$.

Step 2

To solve for x in the diagram, identify the proper trigonometric ratio to use. As the diagram shows, x represents the distance of the sailboat from the base of the cliff.

The height of 25 m is the side adjacent to the 65° angle, and the distance of the sailboat from the base of the cliff, x, is the side opposite to the 65° angle. Since the opposite side and the adjacent side are involved, the tangent ratio should be used.

$$\tan \theta = \frac{O}{A}$$

Step 3

Substitute the variables into the equation, and solve for x.

$$\tan 65° = \frac{x}{25}$$
$$25 \tan 65° = x$$
$$53.6 \approx x$$

The sailboat is approximately 53.6 m from the base of the cliff.

3. 36.7

Step 1

Draw a diagram to represent the given information. Let x represent the distance from the crow's-nest to the lifeboat. The angle of depression from the crow's-nest is equal to the angle of elevation from the lifeboat since both angles are measured from the horizontal.

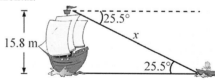

Step 2

Identify which trigonometric ratio to use to solve for x.

The height of the crow's-nest above the ocean, 15.8 m, is the side opposite to the 25.5° angle. The distance from the crow's-nest to the lifeboat, x, is the hypotenuse. Since the opposite side and the hypotenuse are involved, the sine ratio should be used.

$$\sin \theta = \frac{O}{H}$$

Step 3

Substitute the variables into the equation, and solve for *x*.

$$\sin 25.5° = \frac{15.8}{x}$$
$$x\sin 25.5° = 15.8$$
$$x = \frac{15.8}{\sin 25.5°}$$
$$x \approx 36.7$$

The lifeboat is approximately 36.7 m from the crow's-nest.

4. A

Step 1

Determine the length of side *AC* of $\triangle ABC$.

Since side *AC* is adjacent to the 40° angle and side *AB* is the hypotenuse, the cosine ratio should be used.

$$\cos \theta = \frac{A}{H}$$
$$\cos 40° = \frac{AC}{6}$$
$$6\cos 40° = AC$$
$$4.596 \approx AC$$

Side *AC* is approximately 4.596 m long.

Step 2

Determine the length of side *CD* of $\triangle BCD$.

$$AC + CD = AD$$
$$4.596 + CD = 7$$
$$CD = 2.404$$

The length of side *CD* is approximately 2.404 m long.

Step 3

Determine the value of θ, which is the measure of $\angle BDC$.

Since side *CD* is adjacent to θ and side *BD* is the hypotenuse, the cosine ratio should be used.

$$\cos \theta = \frac{A}{H}$$
$$= \frac{CD}{BD}$$
$$\approx \frac{2.404}{4.5}$$
$$\theta \approx \cos^{-1}\left(\frac{2.404}{4.5}\right)$$
$$\approx 57.7°$$

The value of θ is approximately 57.7°.

5. 249

Step 1

Determine the perpendicular height of the triangle using the Pythagorean Theorem.

$$h^2 = 24^2 - 12^2$$
$$h^2 = 576 - 144$$
$$h^2 = 432$$
$$h = \sqrt{432}$$
$$h = 12\sqrt{3}$$

Step 2

Calculate the area of the triangle.

$$A = \frac{bh}{2}$$
$$A = \frac{24 \cdot 12\sqrt{3}}{2}$$
$$A = 249.4153$$

The area of the bracket, rounded to the nearest square centimetre, is 249 cm^2.

6. WR

Step 1

Substitute the known values into the Pythagorean theorem.

Substitute the values in for *b* and *c*.

$$a^2 + b^2 = c^2$$
$$a^2 + 9^2 = 17^2$$

Step 2

Solve for the missing side.

Follow order of operations by calculating the exponents.

$$a^2 + 81 = 289$$

Solve for *a*. Subtract 81 from both sides of the equation to isolate *a*.

$$a^2 + 81 - 81 = 289 - 81$$
$$a^2 = 208$$

Take the square root of both sides to solve for *a*.

$$\sqrt{a^2} = \sqrt{208}$$
$$a = 14.422\,2051$$

The missing side of the triangle is 14.4 m long.

7. B

The scale the boys used for their drawing says that 1 square equals 1 ft^2, which means that each side of a square is equal to 1 ft.

Since the window in the scale drawing is 6 squares long, the length of the window is 6 ft.

8. C

From the diagram the radius of circle C is 2 units, and the radius of circle D is 6 units.

The scale factor can be determined by finding the ratio of the corresponding radii. Because the transformation from circle C to circle D is an enlargement, the scale factor is greater than one.

$$\text{Scale factor} = \frac{\text{image length}}{\text{original length}}$$
$$= \frac{6}{2}$$
$$= 3$$

9. 3

Step 1

Determine the height of the original shape.

The tomato plant is 75 cm tall.

Step 2

Use the formula for scale factor to find the height of the image.

The scale factor can be written as a fraction of $\frac{1}{25}$.

Set up a proportion.

$$\text{scale factor} = \frac{\text{image length}}{\text{original length}}$$
$$\frac{1}{25} = \frac{x}{75}$$
$$25x = 75$$
$$\frac{25x}{25} = \frac{75}{25}$$
$$x = 3$$

The tomato plant in the diagram is 3 cm high.

10. WR

Step 1

Draw the plan view.

Identify the tiles that are on the top of the diagram.

To make it clear, shade the tiles that are on the top.

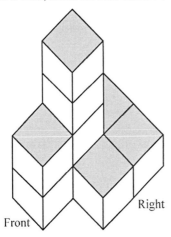

Step 2

Draw the shaded tiles in two dimensions.

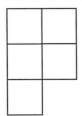

Step 3

Draw the elevation view from the front.

Identify the tiles you would see if you were standing in front of the object.

To make it clear, shade the tiles that are seen from the front.

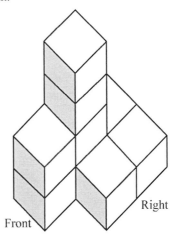

Step 4

Draw the shaded tiles in two dimensions.

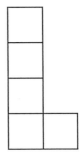

Step 5

Draw the elevation view from the right side.
Identify the tiles you would see if you were standing on the right side of the object.
To make it clear, shade the tiles that are seen from the right.

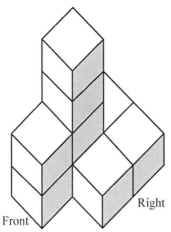

Step 6

Draw the shaded tiles in two dimensions.

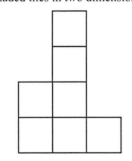

11. **C**

Step 1

Examine the side view.

When the object is looked at from the side, it can be seen that there are three blocks on the bottom level, and the middle column is three blocks high.

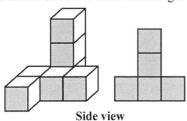

Side view

Step 2

Examine the top view.

When the object is looked at from the top, it can be seen that the object is three blocks wide. The first column is two blocks deep, the second column is three blocks deep, and the third column is one block deep.

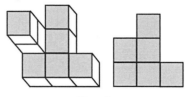

Top view

Step 3

Examine the front view.

When the object is looked at from the front, it can be seen that the object is three blocks wide, and the column farthest to the left is three blocks tall.

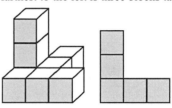

Front view

Therefore, the given diagram of the front view matches the front view of the object.

12. **B**

Step 1

Draw the front view. Identify the tiles that are on the front of the drawing.

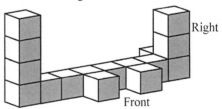

Step 2

Draw the two-dimensional view of the front of the drawing.

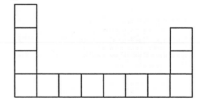

NOTES

Number

NUMBER

Table of Correlations			
Outcome	**Practice Questions**	**Unit Test Questions**	**Practice Test**
20N Number			
20N.1 *Analyze puzzles and games that involve numerical reasoning, using problem-solving strategies. Standard*	1, 2	1, 2	1, 2, 3
20N.2 *Solve problems that involve personal budgets.*	3, 4	3	4, 5, 6
20N.3 *Demonstrate an understanding of compound interest.*	5, 6, 7, 8	4, 5, 6, 7	7, 8, 9
20N.4 *Demonstrate an understanding of financial institution services used to access and manage finances.*	9, 10	8	10
20N.5 *Demonstrate an understanding of credit options, including: credit cards, loans.*	11		11

20N.1 Analyze puzzles and games that involve numerical reasoning, using problem-solving strategies. Standard

APPLYING A VARIETY OF MATHEMATICAL PROBLEM-SOLVING TECHNIQUES

You can apply a variety of mathematical techniques to help you solve problems. One of these problem-solving techniques is guess and check. For this technique, you determine a reasonable guess, select a number, and then check to see if the number is correct by substituting it into the equation.

Example

Laura is asked to find the value of x in the equation $84.25 + x = 102$ by using guess and check.

The steps in Laura's partial solution for determining the value of x are shown:

1. Round the decimal number in the equation to the nearest whole number.
   $84 + x = 102$
2. Since $84 + 18 = 102$, a reasonable guess is a number less than 18.
3. A possible number could be 17. Substitute 17 for x.
   $84.25 + 17 = 101.25$ The guess of 17 gives a number less than 102.

Complete Laura's partial solution to find the value of x.

Solution

Since the guess of 17 gives a number less than 102, a reasonable number for x will be between 17 and 18.

Step 1
Add 0.75 to the last guess of 17.
$17 + 0.75 = 17.75$

Step 2
Substitute for x.
$84.25 + 17.75 = 102$

The value of x in the given equation is 17.75.

Another problem-solving technique is to identify the relevant information from the given information and write a simple equation to solve the problem.

Example

Kyle wants to build a rectangular pool and would like it to fit in his backyard. His backyard has an area of 252 m^2 and a width that is 9 m less than its length. The width of the pool is 3 m. The length of the pool is two times the width of the pool, and the depth of the pool is half the width. Along the perimeter of the pool, there is a walking path that is 2 m longer than the length and width of the pool.

Write and solve an equation to determine the total volume of water that Kyle will need to fill his swimming pool.

Solution

To find the volume of water needed to fill the pool, find the volume of the rectangular pool.

Step 1
Identify the relevant information.
To find the volume of the rectangular pool, only the length, width, and depth of the pool are needed.
The given diagram shows the relevant information, where l is the length, w is the width, and d is the depth.

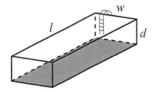

Step 2
Write an equation.
Since the shape of the pool is a rectangular prism, use the formula for the volume of a rectangular prism, which is $V_{\text{rectangular prism}} = lwh$. Thus, $V_{\text{pool}} = lwd$.
The width of the pool equals 3 m. The length of the pool is two times the width, so $l = 2 \times 3 = 6$ m.
The depth of the pool is half the width, so $d = \dfrac{1}{2}(3) = 1.5$ m. Substitute the values into the equation $V_{\text{pool}} = lwd$.
$V_{\text{pool}} = 3(6)(1.5)$

Step 3

Determine the volume of the pool by solving the equation.

$$V_{pool} = 3(6)(1.5)$$
$$= 27 \text{ m}^3$$

The volume of water that Kyle will need to fill the pool is 27 m³.

20N.1 Analyze puzzles and games that involve numerical reasoning, using problem-solving strategies. Standard

APPLYING A VARIETY OF VISUAL PROBLEM-SOLVING STRATEGIES

You can use a variety of visual strategies to solve problems. Some of these visual strategies include drawing a diagram, making a chart, and creating a table. These problem-solving strategies can make it easier for you to find solutions to various problems.

Example

The first four diagrams in a series of diagrams that form a particular pattern are given.

Diagram 1   Diagram 2

Diagram 3   Diagram 4

If the pattern continues, determine how many dots there will be in diagram 5.

Solution

Step 1

Create a table to organize the information from the given diagrams.

Diagram	Number of Dots
1	3
2	6
3	10
4	15

Step 2

Identify the pattern from the given diagrams.

From the table, the number of dots in diagram 2 increases by 3 from the number of dots in diagram 1 (3 + 3 = 6). The number of dots increases by 4 in diagram 3 (6 + 4 = 10). The number of dots in diagram 4 increases by 5 (10 + 5 = 15).

The pattern is that the number of dots added to each diagram increases by 1, or is 1 more than the number of dots added to the previous diagram. For example, 5 dots were added from diagram 3 to diagram 4. Therefore, 6 dots will be added to diagram 5.

$$15 + 6 = 21$$

Diagram 5 will have 21 dots.

Diagram 5

Example

John and Sara are going to have a 60 m race at lunch hour. They want to set up pylons every 8 m to see who can make it to each pylon first.

Which visual problem-solving strategy would John and Sara **most likely** use to determine how many pylons they need for their race?

Solution

Step 1

Choose an appropriate problem-solving strategy.

An effective way to solve this problem is to draw a picture. Drawing a picture can limit the calculations that need to be made, so there is less chance of making an error. Seeing this problem visually will simplify the solution.

Step 2

Draw the picture.

Begin by drawing a line to represent the 60 m race.

Place a pylon that is 8 m away from the start line, the start line being 0.

Next, add another pylon 8 m from the first pylon's location. To identify where the second pylon should be, calculate 8 + 8 = 16.

The second pylon will be 16 m from the start line.

For the third pylon, add another 8 m from the second pylon's location, which is 16 + 8 = 24. Continue in this way until you reach 60 m.

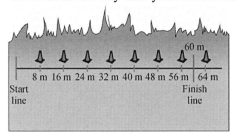

At 56 m, it is not necessary to place another pylon 8 m away, but doing so will help clarify how many pylons will be within the 60 m race.

Step 3

Count the number of pylons.

There are 7 pylons in the 60 m race.

John and Sara would most likely choose to draw a picture to solve this problem because the specific objects, the pylons, and the straight line can be easily drawn in a diagram. The picture also limits the calculations needed to solve this problem. Visually seeing this question makes it easy to simply count the pylons that are within the 60 m.

20N.2 Solve problems that involve personal budgets.

Solving Budget Problems Using Tables and Circle Graphs

Personal budgets are used to keep track of income and expenditures. When total income is greater than total expenditures over a time period, it is said that there is a surplus. When total expenditures are greater than total income, there is a deficit.

A budget worksheet is used to record and categorize income and expenditures. The categories are determined by what is most appropriate for each individual.

The portion of a budget worksheet showing income could look like this:

Category	Budget Amount	Actual Amount	Difference
Net income			
Salary			
Investment			
Other			
Total			

The budgeted amount is how much the person thinks they will earn or spend in each category. The actual amount is the amount earned or spent.

The difference is calculated by subtracting the actual amount from the budgeted amount. Deficits are placed in brackets.

The portion of the budget worksheet showing expenses may include the following categories:

• Housing
• Transportation
• Food
• Clothing
• Health care
• Recreation
• Miscellaneous
• Debt payments
• Savings and investments

When solving problems that involve budget worksheets, you may be asked to determine the following information:

1. Determine the difference between the amount budgeted for an item and the actual cost of the item
2. Determine the percentage of the total budget made up by each category. Comparing the budgets for different time periods may help you to identify changes in spending habits.
3. Determine the percentage of the total budget spent in each category.
4. Represent budgeted amounts using a circle graph

Example

A portion of Braden's budget worksheet showing his expenditures on food and clothing is given.

Category	Budget Amount	Actual Amount	Difference
Groceries	380.00	365.00	
Eating out	175.00	188.00	
Clothing	100.00	70.00	
Total			

Calculate the surplus or a deficit between the amounts Braden budgeted for food and clothing and the actual amount he spent.

Solution

Step 1

Calculate the surplus or deficit for each category by subtracting the actual amount from the budgeted amount.
Groceries: $380 – $365 = $15.00
Eating out: $175 – $188 = –$13
Clothing: $100 – $70 = $30
The completed budget worksheet will look like this:

Category	Budget Amount	Actual Amount	Difference
Groceries	380.00	365.00	15.00
Eating out	175.00	188.00	(13.00)
Clothing	100.00	70.00	30.00
Total			

To determine Braden's surplus or deficit at the end of the month, determine the total in every column, and find the difference in the totals.

Category	Budget Amount	Actual Amount	Difference
Groceries	380.00	365.00	15.00
Eating out	175.00	188.00	(13.00)
Clothing	100.00	70.00	30.00
Total	655.00	623.00	32.00

Braden has a surplus of $32.00 in the food and clothing section of his budget worksheet

Example

Donald kept track of his income and expenses for the month of June. A portion of his budget worksheet showing his household expenses is given below.

Category	Budget Amount	Actual Amount	Difference
Salary	3 250.00	3 250.00	
Mortgage	420.00	420.00	
Insurance	58.00	58.00	
Water/ Power	170.00	180.00	(10.00)
Heat	70.00	68.00	2.00
Cable	80.00	80.00	
Phone	65.00	62.00	3.00
Total			

If Donald's budget consists of his entire salary, what percentage of Donald's budget is set aside for household expenses?

Solution

Step 1

Calculate the total amount budgeted for household expenses.

$= 420.00 + 58.00 + 170.00$
$+ 70.00 + 80.00 + 65.00$
$= \$863.00$

Step 2

Determine the total amount of budgeted income.
$3\ 250.00$

Step 3

Determine the percentage of the budget spent on household expenses.

$$\frac{863.00}{3\ 250.00} \times 100 = 26.6\%$$

Donald budgeted 26.6% of his income for household expenses.

Example

A portion of Glen's budget worksheet that includes transportation expenses is shown.

Category	Budget Amount	Actual Amount	Difference
Salary	3 250.00	3 250.00	
Other income		350.00	
Car Payment	340.00	340.00	
Gas/Oil	210.00	222.00	(12.00)
Insurance	180.00	180.00	
Repairs	87.00	50.00	37.00
Other (bus, taxi)	30.00	35.00	(5.00)
Total			

What percentage of Glen's budget did he actually spend on transportation?

Solution

Step 1

Calculate the actual amount spent on transportation.
$340.00 + 222.00 + 180.00 + 50.00 + 35.00$
$= \$827.00$

Step 2

Calculate the actual amount of income.
$3\ 250.00 + 350.00 = \$3\ 600.00$

Step 3

Calculate the percentage of the total actual income that was spent on transportation.

$$\frac{827.00}{3\ 600.00} \times 100 = 23\%$$

Glen actually spent 23% of his budget on transportation.

Example

Manuela earned $68 000 last year. She made this circle graph to illustrate how she spent last year's income.

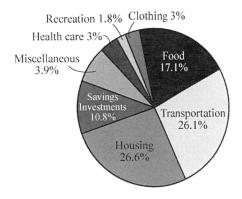

How much money did Manuela spend on housing?

Solution

The circle graph shows that Manuela spent 26.6% of her income on housing.

Calculate 26.6% of Manuela's total income.

= 26.6% of 68 000
= 0.266 × 68 000
= $18 088

20N.3 Demonstrate an understanding of compound interest.

COMPARING SIMPLE AND COMPOUND INTEREST USING A TABLE OF VALUES AND A GRAPH

When you invest money in a financial institution such as a bank, the bank pays you interest. The rate of interest and the terms by which this rate is paid often vary, depending on the banking institution, the current economic conditions, the size of the investment, and the length of time during which the money may not be withdrawn.

The amount that you initially invest is usually referred to as the **principal** (*P*) or the **present value** (*PV*). The annual **interest rate**, *i* or *r*, is usually given as a percentage (%) per year. For calculations, *i* (or *r*) is usually converted to a decimal.

The **total interest**, I_T, that you receive depends on the length of **time** (*t*). Time is often described in terms of the number of months or years, or the number of times interest is calculated (*n*). For example, if interest is calculated semi-annually, *n* is the number of years times 2. If interest is calculated quarterly or monthly, *n* is the number of years times 4 or times 12, respectively.

The total **amount** (*A*) or the **final value** (*FV*) is the sum of the principal and total interest, $FV = P + I_T$.

Simple interest and **compound interest** are two different methods for calculating the total interest earned.

Simple interest is only earned on the principal. To calculate the interest, *I*, each time interest is earned, use the formula $I = P \cdot r$, in which *P* is the principal and *r* is the interest rate.

The total interest can be calculated using the formulas $I_T = I \cdot t$, in which *t* is the number of years (if interest is calculated annually), or $I_T = I \cdot n$, in which *n* is the number of times the interest is calculated.

With simple interest, the following simplified formula for calculating total interest directly may be used:

$I_T = Prt$, in which I_T is the total simple interest, *P* is the principal, *r* is the interest rate per year as a decimal, and *t* is the time in years.

If simple interest is calculated more than once per year (i.e., semi-annually, quarterly, or monthly), the simplified formula is $I_T = Prn$, in which I_T is the total simple interest, *P* is the principal, *r* is the interest rate per time period, and *n* is the number of times interest is calculated.

The amount of interest earned (usually in $) is represented by *I*. The rate of interest (usually a percentage or a decimal) is represented by *i* or *r*.

Compound interest is calculated on the principal amount as well as previously accumulated interest. Therefore, use the formula $I = Pr$ to determine the amount of interest after each time period.

Under compound interest, the principal, P, increases from year to year, as does the interest, I, after each time interest is calculated. To determine the total interest, I_T, the calculation of interest, I, is repeated n times. Then, I_T is the sum of all I's.

When previously calculated values are used to calculate new values, a **recursive relationship** is formed between the two values. A table showing a recursive relationship is called a **recursive table**.

When interest is compounded monthly (12 times per year), quarterly (four times per year), or semi-annually (twice per year), the annual interest rate, r, is divided into 12, 4, or 2, respectively, and the number of years, t, is multiplied by 12, 4, or 2 to determine n.

Unless stated otherwise, the rate of interest, i (or r), is always the same.

Example

Compare simple interest and compound interest earned on a $1 000 investment that receives 10% interest per year over a five-year period. Illustrate the interest growth using a table of values (time versus total interest) and a graph.

Solution

Legend

- t—Time in years
- P—Principal
- I—Interest earned
- I_T—Total interest

The interest rate, r, as a decimal is 0.10.

Simple Interest Table

t	P	I	I_T
0	$1 000	n/a	0
1	$1 000	$1 000 × 0.10 = $100	$100
2	$1 000	$1 000 × 0.10 = $100	$200
3	$1 000	$1 000 × 0.10 = $100	$300
4	$1 000	$1 000 × 0.10 = $100	$400
5	$1 000	$1 000 × 0.10 = $100	$500

The total simple interest after 5 years is $500.
$I_T = \$500.00$

Compound Interest Table

t	P	I	I_T
0	$1 000	n/a	0
1	$1 000	$1 000 × 0.10 = $100	$100
2	$1 100	$1 100 × 0.10 = $110	$210
3	$1 210	$1 210 × 0.10 = $121	$331
4	$1 331	$1 331 × 0.10 = $133.10	$464.10
5	$1 464.10	$1 464.10 × 0.10 = $146.41	$610.51

Total compound interest after five years:
$I_T = \$610.51$.

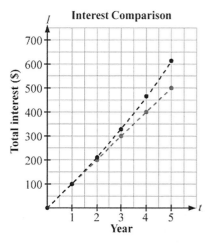

The points representing simple interest follow a linear pattern of growth, while the points representing compound interest follow a non-linear pattern of growth. This pattern is also evident in the table of values.

In the first year, the simple and compound interest is the same. However, after the first year, the compound interest is greater than the simple interest, and this difference increases more and more each year. Money invested in a compound-interest account grows more rapidly than in a simple-interest account.

20N.3 Demonstrate an understanding of compound interest.

CALCULATING SIMPLE AND COMPOUND INTEREST ALGEBRAICALLY AND USING TECHNOLOGY

When you invest money to reach your financial goals, you should make investments that are safe and provide high rates of interest. As well, when you are borrowing money to make a purchase, you should look for the lowest interest rate possible.

Interest is money that is paid for the use of money. It is described as a percentage, usually as a rate per year (annum).

CALCULATING SIMPLE INTEREST

Simple interest is calculated by applying the interest rate only to the initial amount borrowed or invested. This initial amount is known as the principal.

Simple interest is based only on the original principal.

Simple interest is calculated using the formula $I = Prt$, in which I represents interest earned or paid, P represents the initial amount, r represents the time period of the interest rate (usually in years), and t represents the time period (usually in years).

Example

James invested \$5 000 by purchasing a bond that pays 4.3% annually, calculated at the end of each month.

Calculate how much interest is earned at the end of the first month and how much the entire investment is worth at that time.

Solution

Calculate the amount of simple interest earned by applying the simple-interest formula, substituting in the known values, and solving.

$$I = Prt$$
$$= (5\ 000)(0.043)\left(\frac{1}{12}\right)$$
$$= \$17.92$$

James earns \$17.92 in interest.

To calculate how much his entire investment is worth, add the interest earned to the initial investment.
5 000 + 17.92 = \$5 017.92

His investment is worth \$5 017.92 at the end of the first month.

When bills are not paid in full, companies usually charge a late penalty on the outstanding balance.

The following example illustrates how interest is calculated on outstanding credit card balances.

Example

Sunil's credit card bill for the month of May was $625.50. The payment was due on May 31. On May 25, Sunil paid $425.50 off his credit card bill. In June, Sunil charged another $340.25 on the credit card. He paid his June bill at the end of the banking day on June 25.

The credit card company charges a penalty of 18% per annum on overdue balances.
The penalty is calculated on the number of days the unpaid balance is overdue.

How much will Sunil need to pay the credit card company on June 25 in order to pay his bill in full? $_____

Solution

The unpaid balance in May is
625.50 − 425.50 = 200.00.

The late payment penalty is calculated on the number of days overdue, which is 25 days in June.

The penalty is $200.00 \times 0.18 \times \dfrac{25}{365} = \$2.47$.

Sunil will need to pay the unpaid balance, the new charges, and the late payment penalty in order to pay his bill in full.

This is $200.00 + 340.25 + 2.47 = \$542.72$.

Sometimes it is helpful to use tables to organize all the calculated data. Tables allow for calculations to be made quickly and efficiently.

Example

ABC utility company charges a penalty of 1.75% per month on unpaid balances. Sheri's utility bill charges and the amounts she paid in January, February, and March are shown in the following table.

Month	Previous Balance	Payment	Unpaid Balance	Overdue Penalty	New Charges	New Balance
Jan	350.00	200.00	150.00	2.63	250.25	
Feb		200.00			175.30	
Mar		200.00			150.55	

Complete the given table to determine the amount that Sheri needs to pay in March to pay the full amount that is due.

Solution

Step 1
Calculate the unpaid balance for January.
Unpaid balance = Previous balance − Payment
= 350.00 − 200.00
= $150.00

Step 2
Calculate the overdue penalty.
Overdue penalty = 1.75% of unpaid balance
= 1.75% × 150.00
= 0.0175 × 150.00
= $2.63

Step 3
Calculate the new balance.
New balance = Unpaid balance
+Overdue charges+New charges
= 150.00 + 2.63 + 250.25
= $402.88

Step 4
In February, the new balance will become the previous balance. Repeat the steps for each month.

The completed table is shown.

Month	Previous Balance	Payment	Unpaid Balance	Overdue Penalty	New Charges	New Balance
Jan	350.00	200.00	150.00	2.63	250.25	402.88
Feb	402.88	200.00	202.88	3.55	175.30	381.73
Mar	381.73	200.00	181.73	3.18	150.55	335.46

Sheri needs to pay $335.46 in March to pay the full amount of her utility bill.

CALCULATING COMPOUND INTEREST

Compound interest is determined from principal amounts that increase at the end of each compounding period by a rate of interest based on the compounding periods. Compound interest is calculated using the formula $A = P(1 + i)^n$, in which A represents the compound amount, P represents the principal or present amount, i represents the interest rate per compounding period, and n represents the number of compounding periods.

The following terms are used when calculating compound interest:

- Annually—once per year
- Semi-annually—twice per year
- Quarterly—four times per year
- Monthly—12 times per year
- Bimonthly—24 times per year
- Weekly—52 times per year
- Daily—365 times per year

Example

John invests $5 000 by purchasing a bond that pays 4.3%, compounded semi-annually. Determine the compound amount at the end of six years. $_____

Solution

Step 1

Determine the amount invested (*P*).
$P = \$5\ 000.00$

Step 2

Calculate the effective interest rate (*i*).

$$i = \frac{\text{Annual interest rate}}{\text{Number of compounding periods/year}}$$

$$i = \frac{4.3\%}{2}$$

$$i = \frac{0.043}{2}$$

Step 3

Calculate the total number of compounding periods (*n*).
$n = $ No. of periods/year $\times$ No. of years
$n = 2 \times 6$
$n = 12$ periods

Step 4

Substitute into the formula, and perform the calculation.

$$A = P(1 + i)^n$$

$$= (5\ 000)\left(1 + \frac{0.043}{2}\right)^{12}$$

$$= 5\ 000(1.0215)^{12}$$

$$= \$6\ 454.02$$

At the end of six years, John will have $6 454.02.

USING THE TVM SOLVER TO CALCULATE COMPOUND INTEREST

The Time-Value-Money (TVM) Solver is a program that is stored in many calculators. Essentially, this program calculates the value of money over a period of time.

To start the program on a TI-83 Plus calculator, press $\boxed{\text{APPS}}$, choose FINANCE, and choose TVM Solver.

When the TVM Solver program is running on a TI-83 or TI-83 Plus, you will see the following window:

- N—number of payment periods
- I%—annual interest rate
- PV—present value
- PMT—payment amount
- FV—future value
- P/Y—number of payment periods per year
- C/Y—number of compound periods per year
- PMT:END BEGIN—the payment made at the end or the beginning of the period

The values for present value (PV) and future value (FV) are given positive (+) or negative (−) signs. Money that is received is considered to be a positive amount, whereas money that is invested is considered to be a negative amount.

Out-of-pocket money is negative. In-pocket money is positive.

To use the TVM Solver, complete the following steps:

1. Enter the known values for the variables.

2. Press $\boxed{\text{ALPHA}}$ $\boxed{\text{ENTER}}$ to solve for the unknown variable.

When using the TVM Solver, a value must be entered for the unknown variable before you can place the cursor at that location and use ALPHA ENTER. Any value will do, including 0.

Example

Fenella invests $5 000.00 by purchasing a bond that pays 4.3%, compounded semi-annually. Using the TVM Solver, calculate the compound amount at the end of six years. $_____

Solution

Step 1

Press APPS, choose FINANCE, and choose TVM Solver.

Enter the following values:

- N = 12
- I% = 4.3
- PV = −5 000 (This value is negative because the money is being invested.)
- PMT = 0
- FV = 0
- P/Y = 2
- C/Y = 2

Step 2

Use the ENTER key or the arrow keys after each entry. Although the FV is not known because it is the required value, a value must be entered for FV in order to proceed to the next entry, so enter 0 for FV. Also, when PMT = 0, use P / Y = C / Y.

Step 3

To solve for the missing future value, place the cursor on FV, then press ALPHA ENTER.

FV = 6 454.02

Fenella will have $6 454.02 at the end of six years.

The TVM Solver can also be used to calculate the amount of interest earned on an investment.

Example

Chris invested $2 000 at 7%, compounded quarterly for five years. Using both the compound interest formula and the TVM Solver, determine how much interest he earned on his investment. $_____

Solution

To use the compound interest formula, first identify the relevant values, which are given as follows:

$$P = 2\ 000,\ i = \frac{0.07}{4},\ n = 5 \times 4 = 20$$

The compound amount is then calculated as follows:

$$A = 2\ 000\left(1 + \frac{0.07}{4}\right)^{20} = \$2\ 829.56$$

The amount of interest earned is 2 829.56 − 2 000 = $829.56.

To use the TVM Solver, enter the values for the variables as shown.

Place the cursor on FV, and press ALPHA ENTER.

The result is as follows.

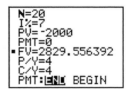

The amount of interest earned is 2 829.56 − 2 000 = $829.56, which agrees with the answer obtained by using the formula.

COMPARING SIMPLE AND COMPOUND INTEREST

In order to see the difference between simple and compound interest, compare the same investment using the two types of interest when the information is organized into a chart and a graph.

Example

Compare the simple and compound interest earned on a $1 000 investment that receives 10% interest per year over a five-year period. To illustrate the interest growth, make a table of values and graph the problem.

- t—time in years
- P—principal
- I—interest earned
- I_T—total interest

The interest rate, r, as a decimal is 0.10.

Simple interest is only earned on the principal, and it is calculated each year using the formula $I = Prt$.

Simple Interest Table

t	P	I	I_T
0	$1 000	n/a	0
1	$1 000	$1 000 × 0.10 × 1 = $100	$100
2	$1 000	$1 000 × 0.10 × 1 = $100	$200
3	$1 000	$1 000 × 0.10 × 1 = $100	$300
4	$1 000	$1 000 × 0.10 × 1 = $100	$400
5	$1 000	$1 000 × 0.10 × 1 = $100	$500

Compound interest can be calculated each year using the formula $I = Prt$, in which $t = 1$. This interest is then added to the principal from the previous year before calculating the interest for the following year. Therefore, the principal, P, increases from year to year, as does the interest, I.

Compound Interest Table

t	P	I	I_T
0	$1 000	n/a	0
1	$1 000	$1 000 × 0.10 × 1 = $100	$100
2	$1 100	$1 100 × 0.10 × 1 = $110	$210
3	$1 210	$1 210 × 0.10 × 1 = $121	$331
4	$1 331	$1 331 × 0.10 × 1 = $133.10	$464.10
5	$1 464.10	$1 464.10 × 0.10 × 1 = $146.41	$610.51

In the graph, the points representing simple interest follow a linear pattern of growth, while the points representing compound interest follow a non-linear pattern of growth. This pattern is also evident in the table of values.

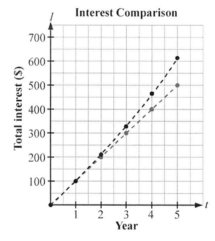

In the first year, the simple and compound interest are the same. However, after the first year, the compound interest is greater than the simple interest, and this difference increases more and more each year. Money invested in a compound interest account grows more rapidly than in a simple interest account.

USING THE TVM SOLVER TO SOLVE ANNUITIES

Usually, a loan is paid by making a series of regular payments rather than one payment at the end of the term of the loan. Similarly, investments are often made by making regular payments into an investment vehicle, such as a savings account.

An **annuity** is a series of payments that are made at regular intervals. Savings plans with regular payments, regular payments on a loan, retirement plans, and loans to acquire mortgages are examples of annuities.

A **mortgage** is a type of loan that uses property as security, and it is often used to purchase the property that is being used as the security. Mortgages are **amortized** over a period of time, meaning that payments are made over this time period. The **amortization period** for a mortgage is often between 25 and 40 years. The **term** of the mortgage is the time period for which a particular interest rate applies. The interest rate is often renegotiated at the end of each term, which is usually much shorter than the amortization period.

The payment features (PMT and P/Y) of the TVM Solver can be used to calculate details of various types of annuities. The following examples and exercises illustrate some of the possible calculations.

Example

Terry has arranged to get a bank loan of $14 000 at 7%/a interest, compounded semi-annually. He wants to pay back the loan by making monthly payments at the end of each month for four years.

What is the amount of his monthly payment?

Solution

Using the TVM Solver, enter the data.

The calculation of his monthly payments for 4 years is as follows. N = 12 × 4 = 48
Interest rate = 7% / a

PV is positive because it is money received.

PMT needs to be found, so enter 0 for now.

FV = 0 when the loan is paid in full.

P / Y = 12 for 12 payments per year.

C / Y = 2 for compounding twice per year.

PMT:END because payments are at the end of the month.

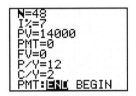

To solve for the monthly payment, move the cursor to PMT, and press | ALPHA | ENTER |.

The result is as follows.

Thus, the amount of the monthly payment is $334.60.

Example

Ken and Laura are planning to buy a condo and are shopping for a mortgage. They want a mortgage of $160 000 that they will amortize over 25 years. They have budgeted $1 200 per month for mortgage payments to be paid at the end of each month.

To the nearest 0.1%, what is the maximum rate of interest compounded annually that would allow Ken and Laura to secure a mortgage?

Solution

N = 12 × 25 = 300

To solve for the interest rate, move the cursor to I%, and press ALPHA ENTER.

Therefore, the maximum rate of interest for the mortgage is 7.9%.

Example

As part of her retirement income, Emma wants to purchase an annuity for $200 000 that will be paid out at the end of each month for 20 years. The interest rate is fixed at 6.5%/a, compounded semi-annually.

What will be Emma's monthly retirement income from the annuity?

Solution

N = 12 × 20 = 240

To solve for the payment, move the cursor to PMT, and press ALPHA ENTER.

Therefore, Emma's monthly retirement income from the annuity will be $1 481.00.

How much interest income will Emma earn over the term of the annuity?

Solution

The total of all the monthly payments that Emma will receive is 240 × 1 481 = $355 440.

The amount of interest income is 355 440 − 200 000 = $155 440.

20N.3 Demonstrate an understanding of compound interest.

CALCULATING THE NUMBER OF COMPOUNDING PERIODS IN AN INVESTMENT OR LOAN

If you put money into an investment or take out a loan, compound interest is added to the principal, which is the initial amount of money invested or borrowed.

Compound interest can be added to the principal more than once a year. The time when interest is calculated and added to the principal is called the **compounding period**.

The following terms are used to describe the different types of compounding periods:

- Annually—once per year
- Semi-annually—twice per year
- Quarterly—4 times per year
- Monthly—12 times per year
- Semimonthly—24 times per year
- Weekly—52 times per year
- Daily—365 times per year

To calculate the number of compounding periods, n, over the total time of an investment or loan, multiply the number of years by the frequency of the compounding periods in a year.

Example

Caleb invests $2 500 in an investment savings account that pays 2.50%/a, compounded annually.

Determine the number of compounding periods at the end of $3\frac{3}{4}$ years.

Solution

To calculate the number of compounding periods, n, over the total time of the investment, multiply the number of years by the frequency of the compounding periods in a year. The time period of the investment is $3\frac{3}{4}$ years.

The interest is compounded annually, which means once per year.

Step 1
Convert the number of years to an improper fraction.
$$3\frac{3}{4} = \frac{15}{4}$$

Step 2
Determine the number of compounding periods, n.

Multiply $\frac{15}{4}$ by 1, and simplify

$$n = \frac{15}{4} \times 1$$
$$n = \frac{15}{4}$$
$$n = 3.75$$

The total number of compounding periods is 3.75.

The letter "a" in the quoted interest rate stands for *annum*, which means year.

Example

Frank is a getting a bank loan for $10 000 at 7.5%/a, compounded monthly.

If Frank wants to pay back the loan at the end of 2 years and 5 months, what is the number of compounding periods?

Solution

To calculate the number of compounding periods, n, over the total time of the investment, multiply the number of years by the frequency of the compounding periods in one year.

The interest rate is compounded monthly, so the frequency equals 12. The time period is 2 years and 5 months, which is equivalent to $2\frac{5}{12}$ years.

Step 1
Convert the number of years into an improper fraction.
$$2\frac{5}{12} = \frac{29}{12}$$

Step 2
Determine the number of compounding periods, n.

Multiply $\frac{29}{12}$ by 12.

$$n = \frac{29}{12} \times 12$$
$$n = 29$$

The number of compounding periods at the end of 2 years and 5 months is 29.

20N.3 Demonstrate an understanding of compound interest.

CALCULATING THE FINAL VALUE AND COMPOUND INTEREST ON AN INVESTMENT OR LOAN

Compound interest is determined from principal amounts that increase at the end of each compounding period by a rate of interest based on the compounding periods.

For compound interest problems, the final value can be found using the compound interest formula $FV = PV(1 + i)^n$. In this formula, FV is the final value, PV is the present value, i is the interest rate (as a decimal) per compounding period, and n is the number of compounding periods over the total time of the investment or loan.

The compound interest formula can appear in several forms. Common alternates use A for the final amount, P for the present value, r for the interest rate, and t for the number of compounding periods over the total time of the investment or loan. For example, you may see the formula $A = P(1 + r)^t$.

The interest rate is usually quoted as an annual rate, but it can be compounded more than once a year. To calculate the interest, i, that is added per compounding period, divide the annual interest rate by the frequency of the compounding periods in a year.

The following terms are used when calculating compound interest:

- Annually—once per year
- Semi-annually—twice per year
- Quarterly—four times per year
- Monthly—12 times per year
- Semimonthly—24 times per year
- Weekly—52 times per year
- Daily—365 times per year

Example

Maryanne invests $9 000 at 5% interest compounded semi-annually.

What is the value of her investment at the end of 5 years?

Solution

The interest on the loan is compound interest collected over 5 years, so the compound interest formula $FV = PV(1 + i)^n$ can be used.

Step 1

Determine the values of the variables in the formula $FV = PV(1 + i)^n$.

The semi-annual rate, i, is $\dfrac{5\%}{2} = 2.5\%$, and the interest, n, is compounded $2 \times 5 = 10$ times. The present value, PV, is $9 000.
Therefore, $i = 0.025$, $n = 10$, and $PV = 9\ 000$.

Step 2

Substitute these values into the formula $FV = PV(1 + i)^n$, and simplify.
$$FV = PV(1 + i)^n$$
$$FV = 9\ 000(1 + 0.025)^{10}$$
$$FV = 9\ 000(1.025)^{10}$$
$$FV \approx \$11\ 520.76$$
Therefore, the final value of Maryanne's investment will be $11 520.76.

Example

Kobe wants to invest $35 000. He has the following two account options:

1. 8%/a, compounded quarterly for 5 years
2. 8%/a, compounded weekly for 5 years

Determine which option is the **best** choice.

Solution

The interest on the loan is compound interest collected over 5 years, so the compound interest formula $FV = PV(1 + i)^n$ can be used.

Step 1

Calculate the value of the investment after 5 years when interest is compounded quarterly.

The quarterly rate, i, is $\dfrac{8\%}{4} = 2\%$, and the interest, n, is compounded $4 \times 5 = 20$ times. The present value, PV, is $35 000.
Therefore, $PV = 35\ 000$, $i = 0.02$, and $n = 20$.
Substitute these values into the formula $FV = PV(1 + i)^n$.
$$FV = PV(1 + i)^n$$
$$FV = 35\ 000(1 + 0.02)^{20}$$
$$FV = 35\ 000(1.02)^{20}$$
$$FV = 35\ 000(1.485\ 94\ldots)$$
$$FV = \$52\ 008.1588\ldots$$
$$FV \approx \$52\ 008.16$$

Step 2

Calculate the value of the investment after 5 years when interest is compounded weekly.

The weekly rate, i, is $\dfrac{8\%}{52} = \dfrac{2}{13}\%$, and the interest, n, is compounded $52 \times 5 = 260$ times. The present value, PV, is $35\ 000.

Therefore, $PV = 35\ 000$, $i = \dfrac{2}{1\ 300}$, and $n = 260$.

Substitute these values into the formula $FV = PV(1+i)^n$.

$FV = PV(1+i)^n$

$FV = 35\ 000\left(1 + \dfrac{2}{1\ 300}\right)^{260}$

$FV = 35\ 000(1.001\ 538...)^{260}$

$FV = 35\ 000(1.491\ 36...)$

$FV = \$52\ 197.817...$

$FV \approx \$52\ 197.82$

The best choice is for Kobe to invest the $35\ 000 into the account with the weekly compounded interest, since more interest accumulates over the 5 years than in the option that is compounded quarterly. You can expect a larger final amount with an option that gives you interest more often during the year.

To determine the amount of compound interest earned on an investment, use the formula $CI = FV - PV$, where CI is the compound interest.

Example

Shanel invests $44\ 000. At the end of 15 years, she has $111\ 775.47.

Calculate the amount of compound interest she earned on her investment.

Solution

Apply the formula $CI = FV - PV$ to calculate the amount of compound interest earned on the investment.

Substitute $111\ 775.47$ for the final value, FV, and $44\ 000$ for the present value, PV.

$CI = FV - PV$

$CI = 111\ 775.47 - 44\ 000$

$CI = \$67\ 775.47$

Shanel made $67\ 775.47 in interest on her investment.

Example

An investment of $12\ 500 has an interest rate of 10.5% per annum.

What is the amount of interest earned when the investment is compounded quarterly for a period of 3.5 years?

Solution

Step 1

Calculate the value of the investment after 3.5 years when interest is compounded quarterly.

The quarterly rate, i, is $\dfrac{10.5\%}{4} = 2.625\%$, and the interest, n, is compounded $4 \times 3.5 = 14$ times. The present value, PV, is $12\ 500.

Therefore, $PV = 12\ 500$, $i = 0.026\ 25$, and $n = 14$.

Substitute these values into the formula $FV = PV(1+i)^n$.

$FV = PV(1+i)^n$

$FV = 12\ 500(1 + 0.026\ 25)^{14}$

$FV = 12\ 500(1.026\ 25)^{14}$

$FV = 12\ 500(1.437\ 28...)$

$FV \approx \$17\ 966.12$

Step 2

Calculate the amount of interest earned on the investment by applying the formula $CI = FV - PV$.

Substitute $17\ 966.12$ for the final value, FV, and $12\ 500$ for the present value, PV.

$CI = FV - PV$

$CI = 17\ 966.12 - 12\ 500$

$CI = \$5\ 466.12$

The amount of interest earned on the investment is $5\ 466.12.

20N.3 Demonstrate an understanding of compound interest.

SOLVING COMPOUND INTEREST PROBLEMS USING A FORMULA

When solving compound interest problems, the resulting amount, A, or final value, FV, can be found using the following compound interest formula:

$A = P(1 + i)^n$ or $FV = PV(1 + i)^n$, in which A or FV is the accumulated amount, P or PV is the principal or original investment, i is the interest rate (as a decimal) per compounding period, and n is the number of compounding periods over the total time of the investment.

Compound interest is often added to the principal more than once a year. The time when interest is calculated and added to the principal is called the **compounding period**.

The interest rate, r, is usually quoted as an annual rate, but can be compounded more than once a year. To calculate the interest, i, that is added per compounding period, divide the annual interest rate by the frequency, f, of the compounding periods in a year.

To calculate the number of compounding periods, n, over the total time of the investment, multiply the number of years by the frequency, f, of the compounding periods in a year.

The following chart illustrates the concept of compounding.

r	f	i	n
5 %/a annually for 3 years	1	$= \dfrac{0.05}{f}$ $= \dfrac{0.05}{1}$ $= 0.05$	$= 3 \times f$ $= 3 \times 1$ $= 3$
6 %/a semi-annually for 4 years	2	$= \dfrac{0.06}{f}$ $= \dfrac{0.06}{2}$ $= 0.03$	$= 4 \times f$ $= 4 \times 2$ $= 8$
12 %/a quarterly for 2 years	4	$= \dfrac{0.12}{f}$ $= \dfrac{0.12}{4}$ $= 0.03$	$= 2 \times f$ $= 2 \times 4$ $= 8$
9 %/a monthly for 6 years	12	$= \dfrac{0.09}{f}$ $= \dfrac{0.09}{12}$ $= 0.0075$	$= 6 \times f$ $= 6 \times 12$ $= 72$
10 %/a daily for 1 year	365	$= \dfrac{0.10}{f}$ $= \dfrac{0.10}{365}$ (leave as fraction)	$= 1 \times f$ $= 1 \times 365$ $= 365$

The designation "a" in the quoted interest rate stands for *annum*, which means "year."

Example

Natasha wants to invest $60 000. She has the following two account options:

1. 10%/a, compounded semi-annually for four years
2. 10%/a, compounded daily for four years

Determine which option is the best choice.

Solution

Use the formula $A = P(1 + i)^n$ to calculate the total amount for each option after four years.

Option 1: Compounded semi-annually
$\Rightarrow f = 2$
$i = 0.10 \div f = 0.10 \div 2 = 0.05$
$n = 4 \times f = 4 \times 2 = 8$
$A = P(1 + i)^n$
$\quad = 60\ 000(1 + 0.05)^8$
$\quad = 60\ 000(1.05)^8$
$\quad = \$88\ 647.33$

Option 2: Compounded daily $\Rightarrow f = 365$
$i = 0.10 \div f$
$\quad = 0.10 \div 365 = \dfrac{0.10}{365}$
$n = 4 \times f = 4 \times 365 = 1\ 460$

Use brackets around i when it is a fraction.
$A = P(1 + i)^n$
$\quad = 60\ 000\left(1 + \left(\dfrac{0.10}{365}\right)\right)^{1\ 460}$
$\quad = \$89\ 504.58$

The best choice is for Natasha to invest the \$60 000 into the account with the daily compounded interest, since more interest accumulates over the four years than in the option that is compounded semi-annually. You can expect a larger final amount with an option that gives you interest more often during the year.

Example

Determine the present value (*PV*) when the future value (*FV*) after 15 years in an investment is \$40 000, and the interest earned is 8%/a, compounded annually.

Solution

Compounded annually $\Rightarrow f = 1$
$\quad i = 0.08 \div f = 0.08 \div 1 = 0.08$
$\quad n = 15 \times f = 15 \times 1 = 15$
$\quad FV = PV(1 + i)^n$
$40\ 000 = PV(1 + 0.08)^{15}$
$40\ 000 = PV(3.172\ 169\ 114)$
$\dfrac{40\ 000}{3.172\ 169\ 114} = PV$
$12\ 609.67 = PV$

The present value is \$12 609.67.

20N.4 Demonstrate an understanding of financial institution services used to access and manage finances.

RECONCILING FINANCIAL STATEMENTS

Managing your finances means keeping track of your money. One aspect of this is reconciling your financial statements.

Reconciling your financial statements involves comparing your records with the statements that the bank or credit card company sends by mail or electronically. The purpose of this process is to make sure the two records match. This process will alert you if the bank or credit card company has made a mistake and will also allow you to bring your records up to date.

There are several different types of financial statements:

- Bank statements are sent from your financial institution. Use your chequebook and debit card receipts to reconcile these statements.
- Credit card statements are sent from each institution with which you have a credit card. Use purchase receipts to reconcile these statements.
- Loan statements are sent from the institutions with which you have outstanding loans. Most often, loan payments will be withdrawn directly from your bank account. Use your loan statements to reconcile your bank statements.

When you receive your statements, check each transaction with your transaction records. When the final balance on each statement matches the final balance in your transaction records (either from your chequebook or your receipts), the financial statements have been reconciled.

Checking your statements is a good way of finding errors made by the bank and of determining how much the bank charges for certain services. For example, when you use your debit card to withdraw money at a private cash machine, you are usually charged two fees: one by the company that owns the cash machine and one by your bank.

If you do not record these fees in your chequebook, your records will not agree with your bank statements, and you may think you have more money in your account than you actually do.

When you use a credit card, it is a good idea to file the receipts from your purchases in a special place so that you can compare them with your credit card statement when it arrives. This process will alert you to any mistakes or extra charges you have incurred.

Your bank statement will also list your loan repayment transactions. You should check these transactions carefully to ensure that the bank has recorded them correctly.

When reconciling your financial statements, follow these steps:

1. Make a note of any credits or debits that appear on the bank statement that you do not have listed in your records.
2. Check all the amounts on your transaction record to ensure that they agree with the bank statement.
3. Determine the final balance on your transaction record.
4. Determine the up-to-date final balance on the bank statement.

Example

Bank Statement

Date	Transaction	Debit ($)	Credit ($)	Balance ($)
	Balance forward			173.45
1/04/11	Deposit		465.20	638.65
3/04/11	Ch. 89	55.65		583.00
4/04/11	Ch. 90	45.89		
4/04/11	Debit	50.00		
4/04/11	Debit fee	2.50		484.61
25/04/11	Ch. 93	142.11		342.50
26/04/11	Ch. 91	68.30		274.20
30/04/11	Service charge	3.00		271.20

Transaction Record

Date	Ch. #	Description	Debit ($)	Credit ($)	Balance ($)
		Balance forward			173.45
1/04/11				465.20	
3/04/11	89	J. Smith	55.65		
4/04/11	90	Upscale Clothing	45.89		
4/04/11		Cash machine	50.00		
20/04/11	91	Valley Ski Centre	68.30		
22/04/11	92	A&M Grocery	72.35		
22/04/11	93	Lamar Sound	142.11		

Assuming the bank statement is correct, reconcile the chequing account for the month.

Solution

Step 1

Determine any credits or debits that appear on the bank statement that have not been recorded in the transaction statement.

- Debit fee: $2.50
- Service charge: $3.00

Step 2

Determine any credits or debits on the transaction statement that have not been recorded in the bank statement.

- A&M Grocery: $72.35

Include the amount in the bank statement.

Step 3

Determine the final balance on the transaction record, including the missing banking fees.

Determine the total for all debits:

$$\begin{array}{r} 55.65 \\ +\quad 45.89 \\ +\quad 50.00 \\ +\quad 68.30 \\ +\quad 72.35 \\ +\quad 142.11 \\ +\quad 2.50 \\ +\quad \underline{3.00} \\ \$439.80 \end{array}$$

Determine the final balance:

Final Balance = Balance Forward + Credits − Debits

$= 173.45 + 465.20 - 439.80$

$= \$198.85$

Step 4

Determine the up-to-date final balance on the bank statement.

The up-to-date final balance is calculated using the following equation:

Final balance = indicated final balance + uncleared deposits − uncleared debts

Final Balance $= 271.20 + 0.00 - 72.35$

$= \$198.85$

Since the final balances match, the statement has been reconciled.

Example

Bank Statement

Date	Transaction	Debit ($)	Credit ($)	Balance ($)
1/09/11	Balance forward			615.00
4/09/11	Ch. 87	55.00		560.00
5/09/11	Ch. 88	110.99		
5/09/11	Bank card fee	2.00		447.01
11/09/11	Deposit		575.20	1 022.21
13/09/11	Ch. 89	425.00		597.21
30/09/09	Service charge	5.50		591.71

Transaction Record

Date	Ch. #	Description	Debit ($)	Credit ($)	Balance ($)
4/09/11	87	Wee Book Store	55.00		
5/09/11	88	The Garage	110.89		
5/09/11		Service charge	2.00		
11/09/11		Paycheque		575.20	
13/09/11	89	Rent: Bayside Apt.	425.00		
20/09/11	90	Mytown Cleaners	56.00		

Assuming the bank statement is correct, reconcile the transaction record of the chequing account for the month of September.

Solution

Step 1

Record any credits or debits that appear on the bank statement that have not been recorded in the transaction record.

- Service charge: $5.50

Step 2

Check all the amounts on the transaction record to ensure that they agree with the bank statement.

- Cheque 88 reads $110.89 on the transaction record, but it should read $110.99. Change the transaction record.
- Mytown Cleaners: $56.00 debit is not recorded on the bank statement.

Step 3

Determine the final balance on the transaction record.

Final balance = balance forward+credits −debits

Determine the total of all the debits first:

$$
\begin{aligned}
& 55.00 \\
& 110.99 \\
& 2.00 \\
& 425.00 \\
& 56.00 \\
+\ & \underline{\ \ \ 5\ 50} \\
& \$654.49
\end{aligned}
$$

Determine the final balance:

Final balance $= 615.00 + 575.20 - 654.49$
$\qquad = \$535.71$

Step 4

Determine the up-to-date final balance on the bank statement.

Final balance = indicated final balance +uncleared deposits−uncleared debts

Final balance $= 591.71 + 0.00 - 56.00$
$\qquad = \$535.71$

Since the final balances match, the statement has been reconciled.

────────────────

20N.5 Demonstrate an understanding of credit options, including: credit cards, loans.

ANALYZING METHODS OF PAYMENT IN RETAIL PURCHASING

There are a few methods of payment available in retail purchasing. A common form of payment is cash. Often, when large purchases are necessary, a form of credit is used. This includes credit cards and personal loans.

CASH

Cash is an immediate form of payment that is normally accepted at almost any retailer.

Paying with cash has the following advantages:

- Convenient for small purchases—it is easy to carry smaller amounts of cash than larger amounts.
- No extra charges incurred—there are no additional fees for using cash at retailers and no outstanding balances.
- Easier to stay out of debt—it is easier to limit your spending and not overspend by using cash rather than a credit card.

Paying with cash has the following disadvantages:

- Stolen or lost—cash can be easily stolen or misplaced. There is no easy way to trace lost or stolen cash.
- Not easy to track spending—you need to retain your receipts to keep track of purchases made with cash to help you manage your budget.
- Online shopping—if purchasing items online, it is not possible to use cash. Another form of payment is required.

CREDIT CARDS

Credit cards are issued by either a financial institution or a retailer. Credit cards usually have a maximum limit. Most credit cards have a revolving charge, which means that purchases can still be made if there is a balance on the card and a minimum payment was made. The balance gets carried over, and interest is charged to the remaining balance.

Credit cards have the following advantages:

- Convenient method of payment—a credit card is useful for large purchases. You may not want to carry large amounts of cash or are purchasing from companies that do not accept cash (such as airlines, hotels, and car rental companies).
- Builds credit history—as long as payments are made on time and purchases made within the given limit, you can build good credit history. Having a good credit history will help in getting future loans and mortgages.
- Reward programs—some credit card companies offer reward programs with other companies in which you can accumulate points and use the points toward travel or selected merchandise.
- Track spending—you can keep track of your spending by looking at your statements.

Credit cards have the following disadvantages:

- Shorter time to pay balance—the time for paying the balance is usually less than a month.
- Higher interest rates—credit cards often have higher interest rates than loans.
- Increases personal debt—often, people spend more than their budget by using credit cards. If payments are not made in full, then interest is accumulated on the outstanding balances until it is completely paid off.
- Risk of credit card fraud—it is possible for your card number to be stolen and misused. Most credit card companies offer insurance so that the cardholder is not responsible for any purchases made after the card was stolen.

LOANS

A loan is a specific amount of money borrowed from a financial institution or a company. There is usually interest that is charged to the amount borrowed, and the amount has to be paid back by a certain date. A loan is paid by making a series of regular payments rather than one payment at the end of the term of the loan. Often, loans can be used to purchase vehicles, furniture, electronics, appliances, and other large items.

Loans have the following advantages:

- Fixed interest rate—the interest rate is set at the time of the loan and will not increase throughout the term.
- Debt slowly decreases—as you make your regular payments, the total amount of debt decreases.
- Extra payments on loan—some lenders give the option for borrowers to make extra payments. This helps repay the loan faster and creates less interest charged on the loan.

Loans have the following disadvantages:

- Long-term commitment—since the debt is long-term, you have to commit to paying the specified amount each month.
- Lots of interest is accumulated—since loans tend to take a long time to pay off, and interest is charged continually throughout the time period of the loan, the total amount of interest charged is sometimes worth more then the initial loan.
- Penalties for missing payments—if you miss a payment, there can be additional fees. Missing payments will also affect your credit score, which affects your ability to borrow money in the future.

Use the following information to answer the next question.

Rachel is asked to find the number of triangles and the number of squares in Level 5 of the given diagram.

Level 1   Level 2

Level 3 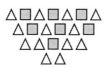   Level 4

She recorded her partial results in a table.

Level	Number of Triangles	Number of Squares
1	1	1
2	3	3
3	7	5
4	13	7
5		

1. What are the two numbers that complete Rachel's table?

A. 14, 8   B. 15, 9

C. 21, 9   D. 26, 8

Use the following information to answer the next question.

Blake is asked to find the value of x in the equation $19 + x = 27.65$ by using guess and check.

The steps in Blake's partial solution for determining the value of x are shown.

1. Round the decimal number in the equation.
   $19 + x = 27$
2. Since $19 + 8 = 27$, a reasonable guess is a number less than 8.
3. Substitute 7 for x.
   $19 + 7 = 26$ The guess of 7 gives a number less than 27.65.
4. Substitute 7.65 for x.
   $19 + 7.65 = 26.65$ The guess of 7.65 gives a number less than 27.65.

2. In which step did Blake make his first error?

A. 1   B. 2

C. 3   D. 4

Use the following information to answer the next question.

Kitwana has a yearly income of $87 560. His yearly budget is represented by the given circle graph.

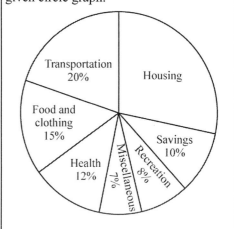

Numerical Response

3. The amount of money, rounded to the nearest dollar, that Kitwana budgeted for housing is $_____.

Written Response

4. Justin has a net monthly income of $2 800. He wishes to set up a monthly budget according to the percentages that are indicated in the following table. Calculate the percentage for savings and investments and the budget amount to the nearest dollar for each of the categories.

Category	Budget Amount	Percentage (%)
Housing		25
Transportation		15
Food		12
Clothing		8
Health care		10
Recreation		8
Miscellaneous		8
Debt payments		10
Savings and investments		

5. If interest is compounded quarterly for 3 years at 5% per annum, how much interest is earned by an investment of $1 100?

　A. $173.39　　**B.** $176.83

　C. $241.33　　**D.** $875.44

Use the following information to answer the next question.

> A loan of $9 850 is taken. At the end of 6.75 years, it is paid off for $13 450.

Numerical Response

6. The amount of compound interest the loan accumulated is $_____.

Use the following information to answer the next question.

> Achmed wanted to compare the growth of the following two interest options over 4 years.
> Simple Interest: $2 000 at 9% per annum
> Compound Interest: $2 000 at 8% per annum compounded annually.
> To compare these two options, he calculated the annual interest, I, and the total amount, A, in the partially completed tables shown below.

Simple Interest (9%)

Year	0	1	2	3	4
I	0	180	180	180	p
A	2 000	2 180	2 360	2 540	q

Compound Interest (8%)

Year	0	1	2	3	4
I	0	160	172.80	186.62	r
A	2 000	2 160	2 332.80	2 519.42	s

7. If the values for p, q, r and s were calculated correctly then the relationship between these values would be.

　A. $r > p$ and $q = s$

　B. $r < p$ and $q > s$

　C. $r > p$ and $q < s$

　D. $r < p$ and $q < s$

Use the following information to answer the next question.

> Julio has taken out a loan of $25 000 at 18% interest compounded semimonthly. He will begin to pay back his loan after 3 years and 9 months.

Numerical Response

8. To the nearest dollar, the value of the loan he has to pay back at the end of 3 years and 9 months is $_____.

Use the following information to answer the next question.

A bank statement for the month of September is given.

Bank Statement

Account/Description	Debits	Credits	Date	Balance
Balance forward			1/9	615.00
Cheque 87	55.00		4/9	560.00
Cheque 88	110.99		5/9	A
Bank card fee	3.00		5/9	B
Deposit		644.49		C
Cheque 89	450.00			D
Service charge	5.50		30/9	E

Numerical Response

9. If cells *A*, *B*, *C*, *D*, and *E* each represent a numerical value, then the numerical value of cell *E* is _____.

Written Response

10. Consider the transaction record and bank statement below. Assuming the bank statement is correct, reconcile the chequing account for August. Identify any errors or omissions, and describe how to correct them.

Bank Statement

Account/Description	Debit	Credit	Date	Balance
Balance forward				75.63
Deposit		564.25	1/8	639.88
Cheque 115	45.75		2/8	594.13
Cheque 116	32.15		4/8	562.00
Debit	25.64		4/8	536.36
Debit fee	2.25		4/8	534.11
Cheque 117	122.25		20/8	411.86
Cheque 118	141.10		25/8	270.76
Service charge	5.00		30/8	265.76

Transaction Record

Date	No	Description	Credit	Debit	Balance
		Balance forward			75.63
1/8			564.25		
2/8	115	Sports R Us		45.75	
4/8	116	Movie Go		32.15	
20/8	117	Hockey registration		122.25	
25/8	118	Football registration		141.10	

Use the following information to answer the next multipart question.

11. A student examined a graph comparing the annual increase in the amount of a $200 investment of a simple and compound interest account.

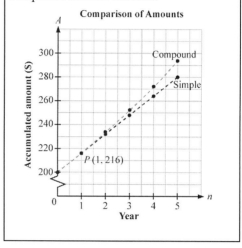

Comparison of Amounts

The point labelled *P*(1, 216) indicates that after 1 year, the accumulated amounts in both accounts is $216. Based on this value, the annual interest rate in both accounts must be

A. 16.0%   **B.** 10.8%

C. 8.0%   **D.** 7.4%

ANSWERS AND SOLUTIONS
NUMBER

1. C	4. WR	7. C	10. WR
2. A	5. B	8. 48977	11. C
3. 24517	6. 3600	9. 635	

1. C

Step 1
Identify the pattern in the number of triangles.

Level	Number of Triangles	Pattern
1	1	
2	3	$3 - 1 = 2$
3	7	$7 - 3 = 4$
4	13	$13 - 7 = 6$

The difference between the number of triangles in one level and the number in the previous level is increasing by 2. Therefore, in Level 5, there will be $13 + 8 = 21$ triangles.

Step 2
Identify the pattern in the number of squares.

Level	Number of Squares	Pattern
1	1	
2	3	$3 - 1 = 2$
3	5	$5 - 3 = 2$
4	7	$7 - 5 = 2$

There is a constant difference of 2 between the number of squares in one level and the number in the previous level. Therefore, in Level 5, there will be $7 + 2 = 9$ squares.

Step 3
Complete the table.

Level	Number of Triangles	Number of Squares
1	1	1
2	3	3
3	7	5
4	13	7
5	21	9

2. A

Blake made his first error in step 1. When the decimal number 27.65 is rounded to the nearest whole number, it becomes 28.
$19 + x = 28$

Steps 2 to 5 of a possible solution are therefore as follows:

2. Since $19 + 9 = 28$, a reasonable guess would be a number less than 9.
3. Substitute 8 for x.
   $19 + 8 = 27$
4. The guess of 8 gives a number less than 27.65. Add 0.65 to 8, and substitute the result for x.
   $19 + 8.65 = 27.65$
5. The value of x is 8.65.

3. 24517

Step 1
Calculate the percentage of Kitwana's yearly income that was budgeted for housing.
Housing
$= 100 - (10 + 8 + 7 + 12 + 15 + 20)$
$= 100 - 72$
$= 28\%$

Step 2
Calculate the amount of money represented by this percentage.
Calculate 28% of $87 560.
$0.28 \times 87\ 560 = \$24\ 517$

4. WR

Step 1

Calculate the percentage that is left for savings and investments.

The percentage that is left for savings and investments is $100 - 96 = 4$.

Category	Budget Amount	Percentage (%)
Housing		25
Transportation		15
Food		12
Clothing		8
Health care		10
Recreation		8
Miscellaneous		8
Debt payments		10
Savings and investments		4

Step 2

Calculate the budget amount for housing.

Budget amount for housing is 25 % of the monthly income.

That is, $\dfrac{25}{100} \times \$2\ 800 = \$700$.

Step 3

Simlarly, calculate the budget amount for the other categories and fill in the table.

Category	Budget Amount	Percentage (%)
H	700.00	25
T	420.00	15
F	336.00	12
C	224.00	8
HC	280.00	10
R	224.00	8
M	224.0	8
DP	280.00	10
S&I	112.00	4

5. B

Step 1

Calculate the accumulated amount of the investment using the compound interest formula.

The principal is $1 100. Since the interest rate is 5 % compounded quarterly, $i = \dfrac{0.05}{4}$. Since the investment is compounded quarterly for 3 years, the number of compounding periods is $n = 3 \times 4 = 12$.

$A = P(1 + i)^n$

$A = 1\ 100\left(1 + \dfrac{0.05}{4}\right)^{12}$

$A = 1\ 100(1.160\ 7545)$

$A = 1\ 276.83$

Therefore, the accumulated value of the investment is $1 276.83.

Step 2

Calculate the interest earned.

Subtract the principal from the accumulated value of the investment.

$1\ 276.83 - 1\ 100 = 176.83$

Therefore, the interest earned is $176.83.

6. 3600

Apply the formula $CI = FV - PV$ to calculate the amount of compound interest accumulated on this loan.

Substitute 13 450 for the final value, FV, and 9 850 for the present value, PV.

$CI = FV - PV$

$CI = 13\ 450 - 9\ 850$

$CI = \$3\ 600$

The loan accumulated $3 600 of interest.

7. C

In a simple interest account, the interest, I, is the same per year, namely, $180. Therefore, $p = 180$, and the amount after 4 years is $q = 2\ 540 + 180 = 2\ 720$.

To find the compound interest, r, take the previous amount $A = 2\ 519.42$, and multiply by the annual interest rate of 8 % or 0.08. Therefore, $r = 2\ 519.42 \times 0.08 = 201.55$.

The total amount is $s = 2\ 519.42 + 201.55 = 2\ 720.97$.

When you examine the values of p, q, r, and s, the following relationships hold true:

$r > p$, since $201.55 > 180$

$q < s$, since $2\ 720 < 2\ 720.97$

8. **48977**

The interest on the loan is compound interest collected over 3 years and 9 months, so the compound interest formula $FV = PV(1 + i)^n$ can be used.

Step 1

Determine the values of the variables in the formula $FV = PV(1 + i)^n$.

The semimonthly rate, i, is $\dfrac{18\%}{24} = 0.75\%$, and the interest, n, is compounded $(3 \times 24) + (9 \times 2) = 90$ times. The present value, PV, is $25\ 000$. Therefore, $i = 0.0075$, $n = 90$, and $PV = 25\ 000$.

Step 2

Substitute these values into the formula $FV = PV(1 + i)^n$.

$FV = PV(1 + i)^n$
$FV = 25\ 000(1 + 0.0075)^{90}$
$FV = 25\ 000(1.0075)^{90}$
$FV = 48\ 977.3115$
$FV \approx \$48\ 977$

To the nearest dollar, the value of Julio's loan when he pays it back will be $48\ 977$.

9. **635**

Debits are subtracted from the balance, and credits are added to the balance.

Step 1

Calculate the amount in cell A.
Cell A is equal to $\$560.00 - \$110.99 = \$449.01$.

Step 2

Calculate the amount in cell B.
Cell B is equal to $\$449.01 - \$3.00 = \$446.01$.

Step 3

Calculate the amount in cell C.
Cell C is equal to $\$446.01 + 644.49 = \$1\ 090.50$.

Step 4

Calculate the amount in cell D.
Cell D is equal to $\$1\ 090.50 - \$450.00 = \$640.50$.

Step 5

Calculate the amount in cell E.
Cell E is equal to $\$640.50 - \$5.50 = \$635.00$.

10. **WR**

Step 1

To check the transaction record, compare the credits and debits that appear on the bank statement with the ones that have been recorded.

The debit charge of 25.64, fee of 2.25, and service charge of 5.00 appear on the bank statement but have not been recorded in the transaction record. These should be included in the debit column of the transaction record to correct the mistake.

11. **C**

Method 1:

Since the total amount after 1 year is $A = \$216$, the interest, I, accumulated is the difference between A and the principal
$P = \$200$. $I = A - P = 216 - 200 = \$16$

Then, if you use the simple interest formula $I = Prt$, you can find the annual interest rate, r:

$\quad I = Prt$
$\quad 16 = 200(r)(1)$
$\dfrac{16}{200} = r$
$0.08 = r$

The rate 0.08 as a percentage is
$0.08 \times 100\% = 8.0\%$.

Method 2:

You can find the growth rate or factor from year 0 to year 1 by dividing the total amount A after 1 year by the principal, P.

$\dfrac{A}{P} = \dfrac{216}{200} = 1.08$

The decimal value 0.08 of this rate represents the annual interest rate, $i = 0.08$ or
$0.08 \times 100\% = 8.0\%$.

UNIT TEST — NUMBER

Tom designs a model of a square-based pyramid for a school project. The surface area of the model is 2 160 cm² with a slant height of 30 cm. The side length of the base of the model is 36 cm, and the height of the model is 24 cm. Tom places the pyramid on a rectangular piece of cardboard that is 10 cm longer and wider than the base of the pyramid.

Tom is then asked to find the volume of the pyramid. The steps in his partial solution are as follows:

1. $V_{pyramid} = \dfrac{1}{3}\left(A_{base} \times h\right)$

2. $V_{pyramid} = \dfrac{1}{3}\left(36^2 \times 30\right)$

3. $V_{pyramid} = \dfrac{1}{3}(38\ 880)$

4. $V_{pyramid} = 12\ 960\,cm^3$

1. In which step did Tom make his first error?

  A. 1   **B.** 2

  C. 3   **D.** 4

Use the following information to answer the next question.

The given image shows the first three diagrams in a series. The series of diagrams illustrates a particular pattern.

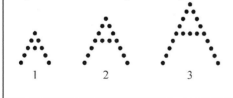

2. How many dots will be in diagram 6?

  A. 20   **B.** 25

  C. 30   **D.** 35

The Tokarek family has set aside $5 000 for a family vacation. Their budget for transportation, food, accommodations, entertainment, and spending money is shown in the chart below.

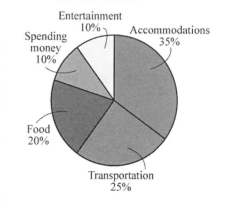

3. If all of their accommodation allowance is spent on 13 nights in a hotel, what is the average daily room rate, to the nearest dollar, for the Tokarek family?

  A. $95   **B.** $135

  C. $175   **D.** $269

Numerical Response

4. Rounded to the nearest hundredth, the amount of interest earned by an investment of $725 when interest is compounded semiannually for 2 years at 6% per year is $_____.

Use the following information to answer the next question.

Shown below is a table indicating the growth patterns for $1 000 invested in a simple interest account compared with the same amount invested in an account that compounds interest annually.

Year	Value (Simple Interest)	Value (Compound Interest)
1	$1 065.00	$1 065.00
2	$1 130.00	$1 134.23
3	$1 195.00	$1 207.95
4	$1 260.00	$1 286.47
5	$1 325.00	$1 370.09
6	$1 390.00	$1 459.14
7	$1 455.00	$1 553.99
8	$1 520.00	$1 655.00
9	$1 585.00	$1 762.57
10	$1 650.00	$1 877.14
11	$1 715.00	$1 999.15
12	$1 780.00	$2 129.10
13	$1 845.00	$2 267.49
14	$1 910.00	$2 414.87
15	$1 975.00	$2 571.84
16	$2 040.00	$2 739.01
17	$2 105.00	$2 917.05
18	$2 170.00	$3 106.65
19	$2 235.00	$3 308.59
20	$2 300.00	$3 523.65

5. How many years does it take before the difference in the two investments is greater than $500?

   A. 13 yrs   **B.** 14 yrs

   C. 15 yrs   **D.** 16 yrs

Use the following information to answer the next question.

Stewart took out a car loan for $25 000 at 1.9%/a, compounded quarterly. He wants to make monthly payments to pay off the loan at the end of 4 years and 3 months.

Numerical Response

6. The number of compounding periods over the total time of the loan is _____.

Use the following information to answer the next question.

Trina has taken out a loan of $18 000 at 3% interest compounded monthly.
She cannot pay back her loan for 6.5 years.

Numerical Response

7. To the nearest cent, the value of the loan she has to pay back at the end of 6.5 years is $_____.

Use the following information to answer the next question.

Laura opens a student bank account by making a deposit of $500. During the month, she makes three withdrawals of $40 each using an automated teller machine. At the end of the month, Laura earns 0.25% interest on the balance of her bank account.

8. If Laura is charged $1.00 for each withdrawal made using her bank card, what will her balance be with interest after one month?

   A. $377.94   **B.** $380.25

   C. $380.95   **D.** $471.25

ANSWERS AND SOLUTIONS — UNIT TEST

1. B	3. B	5. B	7. 21870.28
2. D	4. 90.99	6. 17	8. A

1. B

Tom made his first error in step 2. The volume, V, of a pyramid can be determined by applying the formula $V = \frac{1}{3}(A_{base} \times h)$, where A_{base} is the area of the base and h is the height of the pyramid. Since the pyramid is square-based, the formula becomes $V = \frac{1}{3}(s^2 \times h)$, where s is the side length of the base and h is the height of the pyramid. Tom used the slant height, 30 cm, instead of the height of the pyramid, which is 24 cm.

The correct solution is as follows:

1. $V = \frac{1}{3}(A_{base} \times h)$

2. $V = \frac{1}{3}(s^2 \times h)$

3. $V = \frac{1}{3}(36^2 \times 24)$

4. $V = \frac{1}{3}(1\ 296 \times 24)$

5. $V = \frac{1}{3}(31\ 104)$

6. $V = 10\ 368$

The volume of the model of a square-based pyramid is 10 368 cm³.

2. D

Step 1
Make a table to organize the information from the given diagrams.

Diagram	Number of Dots
1	10
2	15
3	20

Step 2
Identify the pattern.
From diagram 1 to diagram 2, there is a difference of 5 dots (15 − 10 = 5). From diagram 2 to 3, there is also a difference of 5 dots (20 − 15 = 5). Therefore, the pattern is that 5 dots are added to each diagram.

Step 3
Determine how many dots will be in diagram 6.
Diagram 4 will have 20 + 5 = 25 dots, and diagram 5 will have 25 + 5 = 30 dots. Therefore, diagram 6 will have 30 + 5 = 35 dots.

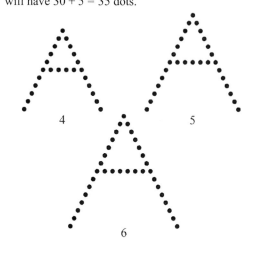

3. B

From the circle graph, we can see that 35% of the Tokarek budget is allocated for accommodations. 35% of $5 000 is equal to $5000 × 0.35 = $1 750. $1 750 is the amount the Tokareks have budgeted for 13 nights' stay at a hotel. Therefore, the average daily room rate, to the nearest dollar, is $135 \left(\dfrac{\$1\ 750}{13} \right)$.

4. 90.99

Step 1
Calculate the accumulated amount of the investment using the compound interest formula.

The principal, P, is $725. Since the interest rate is 6% compounded semiannually, $i = \dfrac{0.06}{2}$. Since the investment is compounded semiannually for 2 years, the number of compounding periods is $n = 2 \times 2 = 4$.

$A = P(1 + i)^n$

$A = 725\left(1 + \dfrac{0.06}{2}\right)^4$

$A \approx 725(1.126)$

$A \approx 815.99$

Therefore, the accumulated amount of the investment is $815.99.

Step 2

Calculate the compound interest.

Subtract the amount of money in the account after 2 years from the principal amount.

$815.99 - 725 \approx 90.99$

Therefore, the compound interest is $90.99.

5. **B**

The word *difference* indicates that the smaller value should be subtracted from the larger table. Calculate the difference in values of the two investments for each year on the table.

The following table shows the calculations of the rows of the investments closest to $500 to find the correct answer:

Year	Value (Simple Interest)	Value (Compound Interest)	Difference
13	$1 845.00	$2 267.49	$422.49
14	$1 910.00	$2 414.87	$504.87
15	$1 975.00	$2 571.84	$596.84

The first year in which the difference between the two investments is greater than $500 is in year 14.

6. **17**

To calculate the number of compounding periods, n, over the total time of the investment, multiply the number of years by the frequency of compounding periods in one year.

The total time of the loan is 4 years and 3 months, which is equivalent to $4\frac{1}{4}$ years. Since the interest is compounded quarterly, it is compounded 4 times per year.

Step 1

Convert the number of years into an improper fraction.

$4\frac{1}{4} = \frac{17}{4}$

Step 2

Determine the number of compounding periods, n.

Multiply $\frac{17}{4}$ by 4.

$n = \frac{17}{4} \times 4$

$n = 17$

The number of compounding periods over 4 years and 3 months is 17.

7. **21870.28**

The interest on the loan is compound interest collected over 6.5 years, so the compound interest formula $FV = PV(1 + i)^n$ can be used.

Step 1

Determine the values of the variables in the formula $FV = PV(1 + i)^n$.

The monthly rate, i, is $\frac{3\%}{12} = 0.25\%$, and the interest, n, is compounded $12 \times 6.5 = 78$ times. The present value, PV, is $18\ 000.

Therefore, $i = 0.0025$, $n = 78$, and $PV = 18\ 000$.

Step 2

Substitute these values into the formula $FV = PV(1 + i)^n$, and simplify.

$FV = PV(1 + i)^n$

$FV = 18\ 000(1 + 0.0025)^{78}$

$FV = 18\ 000(1.0025)^{78}$

$FV = 21\ 870.2751...$

$FV \approx \$21\ 870.28$

To the nearest cent, the value of Trina's loan when she pays it back will be $21\ 870.28.

8. **A**

Step 1

Calculate the total amount of money Laura withdraws.

Laura's opening balance was $500. She made 3 withdrawals of $40.

$40 \times 3 = \$120$

Step 2

Calculate the total service charge on the withdrawals.

She is charged $1.00 for each withdrawal.

$1 \times 3 = \$3$

Step 3

Determine Laura's closing balance before interest.

$\$500.00 - \$120.00 - \$3.00 = \$377.00$

Step 4

Calculate the balance of Laura's account, including interest.

$\$377.00 \times 1.0025 = \$377.94$

Rounded to the nearest cent, Laura's final closing balance is $377.94.

NOTES

Algebra

$a + b$

$a^2 + 2ab + b^3 +$

$3a^2b + 3ab^3 +$

$a^3b + 6a^2b^2 +$

$a^3b + 10a^3b^3 +$

ALGEBRA

	Table of Correlations			
	Outcome	**Practice Questions**	**Unit Test Questions**	**Practice Test**
20A	Algebra			
20A.1	*Solve problems that require the manipulation and application of formulas related to: volume and capacity; surface area; slope and rate of change; simple interest; and finance charges.*	1, 2, 3	1, 2, 3	12, 13, 14
20A.2	*Demonstrate an understanding of slope: as rise over run; as rate of change; and by solving problems.*	4, 5, 6	4, 5, 6	15, 40
20A.3	*Solve problems by applying proportional reasoning and unit analysis.*	7, 8, 9, 10, 11, 12, 13, 14, 15, 16, 17, 18, 19	7, 8, 9, 10, 11, 12, 13, 14, 15, 16, 17, 18, 19	16, 17, 18, 19

20A.1 Solve problems that require the manipulation and application of formulas related to: volume and capacity; surface area; slope and rate of change; simple interest; and finance charges.

EVALUATING POLYNOMIAL EXPRESSIONS

Algebraic expressions contain both variables and numbers.

Follow these steps when evaluating expressions:

1. Replace the variable with the given value.
2. Evaluate the expression following the order of operations.

Example

Evaluate the polynomial expression $3x^2 + 4x - 6$ when $x = -2$.

Solution

Step 1
Replace the variable with the given value. Place brackets around the numbers being substituted into the equation so that the negative sign is included.
$$3(-2)^2 + 4(-2) - 6$$

Step 2
Evaluate the expression following the order of operations. Calculate the exponents first.
$$= 3[(-2)(-2)] + 4(-2) - 6$$
$$= 3(4) + 4(-2) - 6$$
When -2 is put in brackets, its square is $+4$. However, if the brackets are omitted, -2 equals -4, which leads to a completely different and incorrect result.

Multiply in order from left to right.
$$= 3(4) + 4(-2) - 6$$
$$= 12 - 8 - 6$$

Subtract in order from left to right.
$$= 12 - 8 - 6$$
$$= 4 - 6$$
$$= -2$$

Some expressions will have more than one variable. This does not change the steps to follow when evaluating polynomial expressions. Substitute the given values for the corresponding variables. Then, solve the expression following the order of operations.

Example

Evaluate $x^{-3} + y^3$, where $x = 3$ and $y = -1$.

Solution

Step 1
Replace the variables with the given values.
$$(3)^{-3} + (-1)^3$$

Step 2
Rewrite the expression with positive exponents.
$$= \frac{1}{(3)^3} + (-1)^3$$

Step 3
Evaluate the expression following the order of operations.
Exponents:
$$= \frac{1}{3 \times 3 \times 3} + (-1 \times -1 \times -1)$$
$$= \frac{1}{27} + (-1)$$
Addition:
$$= \frac{1}{27} + \left(-\frac{27}{27}\right)$$
$$= \frac{1}{27} - \frac{27}{27}$$
$$= -\frac{26}{27}$$

20A.1 Solve problems that require the manipulation and application of formulas related to: volume and capacity; surface area; slope and rate of change; simple interest; and finance charges.

REARRANGING FORMULAS

Sometimes you will be asked to solve for a variable in an equation that has multiple variables in it, like in a formula. A formula can be used to find the value of any of its variables if you know how to manipulate it.

Follow the same steps to solve these types equations as those used for solving single-variable equations.

1. Identify the variable that is to be isolated.
2. Isolate that variable by performing inverse operations to both sides of the equation.

Example

Solve the equation $P = 2l + 2w$ for w.

Solution

Step 1

Identify the variable that is to be isolated.

In this case, w needs to be isolated.

Step 2

Isolate the variable by performing inverse operations on both sides of the equation.

To isolate the term containing w, subtract both sides of the equation by $2l$.

$P - 2l = 2l + 2w - 2l$
$P - 2l = 2w$

Divide both sides of the equation by 2, the numerical coefficient of w.

$$\frac{P - 2l}{2} = \frac{2w}{2}$$

$$\frac{P - 2l}{2} = w$$

Since w is alone on one side of the equation, the equation is solved for w.

Example

The circumference of a circle is given by the formula $C = 2\pi r$. Solve for r.

Solution

Step 1

Identify the variable that is to be isolated.

In this case, r is to be isolated.

Step 2

Isolate r by performing the inverse operation on both sides of the equation.

Divide both sides by 2π so that r remains on the right side of the equation by itself.

$$\frac{C}{2\pi} = \frac{2\pi r}{2\pi}$$

$$\frac{C}{2\pi} = r$$

Since r is alone on one side of the equation, the equation has been solved for r.

Example

Solve the equation $h(a - k) = y$ for a.

Solution

Step 1

Identify the variable that is to be isolated.

In this case, a is to be isolated.

Step 2

Isolate the variable by performing inverse operations on both sides of the equation.

Divide both sides of the equation by h.

$$\frac{h(a - k)}{h} = \frac{y}{h}$$

$$a - k = \frac{y}{h}$$

Add k to both sides of the equation.

$$a - k + k = \frac{y}{h} + k$$

$$a = \frac{y}{h} + k$$

Since a is alone on one side of the equation, the equation has been solved for a.

20A.2 Demonstrate an understanding of slope: as rise over run; as rate of change; and by solving problems.

IDENTIFYING A RATE OF CHANGE

Rate of change is a ratio between the change of two related variables.

$$\text{rate of change} = \frac{\Delta \text{in dependent variable}}{\Delta \text{in independent variable}}$$

Some common examples of a rate of change are:

- Speed/Velocity (distance versus time)
- Rate of pay (earning versus time)
- Cost per item (cost versus number of items)

Two variables are related by a **constant** rate of change if the relation is linear. That is, when corresponding pairs of independent and dependent variables are graphed, the points form a straight line.

When the data of a linear relation is graphed as ordered pairs (x, y) on the Cartesian plane, the change in the dependent variable (rise) is the same for a consistent change in the independent variable (run).

constant rate of change

$$= \frac{\Delta \text{in dependent variable}}{\Delta \text{in independent variable}}$$

$$= \frac{\text{rise}}{\text{run}}$$

$$= \text{slope}$$

Example

Susan worked at a golf course and made $49.00 after working 7 hours.

Assuming Susan's wage is a constant hourly rate, determine Susan's rate of pay.

Solution

The rate is comparing money and hours worked. The dependent variable is the amount of money made (y-value), and the independent variable is the number of hours worked (x-value):

constant rate of change

$$= \frac{\Delta \text{ in dependent variable}}{\Delta \text{ in independent variable}}$$

$$= \frac{\Delta \$}{\Delta t}$$

$$= \frac{49}{7}$$

$$= \$7/h$$

Example

Graph the relation.

Solution

You are given one ordered pair $(7, 49)$. If Susan did not work any hours, her pay would be $0.00. Thus, the second ordered pair is $(0, 0)$.

The constant rate of change is the slope of the graph. Use the slope to place other points located on the line. To find a point that would occur after point $(0, 0)$ on the line, increase the y-coordinate by 7 (rise) and increase the x-coordinate by 1 (run). This will give you the new point $(0 + 1, 0 + 7) = (1, 7)$. Continue this along the graph. When the rate of change between each pair of successive points is the same, the slope is called the constant rate of change.

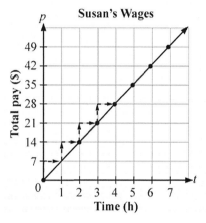

Notice that the data is continuous, so the points are joined in a straight line. Typically, when the independent variable is time, the data is continuous. In practice, however, employers often round hours worked to the nearest hour, half-hour or quarter of an hour. Continuous data includes all the values between the measured points. Discrete data excludes all the data between the measured points.

Another way to determine if two variables have a constant rate of change is to find the first differences of y-coordinates in a table of values.

First differences are differences between *successive y*-values in a table with evenly spaced *x*-values. To find the first differences, subtract each *y*-value by the previous *y*-value in the table.

To find the constant rate of change, divide the first differences of the *y*-values by the change in the *x*-values.

constant rate of change
$$= \frac{\text{first differences of the } y\text{-values}}{\Delta \text{ in the } x\text{-values}}$$

Example

To maintain a hot water tank, it is a good idea to drain it once a year.

The table shows the volume of water remaining after an elapsed time when a hot water tank is drained.

Time (min)	Volume (L)
0	50
2	40
4	30
6	20
8	10
10	0

What is the constant rate of change using first differences? Show your work.

Solution

Time (min)	Volume (L)	First Differences
0	50	
2	40	$40 - 50 = -10$
4	30	$30 - 40 = -10$
6	20	$20 - 30 = -10$
8	10	$10 - 20 = -10$
10	0	$0 - 10 = -10$

constant rate of change
$$= \frac{\text{first differences of the } y\text{-values}}{\Delta \text{ in the } x\text{-values}}$$
$$= \frac{-10}{5}$$
$$= -5 \text{ L/min}$$

Graph the data of this relation.

Solution

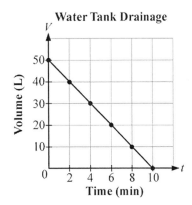

The rate of change can be positive or negative. It is logical here that the rate of change is negative because the tank is losing its water.

Even though the data is continuous, there are no arrows on either end of the line. The tank is full at 50 L and cannot increase in volume. Once the tank is empty at 0 L, it cannot empty any more.

20A.2 Demonstrate an understanding of slope: as rise over run; as rate of change; and by solving problems.

PROPERTIES OF SLOPES

A property is an attribute, quality, or characteristic of something.

The properties of slope describe the characteristics of a line.

DIRECTION

Whether the slope of the line is positive, negative, zero, or undefined dictates the direction (or orientation) of the line.

POSITIVE SLOPE

Property: A positive horizontal change corresponds to a positive vertical change ($y = mx + b$, in which m is positive).

A positive slope rises toward the right, indicating that as the x-values increase, the y-values also increase.

Example

What is the slope of the line passing through the points $A(3, -4)$ and $B(5, -1)$?
Justify your answer.

Solution

Find the slope of the line.

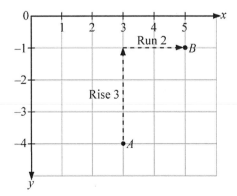

Starting at point A move three steps upward (positive direction) and two steps across (positive direction) to get to point B. Therefore, the slope is:

$$\text{slope} = \frac{\text{rise}}{\text{run}} = \frac{3}{2}$$

Since the slope is positive, the line goes upward from left to right.

Therefore, this line has a positive slope.

NEGATIVE SLOPE

Property: A positive horizontal change corresponds to a negative vertical change ($y = -mx + b$, in which m is negative).

A negative slope falls toward the right, indicating that as the x-values increase, the y-values decrease.

ZERO SLOPE

Property: A constant y-value corresponds to a horizontal line ($y = b$).

A horizontal line runs straight left and right, indicating that the horizontal or x-value changes, while the vertical or y-value remains constant.

UNDEFINED SLOPE

Property: A constant x-value corresponds to a vertical line ($x = a$).

A vertical line runs up and down, indicating that the vertical or y-value changes, while the horizontal or x-value remains constant.

STEEPNESS

Property: The larger the slope value (m), the steeper the line. In the case of negative slopes, the larger the absolute value of the slope, the steeper the line.

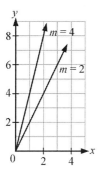

A line with a slope of 4 is steeper than a line with a slope of 2.

PARALLELISM

Property: Parallel lines have the same slope.

Parallel lines ($\parallel$) are straight lines that never meet; they always remain the same distance apart.

Consider the given graph of two parallel lines.

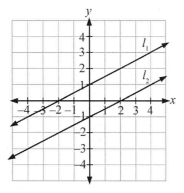

Notice that the slopes of l_1 and l_2 are both $\dfrac{1}{2}$.

In order to stay parallel, the lines must rise and run by the same value. In other words, they must have equal slopes. Conversely, lines with equal slopes are parallel.

Example

Find the slope of a line, l_a, that is parallel to line, l_b, that has a slope of $-\dfrac{2}{3}$.

Solution

Since the lines are parallel to one another, the slope of l_a is equal to the slope of l_b.

If the slope of $l_b = -\dfrac{2}{3}$, the slope of $l_a = -\dfrac{2}{3}$.

PERPENDICULARITY

Property: Perpendicular lines have slopes with products that equal -1.

Perpendicular lines ($\perp$) are lines that meet at a 90° angle. Consider the given graph of perpendicular lines.

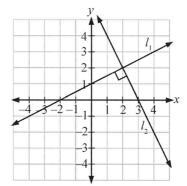

In order for l_2 to be perpendicular to l_1, the slope of l_2 must be the negative reciprocal of l_1.

To determine the slope of l_2, start with the slope of l_1, multiply it by -1, and then write the reciprocal of the result.

Notice that the slope of l_1 is $\dfrac{1}{2}$. The slope of l_2 is $\dfrac{-2}{1}$ or -2.

Example

Find the slope of a line, l_a, that is perpendicular to a line, l_b, that has a slope of $-\dfrac{2}{3}$.

Solution

Since the lines are perpendicular, the slope of l_a must be the negative reciprocal of l_b.

If the slope of $l_b = -\dfrac{2}{3}$, then the slope of $l_a = -1 \times \dfrac{-3}{2} = \dfrac{3}{2}$.

20A.2 Demonstrate an understanding of slope: as rise over run; as rate of change; and by solving problems.

SOLVING CONTEXTUAL SLOPE PROBLEMS

The slope of a linear relation can be referred to as the **rate of change**.

The rate of change is a ratio that represents the change in one variable relative to a corresponding change in another variable.

For any continuous relation whose graph contains a line segment, the slope of the line segment is the rate of change of the dependent variable with respect to the independent variable for the ordered pairs included in the line segment.

Travelling a certain distance over a period of time, being paid a certain wage per hour, and the cost of something per hour are examples of situations that can be described using the rate of change.

Example

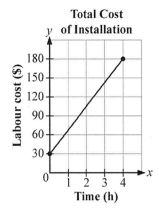

The graph shows the total labour cost of a plumber for the installation of a new water tank.

Determine the plumber's hourly rate of pay.

Solution

Step 1

Determine the slope of the linear relation. Choose two points on the graph to use in the slope formula. Two points that can be chosen are $(0, 30)$ and $(4, 180)$.

Step 2

Substitute the points into the slope formula, and solve for the slope.

$$m = \dfrac{y_2 - y_1}{x_2 - x_1}$$
$$= \dfrac{180 - 30}{4 - 0}$$
$$= \dfrac{150}{4}$$
$$= 37.5$$

Since the slope is 37.5, the plumber's hourly rate of pay is \$37.50 /h.

Example

Amorita is travelling away from home for 5 h. The function $d = 80t + 40$ defines her distance (d) from home in kilometres as a function of time (t) in hours.

Determine the slope of the given function.

Solution

The equation $d = 80t + 40$ is of the form $y = mx + b$, in which m represents the slope of the line.

Therefore, the slope of the line is 80.

What does the slope of the given function represent?

Solution

The slope of the given function represents the speed Amorita is travelling, which is 80 km/h.

Example

The given table of values represents David's earnings as a function of the number of hours he worked.

Number of Hours	Earnings ($)
2	15.90
4	31.80
6	47.70
8	63.60

Determine the slope of the graph of the function.

Solution

Apply the slope formula using any two ordered pairs from the table of values.

If the points (2, 15.9) and (4, 31.8) are used, the calculation is:

$$m = \frac{y_2 - y_1}{x_2 - x_1}$$
$$= \frac{31.8 - 15.9}{4 - 2}$$
$$= \frac{15.9}{2}$$
$$= 7.95$$

The slope of the graph of the given function is 7.95.

What does the slope of the given situation represent?

Solution

The slope of the given situation represents David's rate of pay, which is $7.95/h.

20A.3 Solve problems by applying proportional reasoning and unit analysis.

CONVERTING BETWEEN METRIC UNITS OF LENGTH

The metric system is based on a decimal system with each unit subdivided into tenths. The base unit for measurement of length is a metre.

This chart is used to summarize the difference between the largest unit and the smallest unit in relationship to the base unit. Prefixes show the relation of a unit to the base unit.

Prefix	Multiplying Factor	Symbol
Kilo	1 000	km
Hecto	100	hm
Deca	10	dam
Base unit	1	m
Deci	$\frac{1}{10}$	dm
Centi	$\frac{1}{100}$	cm
Milli	$\frac{1}{1\ 000}$	mm

Sometimes, it is easier to visualize the conversions using a horizontal conversion chart. The larger units are on the left, and the smaller units are on the right.

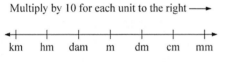

CONVERTING FROM LARGER TO SMALLER UNITS

When converting from kilometres to hectometres, the change is from a larger unit to a smaller measurement unit; therefore, you multiply by 10 (there are 10 hm in 1 km). If you were to convert from kilometres to decametres, the change is to a unit that is two positions to the right on the converter (there are 10×10 dam in 1 km).

When converting from larger units to smaller units, multiply by 10 for each unit to the right.

Example

Multiply by 10 for each unit to the right ⟶

km   hm   dam   m   dm   cm   mm

⟵ Divide by 10 for each unit to the left

Use the chart or the metric converter above to convert 15 hm to dm (three units to the right). _____ dm

Solution

$$15 \times 10 \times 10 \times 10 = 15 \times 1\ 000$$
$$= 15\ 000 \text{ dm}$$

Use the chart or the metric converter above to convert 0.3 m to cm (two units to the right). _____ cm

Solution

$$0.3 \times 10 \times 10 = 0.3 \times 100 = 3 \times 10 = 30 \text{ cm}$$

CONVERTING FROM SMALLER TO LARGER UNITS

When converting from metres to decametres, the change is from a smaller unit to a larger unit; therefore, you divide by 10 or multiply by $\frac{1}{10}$.

If you were to convert from decametres to kilometres, the change is to a unit that is two positions to the left on the converter; therefore, you divide by 10×10, or 100.

When converting from smaller units to larger ones, divide by 10 for each unit to the left.

Example

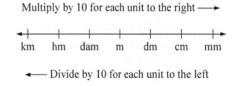

Use the given metric converter to convert 1 753 dm into hectometres.

Solution

Step 1
Determine the divisor or multiplier.
A hectometre (hm) is three positions to the left of the decimetre (dm) on the converter.
The change is from a small unit to a larger unit, so you divide.
The divisor is $10 \times 10 \times 10$, or 1 000.

Step 2

Convert. $1\ 753 \div 1\ 000 = 1.753$

There are 1.753 hm in 1 753 dm.

Example

The number of metres equal to 23 centimetres is _____ m.

Solution

Smaller unit → larger unit = smaller number
This means you should divide.

Since 100 cm = 1 m, divide 23 cm by 100.
$23 \text{ cm} \div 100 = 0.23 \text{ m}$
$\qquad 23 \text{ cm} = 0.23 \text{ m}$
A quick way to divide by 100 is to move the decimal point 2 places to the left.

20A.3 Solve problems by applying proportional reasoning and unit analysis.

CONVERTING BETWEEN METRIC UNITS OF CAPACITY

The **capacity** of a container is the amount of liquid the container can hold, or the amount of space inside a container. This is measured in litres.

You may need to compare or order objects according to their capacity. However, the capacity of the objects may not be expressed in the same units.

For example, one object may be measured in litres (L), while another may be measured in millilitres (mL). To compare different objects according to their capacities, all measurements must be converted into the same units.

Prefix	Symbol	Unit
kilo	k	kL
hecto	h	hL
deca	da	daL
base unit	the unit	L
deci	d	dL
centi	c	cL
milli	m	mL

Capacity is a one-dimensional measure. To convert capacities into different units, multiply or divide by 10.

CONVERTING FROM LARGER UNITS TO SMALLER UNITS

Sometimes, it is easier to visualize conversions using a horizontal conversion chart. The larger units are on the left of the chart, and the smaller units are on the right.

When converting from a larger unit of capacity to a smaller unit, multiply by 10 for each step.

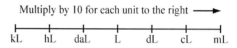

Example

How many litres are there in 14 kL?

Solution

Convert the units of capacity.
kL → L

You are moving 3 places to the right. Multiply by 10 for each step.
$14 \times 10 \times 10 \times 10 = 14\ 000$

There are 14 000 L in 14 kL.

CONVERTING FROM SMALLER UNITS TO LARGER UNITS

When converting a smaller unit of capacity to a larger unit, divide the value by 10 for each step.

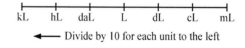

Example

How many litres are there in 53 000 mL?

Solution

Convert the units of capacity.

mL → L

You are moving 3 places to the left. Divide by 10 for each step.

$$\frac{53\ 000}{10 \times 10 \times 10} = \frac{53\ 000}{1\ 000} = 53$$

There are 53 L in 53 000 mL.

20A.3 Solve problems by applying proportional reasoning and unit analysis.

Converting between Metric Units of Mass

Grams are used to describe the mass or weight of an object. A prefix is added to the unit to indicate the size. For example, 1 kilogram means 1 000 grams.

The information in the given chart shows the relationship between some of the most common units of metric measurement.

Prefix	Abbreviation	Number of grams
Kilo	kg	1 000
Hecto	hg	100
Deca	dag	10
Unit	g	1
Deci	dg	0.1
Centi	cg	0.01
Milli	mg	0.001

The largest units of measure appear on the left side of the chart, and the smallest units appear on the right. The order of these measurements is important because it allows for conversions from one measure to another.

There is a pattern in this chart: the units of measurement are based on multiples of 10. For example, there are 1 000 g in 1 kg. This pattern makes unit conversion simple:

- To convert a smaller unit to a larger unit, such as milligrams to grams, divide by a multiple of 10 for each step in the table.
- To convert a larger unit to a smaller unit, such as grams to centigrams, multiply by a multiple of 10 for each step in the table.

The multiple of 10 is determined by how many spaces away the desired unit of measure is.

The conversion rule is logical because it takes fewer litres than milligrams of water to fill a bathtub, for example, and more centigrams than grams to have the same mass.

Example

At Nadia's local deli, ham is on sale for $9.50 for 1 kg.

How much will it cost Nadia to buy 120 g of ham?

Solution

To convert kilograms to grams, the mass in kilograms is multiplied by 1 000.

1 kg × 1 000 = 1 000 g

Step 1

Write a proportion to represent the problem.

$$\frac{\$9.50}{1\ 000\ g} = \frac{x}{120\ g}$$

Step 2

Use cross products to calculate the value of x.

$$x = \frac{9.50 \times 120}{1\ 000}$$

$$x = 1.14$$

It will cost Nadia $1.14 to buy 120 g of ham.

20A.3 Solve problems by applying proportional reasoning and unit analysis.

Converting between Metric Units of Area

The **area** of a shape is the space taken up by the two-dimensional object. Area is measured in square units such as m^2 or cm^2.

You may need to compare or order objects according to their area. However, the areas may not be expressed in the same units.

For example, one object may be measured in square metres (m^2), while another may be measured in square centimetres (cm^2). To compare different objects according to their areas, all measurements must be converted into the same unit.

Prefix	Symbol	Unit
kilo	k	km^2
hecto	h	hm^2
deca	da	dam^2
base unit	the unit	m^2
deci	d	dm^2
centi	c	cm^2
milli	m	mm^2

Since area is a two-dimensional measurement, multiply or divide by 102 or 100 to convert between units.

CONVERTING FROM LARGER TO SMALLER UNITS

The given diagram represents an area of 1 km^2:

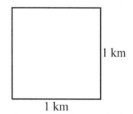

When the measurements are expressed in hm^2, the given diagram will look like this:

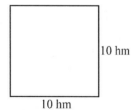

The area of the square is
10 hm × 10 hm = 100 hm^2. This means that 1 km^2 = 100 hm^2.

Sometimes, it is easier to visualize the conversions using a horizontal conversion chart. The larger units are on the left and the smaller units are on the right.

When converting from a larger unit of area to a smaller unit, multiply by 100 for each step.

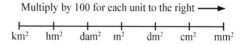

Example

What is the value of 15 hm^2, expressed in dm^2?

Solution

Convert the units of area.
$hm^2 \rightarrow dm^2$

You are moving three places to the right. Multiply by 100 for each step.
$15 \times 100 \times 100 \times 100 = 15\ 000\ 000$

The value of 15 hm^2, expressed in dm^2, is 15 000 000 dm^2.

CONVERTING FROM SMALLER TO LARGER UNITS

The given diagram represents an area of 1 m^2:

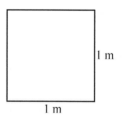

When the measurements are expressed in dam^2, the given diagram will look like this:

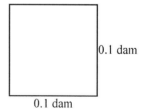

The area of the square is
0.1 dam × 0.1 dam = 0.01 dam^2. This means that 1m^2 = 0.01dam^2.

Sometimes, it is easier to visualize the conversions using a horizontal conversion chart. The larger units are on the left and the smaller units are on the right.

When converting from a smaller unit of area to a larger unit, divide by 100 for each step.

← Divide by 100 for each unit to the left

Example

What is the value of 25 cm², expressed in m²?

Solution

Convert the units of area.

$$cm^2 \rightarrow m^2$$

You are moving two places to the left. Divide by 100 for each step.

$$\frac{25}{100 \times 100} = \frac{25}{10\ 000} = 0.0025\ m^2$$

The value of 25 cm², expressed in m², is 0.0025 m².

20A.3 Solve problems by applying proportional reasoning and unit analysis.

CONVERTING BETWEEN UNITS OF MEASURE FOR CAPACITY

The **capacity** of a container is the amount of liquid the container can hold. In the customary system, capacity is measured in gallons, quarts, pints, cups, and fluid ounces to describe how much liquid the object can hold.

Capacity Conversion	
1 gallon	4 quarts
1 quart	2 pints
1 pint	2 cups
1 cup	8 ounces

When you want to convert amounts between different units, first you need to determine the relationship between those units. For example, to convert pints to quarts, you need to know that there are 2 pt in 1 qt.

Once you know the relationship, then you can do the conversion. If you are converting from smaller units to larger units, you will use division. So to convert pints to quarts, you divide by two. To convert from larger to smaller units, you need to multiply. To convert quarts to pints, multiply by two.

Example

How many pints are there in 64 oz?

Solution

Step 1

The table does not list the conversion for ounces to pints. You will have to make this conversion in two steps. Start by converting from ounces to cups.

There are 8 oz in 1 c.

You are converting from a smaller unit to a larger one, so you need to divide.

$64 \div 8 = 8$

There are 8 c in 64 oz.

Step 2

Convert from cups to pints.

There are 2 c in 1 pt.

You are converting from a smaller unit to a larger on, so you need to divide.

$8 \div 2 = 4$

There are 4 pints in 64 oz.

Example

Christopher bought 1 gallon of milk from the supermarket. He wants to distribute that milk into one-quart bottles.

How many bottles does Christopher need?

Solution

Convert gallons to quarts.
1 gallon = 4 quarts

Since each individual bottle can hold 1 quart, Christopher needs 4 bottles.

Example

How many cups equal 10 quarts?

Solution

Step 1

Choose the correct conversion ratios.

1 qt = 2 pt

1 pt = 2 c

Step 2

Convert quarts to cups.

First, convert quarts to pints. Multiply 10 by 2 to convert 10 quarts to 20 pints.

Next, convert pints to cups. Multiply 20 by 2 to convert 20 pints to 40 cups.

10 quarts is equal to 40 cups.

20A.3 Solve problems by applying proportional reasoning and unit analysis.

CONVERTING BETWEEN UNITS OF VOLUME AND CAPACITY

Volume is the amount of space occupied by a three-dimensional object. Volume is measured in cubic units such as cubic metres (m^3) or cubic centimetres (cm^3).

Capacity is the amount of liquid a container can hold. This can be measured in litres.

You may need to convert between units of volume and capacity. Knowing the equivalents of common units can be useful. Remember that $1\ cm^3 = 1\ mL$, which means that $1\ 000\ cm^3 = 1\ 000\ mL$ and $1\ 000\ mL = 1\ L$. Therefore, $1\ 000\ cm^3 = 1\ L$.

Example

Determine how many litres are in $1\ m^3$.

Solution

Since $1\ 000\ cm^3 = 1\ L$ and $1\ m^3 = 1\ 000\ 000\ cm^3$, multiply both sides of $1\ 000\ cm^3 = 1\ L$ by $1\ 000$.

$$1\ 000\ cm^3 = 1\ L$$
$$1\ 000 \times 1\ 000\ cm^3 = 1\ L \times 1\ 000$$
$$1\ 000\ 000\ cm^3 = 1\ 000\ L$$
$$1\ m^3 = 1\ 000\ L$$

There are $1\ 000\ L$ in $1\ m^3$.

Example

How many cubic metres are in $12\ 500\ mL$?

Solution

Step 1

Convert millilitres (mL) to litres (L).

Use the horizontal conversion chart for capacity.

kL	hL	daL	L	dL	cL	mL

← Divide by 10 for each unit to the left

To convert millilitres to litres, move three steps to the left. Divide by 10 for each step.

$$\frac{12\ 500}{10 \times 10 \times 10} = \frac{12\ 500}{1\ 000}$$
$$= 12.5\ L$$

Step 2

Convert litres (L) to cubic metres (m^3).

If $1\ m^3 = 1\ 000\ L$, solve for cubic metres by setting up a proportion.

$$\frac{1}{x} = \frac{1\ 000}{12.5}$$
$$12.5 = 1\ 000x$$
$$\frac{12.5}{1\ 000} = x$$
$$0.0125 = x$$

There are $0.0125\ m^3$ in $12\ 500\ mL$.

Example

How many litres are in 150 000 cm³?

Solution

Step 1

Convert cubic centimetres (cm³) into millilitres (mL).

1 cm³ = 1 mL

150 000 cm³ = 150 000 mL

Step 2

Convert millilitres (mL) to litres (L).

Since 1 000 mL = 1 L, divide 150 000 mL by 1 000.

$$\frac{150\ 000}{1\ 000} = 150$$

The volume 150 000 cm³ represents a capacity of 150 L.

20A.3 Solve problems by applying proportional reasoning and unit analysis.

CONVERTING BETWEEN METRIC UNITS OF VOLUME (KM³, HM³, DAM³, M³, DM³, CM³, MM³)

The **volume** of a container is the amount of space occupied by a three-dimensional object. Volume is measured in cubic units such as m³ or cm³.

You may need to compare or order objects according to their volume. However, the volume of objects are not always expressed in the same units.

For example, one object may be measured in cubic metres (m³), while another may be measured in cubic centimetres (cm³). All measurements must be converted to the same units so that the volumes can be compared.

Prefix	Symbol	Unit
kilo	k	km³
hecto	h	hm³
deca	da	dam³
base unit	the unit	m³
deci	d	dm³
centi	c	cm³
milli	m	mm³

Since volume is a three-dimensional measure, multiply or divide by 10³, or 1 000, to convert between units.

Sometimes, it is easier to visualize the conversions using a horizontal conversion chart. The larger units are on the left of the chart and the smaller units are on the right.

When converting from a larger unit of volume to a smaller unit, multiply by 1 000 for each step.

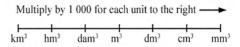

Multiply by 1 000 for each unit to the right ⟶

km³   hm³   dam³   m³   dm³   cm³   mm³

Example

What is the value of 32 m³, expressed in cm³?

Solution

Convert the units of volume.

m³ → cm³

You are moving two places to the right. Multiply by 1 000 for each step.

32 × 1 000 × 1 000 = 32 000 000

The value of 32 m³, expressed in cm³, is 32 000 000 cm³.

When converting from a smaller unit of volume to a larger one, divide the value by 1 000 for each step.

km³   hm³   dam³   m³   dm³   cm³   mm³

⟵ Divide by 1 000 for each unit to the left

Example

What is the value of 12.7 m³, expressed in hm³?

Solution

Convert the units of volume.

m³ → hm³

You are moving two places to the left. Divide by 1 000 for each step.

$$\frac{12.7}{1\ 000 \times 1\ 000} = \frac{12.7}{1\ 000\ 000}$$

$$= 0.000\ 0127\ \text{hm}^3$$

The number 12.7 m³, expressed in hm³, is 0.000 0127 hm³.

20A.3 Solve problems by applying proportional reasoning and unit analysis.

CONVERTING BETWEEN METRIC UNITS OF SPEED

Speed is the measurement of how much distance is travelled in a period of time. In order to convert between metric units of speed, it is important to remember how to convert between metric units of length.

- When converting from a larger unit to a smaller unit, multiply the number by 10 for each step.
- When converting from a smaller unit to a larger unit, divide the number by 10 for each step.

The given chart shows the conversion steps.

km	hm	dam	m	dm	cm	mm
÷ 10	÷ 10	÷ 10	÷ 10	÷ 10	÷ 10	
	× 10	× 10	× 10	× 10	× 10	× 10

Example

A car is travelling at a speed of 80 km/h.

What speed is the car travelling in metres per hour?

Solution

Step 1

Convert kilometres to metres by multiplying by 10 for each step. Both units are per hour, so there is no time conversion necessary.

There are three steps down from kilometres to metres, so multiply 80 km/h by 10 three times.
$80 \times 10 \times 10 \times 10 = 80\ 000$
Therefore, 80 km is 80 000 m.

Step 2

Rewrite the speed in the converted units.
The speed the car is travelling in metres per hour is 80 000 m/h.

Example

A tennis serve is recorded travelling at a speed of 198 km/h.

How fast is the tennis ball moving in metres per second (m/s)?

Solution

Use the relationships between the units to solve the problem.

Step 1

Find the relationship between the units of length. Since converting from kilometres to metres is moving from a larger unit to a smaller unit, use multiplication. Since there are three steps between kilometres and metres, the number should be multiplied by 10 three times.
$198 \text{ km} \times 10 \times 10 \times 10 = x \text{ m}$
$198 \times 1\ 000 = x$
$198\ 000 = x$
Therefore, 198 km = 198 000 m.

Step 2

Find the relationship between the units of time using a proportion.
There are 60 min in 1 h, and there are 60 s in 1 min.
$60 \times 60 = 3\ 600$
Therefore, 1 h = 3 600 s.

Step 3

Convert to metres per second.
According to the given relationships between the units, 198 km/h is the same as 198 000 m per 3 600 s.
Simplify by dividing the units.
$$\frac{198\ 000 \text{ m}}{3\ 600 \text{ s}} = 55 \text{ m/s}$$
The tennis ball is moving at a speed of 55 m/s.

20A.3 Solve problems by applying proportional reasoning and unit analysis.

CONVERTING BETWEEN CUSTOMARY UNITS OF LENGTH

In order to convert between different units of measurement for length, you should use a table of ratios that shows the relationships between the different units.

Relationships between Customary Units of Length

1 mile: 1760 yards	1 yard: 3 feet	1 foot: 12 inches
1 mile: 5280 feet	1 yard: 36 inches	

Follow these steps to convert between two different units:

1. Identify the units involved in the conversion.
2. Choose the ratio from the table that involves these units.
3. Rearrange the ratio to solve for the unknown measurement.

Example
Convert 5 feet into inches.

Solution

Step 1
Identify the units required in the conversion.
The conversion is from feet into inches.

Step 2
Choose the ratio that converts feet into inches from the table of customary units ratios for length.

The conversion of feet into inches is
1 foot = 12 inches.

Relationships between Customary Units of Length

1 mile = 1760 yards = 5280 feet	1 yard = 3 feet = 36 inches	1 foot = 12 inches

Step 3
Rearrange the ratio to solve for the unknown measurement in inches.
$$\frac{12 \text{ inches}}{x} = \frac{1 \text{ foot}}{5 \text{ feet}}$$
$$5 \times 12 = x$$
$$60 \text{ inches} = x$$

Therefore, 5 feet = 60 inches.

Example
Convert 207 inches into yards.

Solution

Step 1
Identify the units required in the conversion.
The conversion is from inches into yards.

Step 2
Choose the ratio that converts inches into yards from the table of customary units ratios for length.

The conversion of inches into yards is
36 inches = 1 yard.

Relationships between Customary Units of Length

1 mile = 1760 yards = 5280 feet	1 yard = 3 feet = 36 inches	1 foot = 12 inches

Step 3
Rearrange the ratio to solve for the unknown measurement in yards.
$$\frac{36 \text{ inches}}{1 \text{ yard}} = \frac{207 \text{ inches}}{x}$$
$$36 \times x = 1 \times 207$$
$$36x = 207$$
$$\frac{36x}{36} = \frac{207}{36}$$
$$x = 5.75$$
207 inches = 5.75 yards
Therefore, 207 inches = 5.75 yards.

Example
Convert 32 506 yards into miles.

Solution

Step 1
Identify the units required in the conversion.
The conversion is from yards into miles.

Step 2
Choose the ratio that converts yards into miles from the table of customary units ratios for length.

The conversion of yards into miles is
1 760 yards = 1 mile.

Relationships between Customary Units of Length

1 mile = 1760 yards = 5280 feet	1 yard = 3 feet = 36 inches	1 foot = 12 inches

Step 3

Rearrange the ratio to solve for the unknown measurement in miles.

$$\frac{1\ 760\ \text{yards}}{1\ \text{mile}} = \frac{32\ 506}{x}$$
$$1\ 760x = 32\ 506 \times 1$$
$$\frac{1\ 760x}{1\ 760} = \frac{32\ 506}{1\ 760}$$
$$x = 18.5$$

32 506 yards = 18.5 miles

Therefore, 32 506 yards = 18.5 miles.

20A.3 Solve problems by applying proportional reasoning and unit analysis.

CONVERTING BETWEEN CUSTOMARY UNITS OF WEIGHT

In the **customary system**, weight is measured in tons (T), pounds (lb), and ounces (oz). A table of ratios showing the relationships between the different units can be used to convert between the different units of weight in the customary system.

**Relationships between
Customary Units of Weight**

1 T	2 000 lb
1 lb	16 oz

When converting between customary units of weight, follow these steps:

1. Choose the correct conversion ratio.
2. Convert. Multiply if you are converting from larger to smaller units, or divide if you are converting from smaller to larger units.

Example

How many pounds equal 352 oz? _____ lb

Solution

Step 1

Choose the correct conversion ratio.
1 lb = 16 oz

Step 2

Convert ounces to pounds.

You are going from a smaller unit to a larger unit, so you need to divide.
352 ÷ 16 = 22

Therefore, 352 oz equals 22 lb.

Example

How many ounces equal 120 lb? _____ oz

Solution

Step 1

Choose the correct conversion ratio.
1 lb = 16 oz

Step 2

Convert pounds to ounces.

To go from a larger unit to a smaller unit, multiply the numbers.
120 × 16 = 1 920

Therefore, 120 lb equals 1 920 oz.

20A.3 Solve problems by applying proportional reasoning and unit analysis.

CONVERTING CUSTOMARY UNITS OF AREA

The area of an object is measured in square units. Square inches (in^2) and square feet (ft^2) are two units that are often used.

The relationship between square inches and square feet is not the same as the relationship between inches and feet.

A square with an area of 1 ft^2 has sides that are each 1 ft long.

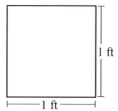

If you convert that to square inches, the sides of the same square are each 12 in long.

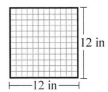

To find the conversion rate from feet to inches, replace 1 ft with 12 in in the area formula for the square.

1 ft^2
$= 1 \text{ ft} \times 1 \text{ ft}$
$= 12 \text{ in} \times 12 \text{ in}$
$= 144 \text{ in}^2$

Notice that the conversion between square units is equal to the conversion rate for length multiplied by itself. The same idea can be used to find the conversions for other customary units.

The following list shows the most common conversions of area when using the customary system.

$1 \text{ ft}^2 = 144 \text{ in}^2$
$1 \text{ yd}^2 = 9 \text{ ft}^2$
$1 \text{ yd}^2 = 1\ 296 \text{ in}^2$
$1 \text{ mi}^2 = 3\ 097\ 600 \text{ yd}^2$

Two common methods used for converting customary units of area are proportional reasoning and cross multiplication.

PROPORTIONAL REASONING

To use proportional reasoning to convert customary units of area, follow these steps:

1. Choose the appropriate conversion rate.
2. Perform the conversion. Multiply if you are converting from larger to smaller units, or divide if you are converting from smaller to larger units.

Example
Convert 10 yd^2 to square feet.

Solution
Step 1
Choose the appropriate conversion rate.
$1 \text{ yd}^2 = 9 \text{ ft}^2$

Step 2
Perform the conversion.
You are going from a larger unit to a smaller one, so you need to multiply.
$10 \times 9 = 90$
Converted to square feet, 10 yd^2 is 90 ft^2.

Example
Convert 576 in^2 to square feet.

Solution
Step 1
Choose the appropriate conversion rate.
$1 \text{ ft}^2 = 144 \text{ in}^2$

Step 2
Perform the conversion.
You are going from a smaller unit to a larger one, so you need to divide.
$576 \div 144 = 4$
Converted to square feet, 576 in^2 is 4 ft^2.

CROSS MULTIPLICATION

To use cross multiplication to convert customary units of area, follow these steps:

1. Choose the correct conversion ratio.
2. Set up a proportion.
3. Solve for the unknown.

Example
Convert 576 in^2 to square feet.

Solution
Step 1
Choose the correct conversion ratio.
$1 \text{ ft}^2 = 144 \text{ in}^2$

Step 2
Set up a proportion.
$$\frac{1 \text{ ft}^2}{144 \text{ in}^2} = \frac{x}{576 \text{ in}^2}$$

Step 3

Solve for the unknown.

$$144 \times x = 1 \times 576$$
$$144x = 576$$
$$x = \frac{576}{144}$$
$$x = 4$$

Converted to square feet, 576 in^2 is 4 ft^2.

20A.3 Solve problems by applying proportional reasoning and unit analysis.

CONVERTING BETWEEN CUSTOMARY UNITS OF VOLUME

Volume is the amount of space occupied by a three-dimensional object. Volume is measured in cubic units such as cubic inches or cubic yards.

When you convert between two units of length, you find out the relationship between the units, and then you multiply or divide by that amount. For instance, to convert from feet to inches, you multiply by 12 because there are 12 in in 1 ft.

When you want to convert units of volume, it is not quite so simple. To convert from cubic feet to cubic inches, you actually need to multiply by 1 728 because there are 1 728 in^3 in 1 ft^3.

Example

A cube that is one cubic foot has sides that are each 1 ft long.

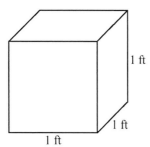

If you convert that to cubic inches, the sides of that same cube are each 12 in long.

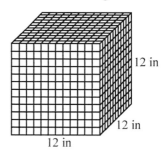

The volume of the cube can be calculated using the formula for the volume of a prism.

$$V = l \times w \times h$$
$$= 12 \text{ in} \times 12 \text{ in} \times 12 \text{ in}$$
$$= 1\ 728 \text{ in}^3$$

This means that 1 ft^3 = 1 728 in^3.

When you want to convert between units of volume, follow these steps:

1. Calculate the relationship between the cubic units by cubing the linear conversion rate. For example, there are 3 ft in 1 yd, so there are $3 \times 3 \times 3$ ft^3 in 1 yd^3.

2. Perform the conversion. Multiply to convert from larger to smaller units, or divide to convert from smaller to larger units.

Example

Convert 432 ft^3 into cubic yards.

Solution

Step 1

Determine the relationship between the units.

1 yd = 3 ft

To find the relationship between cubic feet and cubic yards, you need to find the cube of 3.

$$1 \text{ yd}^3 = 3 \times 3 \times 3 \text{ ft}^3$$
$$= 27 \text{ ft}^3$$

Step 2

Perform the conversion.

You are going from a smaller unit to a larger one, so you need to divide.

$$432 \div 27 = 16 \text{ yd}^3$$

Example

Convert 5 ft³ into cubic inches.

Solution

Step 1

Determine the relationship between the units.

1 ft = 12 in

To find the relationship between cubic feet and cubic inches, you need to find the cube of 12.

$$1 \text{ ft}^3 = 12 \times 12 \times 12 \text{ in}^3$$
$$= 1\ 728 \text{ in}^3$$

Step 2

Perform the conversion.

You are going from a larger unit to a smaller one, so you need to multiply.

$$5 \times 1\ 728 = 8\ 640 \text{ in}^3$$

20A.3 Solve problems by applying proportional reasoning and unit analysis.

CONVERTING BETWEEN CUSTOMARY UNITS OF SPEED

When you are converting customary units of speed, it is important to remember the correct way to convert between units of length and between units of time. You must use the relationships between the various units to set up the proportions required to solve the problem. The given table shows the most important conversions to remember.

Original Unit	Conversion
1 foot (ft)	12 inches (in)
1 yard (yd)	3 feet
	36 inches
1 mile (mi)	5 280 feet
	1 760 yards
	63 360 inches
1 minute (min)	60 seconds(s)
1 hour (h)	60 minutes
	3 600 seconds

Example

A car is travelling at a speed of 85 mph.

How fast is the car travelling in feet per second?

Solution

Convert the given speed of miles per hour to feet per second.

Step 1

Use relationships between various units to set up proportions required to solve the problem.

- In 1 mi, there are 5 280 ft.
- In 1 h, there are 60 min.
- In 1 min, there are 60 s.

$$\frac{1 \text{ mi}}{5\ 280 \text{ ft}} = \frac{85 \text{ mi}}{x \text{ ft}}$$
$$x = 85 \times 5\ 280$$
$$x = 448\ 800 \text{ ft}$$

$$\frac{1 \text{ h}}{60 \text{ min}} = \frac{1 \text{ h}}{x \text{ min}}$$
$$x = 1 \times 60$$
$$x = 60 \text{ min}$$

$$x = 60 \times 60$$
$$x = 3\ 600 \text{ s}$$

Step 2

Find the answer in feet per second.

Since you know that 85 mph becomes 448 800 ft per 3 600 s, simplify this ratio by dividing so the units will be per second.

$$\frac{448\ 800 \text{ ft}}{3\ 600 \text{ s}} = 124.6\bar{6}$$
$$= 125 \text{ ft/s}$$

The answer is rounded up because of the repeating decimal in the quotient.

Therefore, the car is travelling at a speed of about 125 ft/s.

20A.3 Solve problems by applying proportional reasoning and unit analysis.

EQUIVALENT UNITS OF LENGTH FOR METRIC AND CUSTOMARY SYSTEMS

Units of length can be converted within the customary system and within the metric system. They can also be converted between the metric and customary systems.

The given table shows the most common conversions between customary and metric units.

Customary System	Metric System
1 in	2.54 cm
1 ft	0.30 m
1 yd	0.91 m
1 mi	1.61 km

To convert between systems, follow these steps:

1. Determine the correct conversion ratio.
2. Calculate.

Example

How many centimetres are there in 24 in?

Solution

Step 1

Determine the correct conversion ratio.
Determine how many centimetres are equal to 1 in.

2.54 cm → 1 in

The conversion ratio is $\dfrac{2.54 \text{ cm}}{1 \text{ in}}$.

Step 2

Calculate.
Convert 24 inches to centimetres.

$2.54 \times 24 = 60.96$

There are 60.96 cm in 24 in.

20A.3 Solve problems by applying proportional reasoning and unit analysis.

CONVERTING UNITS OF MASS BETWEEN METRIC AND CUSTOMARY SYSTEMS

Equivalencies showing the relationships between the different units can be used to convert between units of mass in the metric and customary systems.

Relationships between Units of Mass in the Customary and Metric Systems
1 lb = 0.45 kg
1 oz = 28.35 g

To convert between two different units, follow these steps:

1. Select the correct conversion ratio.
2. Set up the appropriate ratios into a proportion. Let x stand for the unknown value. Be sure to place the units used for each system in the same place. For example, pounds to kilograms equals pounds to kilograms becomes $\dfrac{\text{pounds}}{\text{kilograms}} = \dfrac{\text{pounds}}{\text{kilograms}}$.
3. Solve for the unknown value using cross products.

Example

Convert 4 kg into pounds, and round the answer to the nearest tenth.

Solution

Step 1

Select the correct conversion ratio.
This question involved conversion between pounds and kilograms, so the correct ratio is $\dfrac{1 \text{ lb}}{0.45 \text{ kg}}$

Step 2

Set up the proportion.
Let x stand for the unknown value. Be sure to place the units used for each system in the same place.

$$\frac{\text{pounds}}{\text{kilograms}} = \frac{\text{pounds}}{\text{kilograms}}$$

$$\frac{1}{0.45} = \frac{x}{4}$$

Step 3

Solve for the unknown value using cross products.

$$\frac{1}{0.45} = \frac{x}{4}$$
$$1 \times 4 = x \times 0.45$$
$$4 = 0.45x$$
$$\frac{4}{0.45} = \frac{0.45x}{0.45}$$
$$8.\overline{8} = x$$

The mass 4 kilograms is approximately 8.9 pounds.

20A.3 Solve problems by applying proportional reasoning and unit analysis.

EQUIVALENT UNITS OF CAPACITY FOR METRIC AND CUSTOMARY SYSTEMS

Units of capacity can be converted within the customary system and within the metric system. They can also be converted between metric and customary systems.

The given table shows the most common conversions between customary and metric units.

Customary System	Metric System
1 fl oz	29.57 mL
1 qt	0.95 L
1 gal	3.79 L

To convert between systems, follow these steps:

1. Determine the correct conversion ratio.
2. Calculate.

Example

Bobby is driving his car. He stops to fill it up with gas. He puts 14.5 gal of fuel in his car. His friend is reading the owner's manual and reads that the tank holds 60 L when full.

If the tank is now full, how many litres of gas were in Bobby's car before he filled up?

Solution

Step 1
Determine the correct conversion ratio.
1 gal = 3.79 L

Step 2
Calculate.
Convert 14.5 gal to litres.
14.5 × 3.79 = 54.955

Step 3
Subtract this amount from the total amount the tank holds to find how much was in the tank before filling.
60 − 54.955 = 5.045
There were 5.045 L of gas in the tank before Bobby filled it up.

20A.3 Solve problems by applying proportional reasoning and unit analysis.

CONVERTING BETWEEN METRIC AND CUSTOMARY UNITS OF VOLUME

Volume is the amount of space occupied by a three-dimensional object. Volume is measured in cubic units, such as cubic metres or cubic inches. Units of volume can be converted within the customary and metric systems. They can also be converted between the metric and customary systems.

This table shows the most common conversions between customary and metric units.

Customary System	Metric System
1 ft	0.3048 m
1 yd	0.9144 m
1 in	2.54 cm

To convert between systems, follow these steps:

1. Determine the correct conversion ratio.
2. Apply the conversion ratio. Let x stand for the unknown value.

Example

To the nearest whole number, determine how many cubic feet are equivalent to 20 m³.

Solution

Step 1
Determine the correct conversion ratio.
1 ft = 0.3048 m
Raise each unit of measurement to the power of 3.
$1 \text{ ft}^3 \approx 0.028\,32 \text{ m}^3$

Step 2
Apply the conversion ratio.
Let x stand for the unknown value.
$$\frac{1}{0.028\,32} \approx \frac{x}{20}$$
$$\frac{20}{0.028\,32} \approx x$$
$$706 \approx x$$

To the nearest whole number, 20 m³ is equivalent to 706 ft³.

Example

To the nearest hundredth, determine how many cubic centimetres are equivalent to 19 in³.

Solution

Step 1

Determine the correct conversion ratio.

1 in = 2.54 cm

Raise each unit of measurement to the power of 3.

$1 \text{ in}^3 \approx 16.387 \text{ cm}^3$

Step 2

Apply the conversion ratio.

Let x stand for the unknown value.

$$\frac{1}{16.387} \approx \frac{19}{x}$$

$$x \approx 311.35$$

To the nearest hundredth, 19 in³ is equivalent to 311.35 cm³.

20A.3 Solve problems by applying proportional reasoning and unit analysis.

SOLVING LINEAR MEASUREMENT PROBLEMS

To estimate a linear measure, it is important to select the most appropriate **imperial** or SI unit of measure. A personal **referent** can then be used to approximate the length of an object or the distance between two points.

Example

To estimate the length of her car, Fiona could use the length of her thumb to the first joint or her stride length.

Which referent and corresponding imperial unit would be the **most appropriate** choice?

Solution

Using the thumb as a referent would be far too tedious, impractical, and prone to measurement error. Therefore, the stride, corresponding approximately to the imperial unit of 1 yd, would be the most appropriate referent to use in order to estimate the length of a car.

When solving problems involving linear measurement, use an appropriate instrument (ruler, tape measure, etc.), use necessary formulas, and use an effective problem-solving strategy.

Example

Conrad wanted to buy enough border material for his circular garden plot. Since he had no measuring instrument, he used his shoe to estimate the diameter of the garden plot to be 9.5 shoe lengths. When he got to the store, he measured his shoe with a tape measure, and determined its length to be $10\frac{3}{8}$ in.

To the nearest inch, what is the approximate length of the border material required?

Solution

Step 1

Calculate the diameter, d, of the garden plot.

d = shoe length × # of shoe lengths

$$d = 10\frac{3}{8} \times 9.5$$

$$= 10.375 \times 9.5$$

$$= 98.5625 \text{ in}$$

Step 2

Determine the length of the border material by calculating the circumference, C, of the garden plot.

$$C = \pi d$$

$$= \pi \times 98.5625$$

$$\approx 309.6432 \text{ in}$$

The approximate length of the border material required is 310 in.

Use the following information to answer the next question.

Christine measures the volume of a box of cereal and of a box of popcorn.

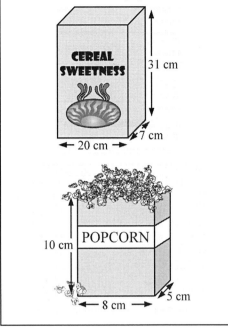

Written Response

1. Find the difference between the volume of the box of cereal and the volume of the box of popcorn.

2. A circular field has a circumference of 515 m. What is the radius of the field, rounded to the nearest whole number?
   A. 82 m   B. 164 m
   C. 258 m   D. 328 m

3. What is the value of $ef - fg + g$ when $e = 7$, $f = 3$, and $g = -5$?
   A. 1   B. 11
   C. 31   D. 41

Numerical Response

4. In the linear relation $14x - 4y + 3 = 0$, what will the rate of change of y with respect to x be, to the nearest tenth? _____

Written Response

5. Will the slopes $3\frac{1}{2}$ and $-\frac{2}{7}$ result in perpendicular lines?

Use the following information to answer the next question.

To hire a cab, Carla has to pay a fixed charge plus an additional constant rate for every kilometre driven.

6. If the cab driver charges $23 for 10 km and $33 for 15 km, what is the fixed charge to hire this cab?
   A. $1   B. $2
   C. $3   D. $4

Numerical Response

7. Samia has a box that is 5 184 in^3. How many cubic feet is the box? _____ ft^3

8. If Daniel buys 5 gal of paint, what is the amount of paint in quarts that he will have?
   A. 3 qt   B. 10 qt
   C. 13 qt   D. 20 qt

Numerical Response

9. How many tons equal 8 000 lb? _____ tons

10. Order these lengths from shortest to longest.

34 cm, 3.3 m, 304 cm, 343 mm

11. The value of 0.3 m^2 expressed in square centimetres is

   A. 0.000 03 cm^2 **B.** 0.03 cm^2

   C. 300 cm^2 **D.** 3 000 cm^2

   Use the following information to answer the next question.

   A mug has a capacity of 750 mL. The mug is filled and emptied into a bottle 12 times, which completely fills the bottle.

12. What is the capacity of the bottle in litres?

   A. 9 000 L   **B.** 900 L

   C. 90 L   **D.** 9 L

   Written Response

13. How many milligrams equals 28.65 hectograms?

   Use the following information to answer the next question.

   An Indy car goes an average of about 360 km/h during a race.

   Numerical Response

14. What is the average speed of an Indy car in metres per minute? _____ m/min

15. To the nearest whole ounce, how many fluid ounces are equal to 5 L?

   A. 169 fl oz   **B.** 145 fl oz

   C. 29 fl oz   **D.** 17 fl oz

16. To the nearest whole number, how many cubic centimetres are in 2.5 yd^3 given that 1 yd equals 0.9144 m?

   A. 31 cm^3 **B.** 191 cm^3

   C. 305 822 cm^3 **D.** 1 911 387 cm^3

   Use the following information to answer the next question.

   A cube has edges that are 27 cm long.

17. What is the volume of the cube expressed in cubic metres?

   A. 19 683 m^3 **B.** 19.683 m^3

   C. 0.019 683 m^3 **D.** 0.000 019 68 3 m^3

18. How many square inches are equal to 59 ft^2?

   A. 531 in^2 **B.** 708 in^2

   C. 5 310 in^2 **D.** 8 496 in^2

   Use the following information to answer the next question.

   A milk container has a length of 2 dm, a width of 2 dm, and a height of 3 dm.

19. What is the capacity of the container in liters?

   A. 120 L   **B.** 12 L

   C. 1.2 L   **D.** 0.12 L

ANSWERS AND SOLUTIONS
ALGEBRA

1. WR	**6.** C	**11.** D	**16.** D
2. A	**7.** 3	**12.** D	**17.** C
3. C	**8.** D	**13.** WR	**18.** D
4. 3.5	**9.** 4	**14.** 6000	**19.** B
5. WR	**10.** WR	**15.** A	

1. WR

Step 1

Determine the volume of the cereal box by substituting the appropriate numbers for the length (20 cm), width (7 cm), and height (31 cm) of the box.

$V = l \times w \times h$
$V = 20 \times 7 \times 31$
$V = 4\ 340 \text{ cm}^3$

Step 2

Determine the volume of the popcorn box by substituting the appropriate numbers for the length (8 cm), width (5 cm), and height (10 cm) of the box.

$V = l \times w \times h$
$V = 8 \times 5 \times 10$
$V = 400 \text{ cm}^3$

Step 3

To determine the difference between the two volumes, subtract the volume of the popcorn box from the volume of the cereal box.

$4\ 340 - 400 = 3\ 940$

The difference between the two volumes is $3\ 940 \text{ cm}^3$.

2. A

To calculate the radius of the field, rearrange the circumference formula to solve for r, substitute the known values into the new formula and solve.

$$C = 2\pi r$$
$$\frac{C}{2\pi} = \frac{2\pi r}{2\pi}$$
$$\frac{C}{2\pi} = r$$

Then substitute 515 for C in the new formula.

$$r = \frac{C}{2\pi}$$
$$= \frac{515}{2\pi}$$
$$= 82 \text{ m}$$

Rounded to the nearest whole number, the radius of the field is 82 m.

3. C

Step 1

Replace the variables with the given values. Place brackets around the numbers being substituted in the equation.

$$ef - fg + g$$
$$(7)(3) - (3)(-5) + (-5)$$

Step 2

Evaluate the expression following the order of operations.

$$= (7)(3) - (3)(-5) + (-5)$$
$$= 21 + 15 - 5$$
$$= 31$$

4. 3.5

The rate of change of a linear equation is the slope of the line.

Write the given linear relation in the slope-intercept form $y = mx + b$, where m is the slope and b is the y-intercept.

$$14x - 4y + 3 = 0$$
$$4y = 14x + 3$$
$$y = \frac{14x + 3}{4}$$
$$y = \frac{7}{2}x + \frac{3}{4}$$
$$y = 3.5x + 0.75$$

The slope of the line $y = 3.5x + 0.75$ is 3.5.

Therefore, the rate of change of y with respect to x is 3.5.

5. WR

Perpendicular lines have slopes with a product that equals −1.

Multiply the two slopes together.

$3\frac{1}{2} \times \left(-\frac{2}{7}\right)$

$= \frac{7}{2} \times \left(-\frac{2}{7}\right)$

$= -\frac{14}{14}$

$= -1$

The product is −1. Therefore, the slopes correspond to perpendicular lines.

6. C

Step 1

Determine the constant rate of change, m.

Constant rate of change $(m) = \dfrac{\text{rise}}{\text{run}}$

The rise is the change in charge.

$33 - 23 = 10$

The run is the change in distance.

$15 - 10 = 5$

Constant rate of change $(m) = \dfrac{\$10}{5 \text{ km}}$ or $2/km$

Step 2

Determine the fixed charge.

The initial value is the charge, C, at the start of the ride when the distance driven is 0 km. Use one of the other charge values and the value of m to find c.

$$m = \frac{\text{rise}}{\text{run}}$$

$$2 = \frac{23 - c}{10 - 0}$$

$$2 = \frac{23 - c}{10}$$

$$10(2) = 10\left(\frac{23 - c}{10}\right)$$

$$20 = 23 - c$$

$$c + 20 - 20 = 23 - c + c - 20$$

$$c = 3$$

The fixed charge, or initial value, is $3.

7. 3

Step 1

Determine the relationship between the units.

1 ft = 12 in

To find the relationship between cubic feet and cubic yards, you need to find the cube of 12.

$1 \text{ ft}^3 = 12 \times 12 \times 12 \text{ in}^3$

$= 1\ 728 \text{ in}^3$

Step 2

Perform the conversion.

You are going from a smaller unit to a larger one, so you need to divide.

$5\ 184 \div 1\ 728 = 3 \text{ ft}^3$

8. D

Step 1

Choose the correct converting ratio.

1 gal = 4 qt

Step 2

Convert gallons to quarts.

Since you are converting from larger units to smaller units, you need to multiply.

$5 \times 4 = 20$

Daniel will have 20 qt of paint.

9. 4

Step 1

Choose the correct conversion ratio.

1 T = 2 000 lb

Step 2

Convert pounds to tons.

You are going from a smaller unit to a larger unit, so you need to divide.

$8\ 000 \div 2\ 000 = 4$

Therefore, 8 000 lb equals 4 T.

10. WR

HINT:

Smaller unit → larger unit: Think division.

Larger unit → smaller unit: Think multiplication.

Step 1

Before you can order the numbers from shortest to longest, all the measures should be in the same unit. Since two of the measures are in centimetres (34 cm and 304 cm), convert the other two measures (3.3 m and 343 mm) to centimetres.

When you convert metres to centimetres, you are converting a larger unit to a smaller unit. This means that the answer will be a larger number. To get a larger number, think multiplication.

Since 1 m = 100 cm, convert 3.3 m to centimetres by multiplying 3.3 m by 100.

$3.3 \times 100 = 330$

$3.3 \text{ m} = 330 \text{ cm}$

When you convert millimetres to centimetres, you are converting a smaller unit to a larger unit. This means that the answer will be a smaller number. To get a smaller number, think division.

Since 10 mm = 1 cm, convert 343 mm to centimetres by dividing 343 by 10.

$343 \div 10 = 34$

$343 \text{ mm} = 34 \text{ cm}$

Step 2

Now that the lengths are all in the same unit (centimetres), they can be ordered from shortest to longest: 34 cm, 34.3 cm (343 mm), 304 cm, 330 cm (3.3 m)

From shortest to longest, the lengths are 34 cm, 343 mm, 304 cm, 3.3 m.

11. D

Convert the units of area.

$m^2 \rightarrow cm^2$

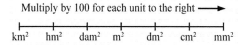

You are moving two places to the right. Multiply by 100 for each step.

$0.3 \times 100 \times 100 = 3\ 000$

The value of 0.3 m² expressed in square centimetres is 3 000 cm².

12. D

Step 1

Determine the total capacity of the bottle.

Multiply the capacity of the mug by the number of times it is poured into the bottle.

$750 \times 12 = 9\ 000 \text{ mL}$

Step 2

Convert millilitres (mL) to litres (L).

Recall the horizontal conversion chart for capacity.

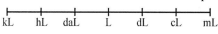

To convert millilitres (mL) to litres (L), move three steps to the left. Divide the capacity by 10 for each step.

$\dfrac{9\ 000}{10 \times 10 \times 10} = \dfrac{9\ 000}{1\ 000} = 9 \text{ L}$

13. WR

Step 1

Choose the correct conversion ratio.

1 hg = 100 000 mg

Step 2

Convert hectograms to milligrams.

$28.65 \times 100\ 000 = 2\ 865\ 000$

Therefore, 28.65 hectograms equals 2 865 000 milligrams.

14. 6000

Step 1

Convert the speed of the car from kilometres per hour to metres per hour.

There are 1 000 m in 1 km.

$360 \text{ km} = (360 \times 1\ 000 \text{ m})$

$= 360\ 000 \text{ m}$

An Indy car travels 360 000 m/h.

Step 2

Convert the speed of an Indy car from metres per hour to metres per minute.

There are 60 min in 1 h.

An Indy car travels 360 000 m/h. You can write this as $\dfrac{360\ 000 \text{ m}}{60 \text{ min}}$. To simplify, divide both numbers by 60.

$\dfrac{360\ 000 \text{ m}}{60 \text{ min}} = \dfrac{360\ 000 \text{ m}}{60} \div \dfrac{60 \text{ min}}{60}$

$= 6\ 000 \text{ m/min}$

An Indy car travels an average of 6 000 m/min during a race.

15. A

Step 1

Determine the conversion ratio.

1 fl oz = 29.57 mL

1 fl oz = 0.029 57 L

Step 2

Apply the conversion ratio.

Let x equal the unknown value.

$$\frac{1}{0.029\ 57} = \frac{x}{5}$$

$$\frac{5}{0.029\ 57} = x$$

$$169 \approx x$$

To the nearest ounce, 5 L is equal to 169 fl oz.

16. D

Step 1

Determine the conversion ratio.

1 yd = 0.9144 m

1 yd = 91.44 cm

Raise each unit of measurement to the power of 3.

1 yd^3 = 764 554.858 cm^3

Step 2

Apply the conversion ratio. Let x stand for the unknown value.

$$\frac{1}{764\ 554.858} = \frac{2.5}{x}$$

$$x = 2.5 \times 764\ 554.858$$

$$x = 1\ 911\ 387.145$$

To the nearest whole number, 2.5 yd^3 is equivalent to 1 911 387 cm^3.

17. C

Step 1

Determine the volume of a cube.

Substitute the known values into the volume formula for a cube, and simplify.

$$V = s^3$$
$$= (27)^3$$
$$= 19\ 683 \text{ cm}^3$$

Step 2

Convert cubic centimetres (cm^3) to cubic metres (m^3).

Use the horizontal conversion chart for volume.

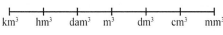

To convert cubic centimetres to cubic metres, move two steps to the left. Divide the volume by 1 000 for each step.

$$\frac{19\ 683}{1\ 000 \times 1\ 000}$$

$$= \frac{19\ 683}{1\ 000\ 000}$$

$$= 0.019\ 683 \text{ m}^3$$

18. D

Method 1

Use cross multiplication to solve the problem.

Choose the correct conversion rate.

1 ft^2 = 144 in^2

Set up a proportion.

Put feet on the top, and inches on the bottom.

$$\frac{1 \text{ ft}^2}{144 \text{ in}^2} = \frac{59 \text{ ft}^2}{x \text{ in}^2}$$

Solve for x.

$$1 \times x = 59 \times 144$$
$$x = 8\ 496$$

Method 2

The problem can also be solved by using proportional reasoning.

Choose the appropriate conversion rate.

1 ft^2 = 144 in^2

Perform the conversion.

When going from larger units to smaller ones, multiply.

$$59 \times 144 = 8\ 496 \text{ in}^2$$

Therefore, 59 ft^2 is equal to 8 496 in^2.

19. B

Step 1

Determine the volume of the milk container.

$$V = lwh$$
$$= 2 \times 2 \times 3$$
$$= 12$$

The volume of the milk container is 12 dm^3.

Step 2

Convert cubic decimeters to cubic centimeters.

The horizontal conversion chart for volume is given as shown.

Multiply by 1 000 for each unit to the right ⟶

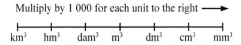

To convert cubic decimeters to cubic centimeters, move one step to the right. Multiply by 1 000.

$12 \times 1\ 000 = 12\ 000$

$$12\ dm^3 = 12\ 000\ cm^3$$

Step 3

Convert cubic centimeters to milliliters.

Recall that $1\ cm^3 = 1\ mL$, so

$12\ 000\ cm^3 = 12\ 000\ mL$.

Step 4

Convert milliliters to liters.

The horizontal conversion table for capacity is given as shown.

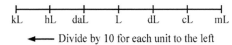

◄— Divide by 10 for each unit to the left

To convert milliliters to liters, move three step to the left. Divide by 10 for each step.

$$\frac{12\ 000}{10 \times 10 \times 10}$$

$$= \frac{12\ 000}{1\ 000}$$

$$= 12$$

The capacity of the milk container is 12 L.

UNIT TEST — ALGEBRA

1. What is the value of $p^3 - 3p^2 + 3p$ when $p = 4$?

   A. 30   **B.** 29

   C. 28   **D.** 27

2. The ratio of the circumference of a circle to its diameter will always equal the
   A. perimeter of the circle

   B. radius of the circle

   C. area of the circle

   D. value of pi

   Written Response
   ---

3. Rewrite the equation $A = \dfrac{bh}{2}$ to isolate h.

Use the following information to answer the next question.

A cylindrical tank with a 200 L capacity is filled with water. The tank has an outlet pipe that drains the water out of the tank at a constant rate.

Rate of Water Draining Out of a Tank

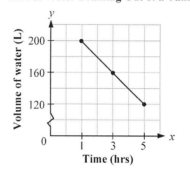

4. At what rate does the water drain out of the tank?

   A. 8 L/h   **B.** 9 L/h

   C. 20 L/h   **D.** 21 L/h

   Written Response
   ---

5. What are the slopes of lines that are parallel and perpendicular to a line with a slope of $m = -\dfrac{1}{5}$?

Use the following information to answer the next question.

Martia, a beginner skier, must choose one of four ski hills to practise on. The given table shows the name of each of the four ski hills she has to choose from as well as the height (the rise) and the horizontal distance from the top to the bottom of each ski hill (the run).

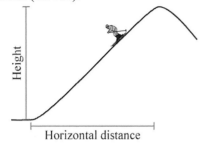

Name	Height (m)	Horizontal Distance (m)
Powder Keg	500	250
Lookout Peak	640	400
Free Fall	760	285
Black Ridge	810	540

6. Considering Martia's skiing abilities, which ski hill would be **best** for her to practise on?

A. Free Fall   B. Black Ridge

C. Powder Keg   D. Lookout Peak

Use the following information to answer the next question.

Mark had 3 pints of orange juice after he ran a marathon.

7. How many cups of orange juice did Mark drink?

A. 4 c   B. 5 c

C. 6 c   D. 7 c

Numerical Response

8. How many pounds are in 14.75 tons? _____ pounds

Use the following information to answer the next question.

To build up his stamina before a 1 500 m race, Jean ran a little bit farther each day as he practised. These are the distances Jean ran for the three days prior to the race:

- Wednesday: 1 460 m
- Thursday: 1 495 m
- Friday: 1 510 m

Written Response

9. How many kilometres did Jean run in total on Wednesday, Thursday, and Friday?

Use the following information to answer the next question.

James has 6bottles of pop, each with a volume of 1.5 L. He pours the contents of all six bottles into a large bowl.

10. How many mL of pop are poured into the bowl?

A. 9 000 mL   B. 90 mL

C. 0.9 mL   D. 0.009 mL

Use the following information to answer the next question.

A table is 96 in long.

11. How many feet are in 96 in?

A. 5 ft   B. 6 ft

C. 7 ft   D. 8 ft

Written Response

12. How many decagrams is equal to 300 decigrams?

Numerical Response

13. What is 250 000 m/h converted into kilometres per hour? _____km/h

14. To the nearest tenth, how many cubic feet are equivalent to 10 m^3 given that 1 ft equals 0.3048 m?

A. 28.3 ft^3 **B.** 32.8 ft^3

C. 304.8 ft^3 **D.** 353.1 ft^3

15. To the nearest tenth, how many fluid ounces are equal to 200 mL?

A. 3.4 fl oz   **B.** 6.8 fl oz

C. 12.5 fl oz   **D.** 25.0 fl oz

16. If the volume of a fuel tanker is 1.125 hm^3, what is its volume expressed in cubic centimetres?

A. 0.000 000 0011 (25) cm^3

B. 1 125 000 000 000 cm^3

C. 1 125 000 000 cm^3

D. 0.001 125 cm^3

17. If the area of a football field is 8 242 560 in^2, how many square yards is the field?

A. 3 664 yd^2 **B.** 6 360 yd^2

C. 57 240 yd^2 **D.** 228 960 yd^2

18. Expressed in kilolitres, what is the capacity of a metal box with dimensions of 1.5 m by 2 m by 3.2 m?

A. 0.96 kL   **B.** 9.6 kL

C. 96 kL   **D.** 960 kL

Use the following information to answer the next question.

Roger used a pencil to trace the circular base of his water bottle. He then laid exactly four quarters in a line across the diameter of the circle. Using a ruler, he measured the diameter of each quarter, and calculated the circumference of his water bottle as 29.78 cm. The quarter could be used as a referent for one ____*i*____, and, according to Roger's measurement, it has a diameter of ____*ii*____ cm.

19. The given statement is completed by the information in which of the following tables?

A.

i	*ii*
centimetre	1.19

B.

i	*ii*
centimetre	2.37

C.

i	*ii*
inch	1.19

D.

i	*ii*
inch	2.37

ANSWERS AND SOLUTIONS — UNIT TEST

1. C	6. B	11. D	16. B
2. D	7. C	12. WR	17. B
3. WR	8. 29500	13. 250	18. B
4. C	9. WR	14. D	19. D
5. WR	10. A	15. B	

1. C

Step 1
Replace the variable p by the given value 4.
Place brackets around the numbers being substituted in the equation.

$p^3 - 3p^2 + 3p$
$(4)^3 - 3(4)^2 + 3(4)$

Step 2
Evaluate the expression following the order of operations.

$= (4)^3 - 3(4)^2 + 3(4)$
$= 64 - 3(16) + 3(4)$
$= 64 - 48 + 12$
$= 28$

2. D

To determine the ratio of the circumference of a circle to its diameter, begin with the circumference formula $C = \pi d$.

Rearrange the formula to isolate π.

$\dfrac{C}{d} = \dfrac{\pi d}{d}$

$\dfrac{C}{d} = \pi$

The ratio of the circumference to the diameter is equal to the value of π.

3. WR

Step 1
Multiply both sides of the equation by 2 to eliminate the fraction.

$A = \dfrac{bh}{2}$

$2(A) = \left(\dfrac{bh}{2}\right)2$

$2A = bh$

Step 2
Divide both sides of the equation by b to isolate h.

$\dfrac{2A}{b} = \dfrac{bh}{b}$

$\dfrac{2A}{b} = h$

4. C

The water drains out at a constant rate. Use the constant rate of change formula to determine the rate of drainage.

Constant rate of change

$= \dfrac{\Delta \text{ in dependent variable}}{\Delta \text{ in independent variable}}$

Rate of drainage $= \dfrac{\text{Change in volume of water}}{\text{Change in time}}$

$= \dfrac{200 - 160}{3 - 1}$

$= \dfrac{40}{2}$

$= 20 \text{ L/h}$

The water drains out of the tank at a rate of 20 L/h.

5. WR

Step 1
Determine the slope of a line parallel to the slope $m = -\dfrac{1}{5}$.

Parallel lines have the same slope. Therefore, $m_\parallel = -\dfrac{1}{5}$ is the slope of a line parallel to the slope $m = -\dfrac{1}{5}$.

Step 2
Determine the slope of a line perpendicular to the slope $m = -\dfrac{1}{5}$.

Perpendicular lines have slopes that are negative reciprocals of each other.

$m_\perp = -1 \times \dfrac{1}{m}$

$m_\perp = -1 \times \left(\dfrac{1}{-\dfrac{1}{5}}\right)$

$m_\perp = -1 \times (-5)$

$m_\perp = 5$

Therefore, $m_\perp = 5$ is the slope of a line perpendicular to the slope $m = -\dfrac{1}{5}$.

6. B

Since Martia is a beginner skier, the easiest hill will be the least steep of the four given ski hills. In other words, the ski hill that has the smallest value for the slope will be the least steep.

Determine the slope of each ski hill by applying the formula $m = \dfrac{\text{rise}}{\text{run}}$, where m represents the slope.

$$\text{Slope of Powder Keg} = \frac{500}{250} = 2$$

$$\text{Slope of Lookout Peak} = \frac{640}{400} = \frac{8}{5}$$

$$\text{Slope of Free Fall} = \frac{760}{285} = \frac{8}{3}$$

$$\text{Slope of Black Ridge} = \frac{810}{540} = \frac{3}{2}$$

Since $\dfrac{3}{2}$ is the smallest of the four values for the slope, the Black Ridge would be the best hill for Martia to practise on.

7. C

Step 1
Choose the correct conversion ratio.
1 pt = 2 c

Step 2
Convert pints to cups.

You are going from a larger unit to a smaller unit, so you need to multiply.
$3 \times 2 = 6$

Therefore, Mark drank 6 cups of orange juice.

8. 29500

Step 1
Choose the correct conversion ratio.
1 ton = 2 000 pounds

Step 2
Convert tons to pounds.

Because tons are larger units than pounds, multiply 14.75 by 2 000.
$14.75 \times 2\ 000 = 29\ 500$

There are 29 500 pounds in 14.75 tons.

9. WR

HINT: Smaller unit→ larger unit
Think division.

Step 1
To determine the total number of metres Jean ran, add the three distances for Wednesday (1 460 m), Thursday (1 495 m), and Friday (1 510 m).
$1\ 460 + 1\ 495 + 1\ 510 = 4\ 465$ m

Step 2
When you convert metres into kilometres, you are converting a smaller unit into a larger unit. This means that the answer will be a smaller number. To get a smaller number, think division.

Since 1 000 m = 1 km, convert 4 465 m to kilometres by dividing 4 465 by 1 000.
$4\ 465 \div 1\ 000 = 4.465$
$\quad 4\ 465$ m = 4.465 km

A quick way to divide by 1 000 is to move the decimal point three places to the left. 4 465→ 4.465 Remember: If a decimal point is not shown, it would be located to the right of the last digit.

Jean ran 4.465 km in total on Wednesday, Thursday, and Friday.

10. A

Step 1
Determine the total volume of pop poured into the bowl.

Multiply the number of bottles of pop by the capacity of each bottle.
$6 \times 1.5 = 9$ L

Step 2
Convert L to mL.

Use the horizontal conversion chart for capacity.

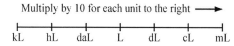

Multiply by 10 for each unit to the right ⟶

| kL | hL | daL | L | dL | cL | mL |

To convert L to mL, move three steps to the right. Multiply the capacity by 10 for each step.
$9 \times 10 \times 10 \times 10 = 9\ 000$ mL

11. D

Step 1
Set up a proportion.

Let x represent the number of feet required.
Since 1 ft = 12 in, set up the following proportion to convert from inches to feet.
$$\frac{x \text{ ft}}{1 \text{ ft}} = \frac{96 \text{ in}}{12 \text{ in}}$$

Step 2
Solve for x.
$$x = \frac{96}{12}$$
$$x = 8$$
The length of the table is 8 ft.

12. WR

Step 1
Choose the correct conversion ratio.
1 dag = 100 dg

Step 2

Convert decigrams to decagrams.

$300 \div 100 = 3$

Therefore, 300 decigrams is equal to 3 decagrams.

13. 250

Step 1

Choose the correct conversion ratio.

$1 \text{ km} = 1\ 000 \text{ m}$

Step 2

Convert metres per hour into kilometres per hour.

$250\ 000 \div 1\ 000 = 250$

The unit of time does not change, so no time conversion is necessary.

Therefore, $250\ 000$ m/h equals 250 km/h.

14. D

Step 1

Determine the conversion ratio.

$1 \text{ ft} = 0.3048 \text{ m}$

Raise each unit of measurement to the power of 3.

$1 \text{ ft}^3 \approx 0.028\ 32 \text{ m}^3$

Step 2

Apply the conversion ratio. Let x stand for the unknown value.

$$\frac{1}{0.028\ 32} \approx \frac{x}{10}$$

$$\frac{10}{0.028\ 32} \approx x$$

$$353.1 \approx x$$

To the nearest tenth, 10 m^3 is equivalent to 353.1 ft^3.

15. B

Step 1

Determine the conversion ratio.

$1 \text{ fl oz} = 29.57 \text{ mL}$

Step 2

Apply the conversion ratio. Let x equal the unknown value.

$$\frac{1}{29.57} = \frac{x}{200}$$

$$\frac{200}{29.57} = x$$

$$6.76 \approx x$$

To the nearest tenth, 6.8 fl oz are equal to 200 mL.

16. B

Recall the horizontal conversion chart for volume.

Multiply by 1 000 for each unit to the right ⟶

km^3 hm^3 dam^3 m^3 dm^3 cm^3 mm^3

To convert from cubic hectometres (hm^3) to cubic centimetres (cm^3), move four steps to the right.

Multiply the volume by 1 000 for each step.

$1.125 \times 1\ 000 \times 1\ 000 \times 1\ 000 \times 1\ 000$
$= 1\ 125\ 000\ 000\ 000$

$1.125 \text{ hm}^3 = 1\ 125\ 000\ 000\ 000 \text{ cm}^3$

Therefore, the volume of the tanker is $1\ 125\ 000\ 000\ 000$ cm^3.

17. B

Method 1

Use cross multiplication.

1. Choose the correct conversion ratio.

   $1 \text{ yd}^2 = 1\ 296 \text{ in}^2$

2. Set up a proportion. Put the yards on the top and the inches on the bottom.

$$\frac{1 \text{ yd}^2}{1\ 296 \text{ in}^2} = \frac{x \text{ yd}^2}{8\ 242\ 560 \text{ in}^2}$$

3. Solve by using cross multiplication.

$$1 \times 8\ 242\ 560 = 1\ 296 \times x$$
$$8\ 242\ 560 = 1\ 296x$$
$$\frac{8\ 242\ 560}{1\ 296} = \frac{1\ 296x}{1\ 296}$$
$$6\ 360 = x$$

Method 2

Use proportional reasoning.

1. Choose the appropriate conversion rate.

   $1 \text{ yd}^2 = 1\ 296 \text{ in}^2$

2. Perform the conversion. To convert from smaller units to larger ones, use division.

   $8\ 242\ 560 \div 1\ 296 = 6\ 360 \text{ yd}^2$

The football field is $6\ 360$ yd^2.

18. B

Step 1

Determine the volume of the box.

$V = lwh$
$V = 1.5 \times 2 \times 3.2$
$V = 9.6 \text{ m}^3$

Step 2

Convert cubic metres (m^3) to cubic centimetres (cm^3).

Recall the horizontal conversion chart for volume.

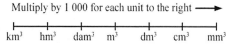

Multiply by 1 000 for each unit to the right ⟶

km³   hm³   dam³   m³   dm³   cm³   mm³

To convert cubic metres to cubic centimetres, move three steps to the right and multiply by 1 000 for each step.

$9.6\ m^3 = 9.6 \times 1\ 000 \times 1\ 000$

$9.6\ m^3 = 9\ 600\ 000\ cm^3$

Step 3

Convert cubic centimetres to millilitres.

Recall that $1\ cm^3 = 1\ mL$.

$9\ 600\ 000\ cm^3 = 9\ 600\ 000\ mL$

Step 4

Convert millilitres (mL) to kilolitres (kL).

Recall the horizontal conversion table for capacity.

kL   hL   daL   L   dL   cL   mL

⟵ Divide by 10 for each unit to the left

To convert millilitres to kilolitres, move six units to the left. Divide by 10 for each step.

$$\frac{9\ 600\ 000}{10 \times 10 \times 10 \times 10 \times 10 \times 10} = 9.6\ kL$$

19. D

Step 1

Draw a sketch of the situation represented in the problem.

- Draw a large circle, and label it "water bottle."
- Draw four small circles side by side across the diameter of the large circle, and label them "quarters."
- Draw a dotted line across the diameter of the circle through the centres of the quarters.

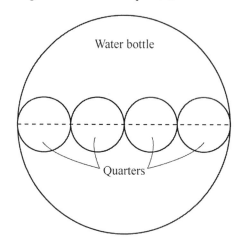

Step 2

Determine the unit of measure that the diameter of the quarter best represents.

A quarter has a diameter of approximately one inch. Therefore, it is a good referent for one inch.

Step 3

Determine the diameter, d_w, of the water bottle.

$C_w = \pi d_w$

$d_w = \dfrac{C_w}{\pi}$

$ = \dfrac{29.78}{\pi}$

$ \approx 9.479\ 27\ cm$

Step 4

Since there are four quarters representing the diameter, d_w, of the water bottle, the diameter of each quarter, d_q, can be determined.

$d_w = 4 \times d_q$

$d_q = \dfrac{d_w}{4}$

$ \approx \dfrac{9.479\ 27}{4}$

$ \approx 2.3698\ cm$

Therefore, each quarter has a diameter of approximately 2.37 cm.

Statistics

STATISTICS

Table of Correlations			
Outcome	**Practice Questions**	**Unit Test Questions**	**Practice Test**
20S Statistics			
20S.1 *Solve problems that involve creating and interpreting graphs, including: bar graphs; histograms; line graphs; and circle graphs.*	1, 2, 3, 4, 5, 6, 7, 8	1, 2, 3, 4, 5, 6, 7, 8	36, 37, 38, 39

20S.1 Solve problems that involve creating and interpreting graphs, including: bar graphs; histograms; line graphs; and circle graphs.

REPRESENTING DATA IN A BROKEN-LINE GRAPH

Broken-line graphs are used to show trends in data over time.

To construct a broken-line graph from a given set of data, follow these steps:

1. Draw and label the horizontal and vertical axes using a scale that includes all the information and that uses at least 75% of the axis. Place any units of measurement in parentheses.
2. Plot the information on the graph using a dot for each piece of data.
3. Connect the dots using straight lines.
4. Give the graph a title.

Example

Randy made a table to represent the amount of money he raised for charity for the week.

Day	Money Raised ($)
Monday	400
Tuesday	550
Wednesday	350
Thursday	600
Friday	850
Saturday	300

Display the given information using a broken-line graph.

Solution

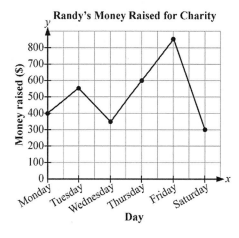

20S.1 Solve problems that involve creating and interpreting graphs, including: bar graphs; histograms; line graphs; and circle graphs.

REPRESENT DATA IN A BAR GRAPH

A **graph** is used to organize and display **data**. The main point of a graph is to present information clearly so it can be compared.

Bar graphs are graphs that use bars to show quantities. When you create a bar graph, you must include the following:

- A title.
- Label on the *x*-axis. This is the horizontal line at the bottom of the bar graph.
- Label on the *y*-axis (vertical line). This is the vertical line that makes a right angle with the *x*-axis.
- Bars to represent the data you are trying to show. The bars may either be horizontal or vertical.

Example

The parents of students in grades 1 to 3 at Lennon Elementary School completed a survey. They wanted to find out their children's favourite burger places. The results are shown in this chart.

Restaurant	Number of Students
Mings	30
Ahmed and Williams	25
Marissa's	15
King Burger	10

Draw a bar graph showing the data in the given chart.

Solution

Step 1

Label the parts of the graph.

To display the burger places in a bar graph, start by writing a title for the graph. Then, label the *x*-axis and the *y*-axis.

A good title for the bar graph might be "Favourite Place for Burgers."

Label the *x*-axis "Restaurant." The *x*-axis is the axis along the bottom of the graph.

Label the *y*-axis "Number of students." The *y*-axis is the axis on the side of the graph.

Step 2

Draw the bars that represent the data.

Start with the first restaurant in the chart, Mings. Since 30 students chose Mings as their favourite burger place, draw the bar up to 30 on the *y*-axis.

Then, draw the bar for the next restaurant, Ahmed and Williams. Since 25 students chose that restaurant, draw the bar up to 25.

Draw the bar for Marissa's to 15 and the bar for King Burger to 10.

This bar graph represents the data found in the survey.

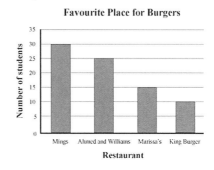

Example

Cathy counts the number of crayons in the art box. There are 4 red crayons, 7 green crayons, 5 blue crayons, and 2 yellow crayons.

Draw a bar graph using the grid below to show the number of each colour of crayons Cathy found in the art box. One square will represent two crayons. Remember to use appropriate labels and a title.

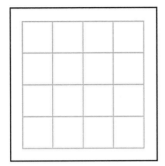

Solution

Step 1

Label the parts of the graph.

To display the crayons in a bar graph, start by writing a title for the graph. Then, label the *x*-axis and the *y*-axis.

A good title for the bar graph might be "Crayons in Art Box."

Label the *x*-axis "Number of crayons."
The *x*-axis is the axis along the bottom of the graph.
Label the *y*-axis "Colours." The *y*-axis is the axis on the side of the graph

Step 2

Draw the bars that represent the data.

Start with the first colour in the chart, yellow. Since 2 crayons were yellow, draw the bar across to 2 on the *x*-axis.

Then, draw the bar for the next colour, blue. Since 5 crayons were blue, draw the bar across to 5.

Draw the bar for green to 7 and the bar for red to 4.

This bar graph represents the crayons in the box.

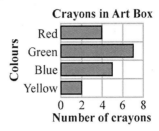

20S.1 Solve problems that involve creating and interpreting graphs, including: bar graphs; histograms; line graphs; and circle graphs.

REPRESENTING DATA IN A HISTOGRAM

A histogram looks similar to a bar graph, but since the data is continuous, there are no gaps between the bars. The bars in a histogram are used to represent continuous data found in a frequency table.
The given graph is an example of a histogram.

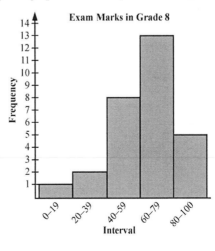

The horizontal axis of a histogram represents the intervals, and the vertical axis represents the frequency of the data.

In order to make a histogram, first collect the necessary data. Suppose that the objective is to try to measure the heights (in centimetres) of all 30 students in a class. The following measurements represent the data that might have been collected: 177 cm, 176 cm, 183 cm, 177 cm, 180 cm, 171 cm, 160 cm, 180 cm, 162 cm, 157 cm, 183 cm, 155 cm, 177 cm, 167 cm, 176 cm, 171 cm, 145 cm, 180 cm, 174 cm, 177 cm, 156 cm, 166 cm, 178 cm, 184 cm, 180 cm, 165 cm, 167 cm, 178 cm, 177 cm, 164 cm

The intervals in a histogram must be defined so that several pieces of data fall into each interval.

Second, the data must be grouped into smaller, more manageable intervals.

The following intervals would be appropriate when organizing the heights of students in a class: 145–149 cm, 150–154 cm, 155–159 cm, 160–164 cm, 165–169 cm, 170–174 cm, 175–179 cm, 180–184 cm

When creating a histogram, the only relevant information is found in the numbers and their frequencies. The number of people in each height category is revealed by creating a frequency table with intervals.

The hardest thing about making a good histogram is choosing the right intervals.

Height (cm)	Tally	Frequency
145–149	|	1
150–154		0
155–159	|||	3
160–164	|||	3
165–169	||||	4
170–174	|||	3
175–179	|||| ||||	9
180–184	|||| ||	7

The number next to each height is the frequency with which that height occurs. The higher the frequency of each interval, the more people there are in that category.

By grouping data into intervals, there will be fewer bars on the graph, and each bar will contain a significant amount of data. More importantly, there is now a continuous range of heights, from 145 cm to 184 cm.

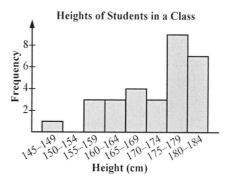

In a histogram, the bars must touch because the set of data is represented by numbers that are grouped to form a continuous range from left to right. There are no gaps in the numbers along the bottom axis because every possible height of the classmates can be located in one of the intervals.

20S.1 Solve problems that involve creating and interpreting graphs, including: bar graphs; histograms; line graphs; and circle graphs.

Selecting Appropriate Graphs to Display Data: Histograms, Bar Graphs, Line Plots, and Stem-and-Leaf Plots

Data can be visually displayed by using a variety of graphs. Knowing what each kind of graph is used for can help you decide which graph to use to display data.

Bar Graphs

Bar graphs are best for displaying **categorical data**. Categorical data are organized according to categories, such as favourite subjects at school or kinds of animals at the zoo.

The names of the categories are usually at the bottom of the graph, and the heights of the bars show how many items fall into each category.

For example, in the bar graph shown here, the different kinds of animals are the categories. The height of each bar shows how many of each animal there are at the zoo.

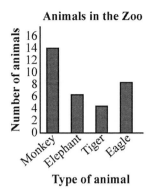

Animals in the Zoo

LINE PLOTS

Line plots look a bit like bar graphs, but they are used to show data that are given as a set of numbers. Examples of this type of data are the number of letters that your friends have in their names and your results when you roll a standard six-sided die.

The bottom of a line plot is a number line. The number of Xs shows how many times that number appeared in the data set. For example, in the line plot shown, all the numbers you can roll on a six-sided die are in the number line on the bottom and the Xs show how many times that number was rolled.

```
×
×  ×      ×      ×
×  ×      ×   ×  ×
×  ×   ×  ×   ×  ×
×  ×   ×  ×   ×  ×
 1  2  3  4  5  6
```

STEM-AND-LEAF PLOTS

A stem-and-leaf plot is another way to show data that are given as a set of numbers. In a stem-and-leaf plot, each value is split into a stem and a leaf. The leaf is usually the last digit of the given number, and the other digits of that number are placed in the stem in numerical order.

For example, the given stem-and-leaf plot shows the data set {45, 50, 60, 60, 65, 70, 75, 75, 75, 75, 75, 75, 75, 80, 80, 80, 85, 85, 90, 100}. The stem shows the tens value of each number, and the leaf shows the ones value. In the first row, the number 45 is shown as a 4 in the stem column and a 5 in the leaf column.

Stem	Leaves
4	5
5	0
6	0 0 5
7	0 5 5 5 5 5 5 5
8	0 0 0 5 5
9	0
10	0

Stem-and-leaf plots are useful because they make it easier to show more data than line plots.

For example, if you wanted to show the data in the given stem-and-leaf plot on a line plot, the number line across the bottom would have to go from 45 to 100. Stem-and-leaf plots can show more data with a wider range than line plots can. Line plots are easier to read, however, so if you have a smaller data set, it is usually a good idea to show it in a line plot.

HISTOGRAMS

A histogram is another kind of graph that looks like a bar graph. Like line plots and stem-and-leaf plots, histograms are used to show data that are given as numbers. To understand how histograms are useful, you need to understand the difference between discrete and continuous data.

Discrete data are always whole numbers. The number of letters in your name or the number you roll on a die are examples of discrete data. You will never have half a letter in your name or roll a quarter of a number on a die.

Copyright Protected

Continuous data can be any number, including a decimal number. Height is an example of continuous data, because a person's height can fall between an exact number of inches or centimetres. For instance, you could be 145.6 cm tall.

Line plots and stem-and-leaf plots are used to show discrete data. If your data are continuous, then you can use a histogram. In a histogram, the bars are always touching and each bar represents a range of data, such as 115 cm to 120 cm. The ranges are listed on the bottom of the histogram, and the bars show how many numbers appear in that range.

Example
In the given graph, height ranges are listed on the bottom and the bars show how many people fall into each height range.

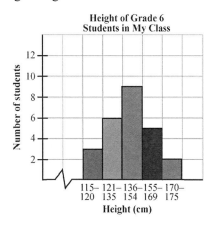

Histograms can also be used to show sets of data that are too large for either line plots or stem-and-leaf plots. If you have more than about 100 numbers in a data set, you should use a histogram, even if the data are discrete.

20S.1 Solve problems that involve creating and interpreting graphs, including: bar graphs; histograms; line graphs; and circle graphs.

CONVERTING DATA INTO DEGREES FOR USE IN A CIRCLE GRAPH

A **circle graph** is used to represent data that are given as parts of a whole. Usually, data that are shown in a circle graph are given as percentages. The graph shown here displays the percentages of the different types of baking that were sold at a school bake sale.

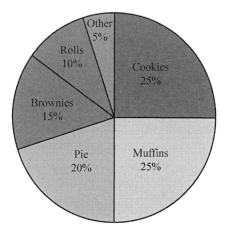

If you use a protractor to measure the angles in this circle graph, you will see that the angle is not the same as the percentage. For instance, 25% of the baking sold was cookies, but the section of the circle that shows this is 90°. This is because a circle has a total of 360°. Remember that 25% is the same as a quarter. A quarter of the circle is 360° ÷ 4 = 90°.

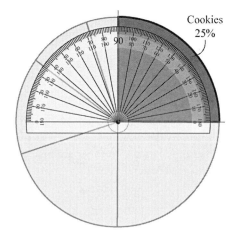

Statistics   212   Castle Rock Research

Whenever you are given a set of data to put into a circle graph, you always need to find out the number of degrees for each percentage. To do this, use the following steps:

1. Convert the percentage into either a decimal or a fraction.
2. Multiply the decimal or fraction by 360°.
3. Check your answer by adding up the degrees. If the total is 360°, then your answer is correct.

Example

Ms. Liu's Grade 6 class is responsible for planning this year's bake sale. They looked at what was sold last year to help them decide what to bake. They decide to represent the data as a circle graph because this will help them see the relationship between the different kinds of baking and the total amount of baking sold.

Kinds of Baking Sold	
Baking	**Percentage of Total**
Cookies	25%
Muffins	25%
Pie	20%
Brownies	15%
Cinnamon Rolls	10%
Other	5%

Convert the data in the table into the degrees of a circle.

Solution

Step 1

Convert the percentages into fractions.

- Cookies: $25\% = \dfrac{25}{100}$

- Muffins: $25\% = \dfrac{25}{100}$

- Pie: $20\% = \dfrac{20}{100}$

- Brownies: $15\% = \dfrac{15}{100}$

- Rolls: $10\% = \dfrac{10}{100}$

- Other: $5\% = \dfrac{5}{100}$

Step 2

Multiply each fraction by 360°.

- Cookies: $\dfrac{25}{100} \times 360° = 90°$

- Muffins: $\dfrac{25}{100} \times 360° = 90°$

- Pie: $\dfrac{20}{100} \times 360° = 72°$

- Brownies: $\dfrac{15}{100} \times 360° = 54°$

- Rolls: $\dfrac{10}{100} \times 360° = 36°$

- Other: $\dfrac{5}{100} \times 360° = 18°$

Step 3

Check the answer.

$90 + 90 + 72 + 54 + 36 + 18 = 360°$

The numbers add up to 360°, so the calculation is correct. This information can now be used to make a circle graph.

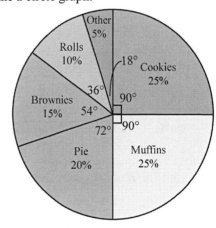

Sometimes, the data are not given as percentages. When this happens, you need to convert the data into decimals before multiplying them by 360°.

Example

The students in Fashanda's Grade 6 class come from three different Grade 5 classes. Fashanda decides to make a circle graph to show the proportion of students that come from each class. She surveys her classmates and puts the information in a frequency table.

Number of Students from Each Grade 5 Class	
Grade 5 Teacher	**Number of Students**
Mr. Moore	卌	
Ms. Cegielny	卌 卌
Mrs. Yim	卌				

Convert the data in Fashanda's table into the degrees of a circle graph.

Solution

Step 1

Change the data into fractions.

Count the total number of students in Fashanda's class this year. There are 25 students in total. This will be the denominator of each fraction. The different numbers of students that came from the Grade 5 classes will be the numerators.

- Mr. Moore: $\dfrac{6}{25}$

- Ms. Cegielny: $\dfrac{10}{25}$

- Mrs. Yim: $\dfrac{9}{25}$

Step 2

Change the fractions into decimals by dividing each numerator by the denominator.

- Mr. Moore: $\dfrac{6}{25} \rightarrow 6 \div 25 = 0.24$

- Ms. Cegielny: $\dfrac{10}{25} \rightarrow 10 \div 25 = 0.40$

- Mrs. Yim: $\dfrac{9}{25} \rightarrow 9 \div 25 = 0.36$

Step 3

Multiply each decimal by 360° to find out how many degrees of the circle each class will take up.

- Mr. Moore: $0.24 \times 360° = 86.4°$
- Ms. Cegielny: $0.40 \times 360° = 144°$
- Mrs. Yim: $0.36 \times 360° = 129.6°$

Step 4

Check the answer.
$86.4 + 144 + 129.6 = 360°$
The degrees add up to 360°, so the calculation is correct.

20S.1 Solve problems that involve creating and interpreting graphs, including: bar graphs; histograms; line graphs; and circle graphs.

REPRESENTING DATA IN A CIRCLE GRAPH

Circle graphs represent data that constitutes parts of a whole. The data is divided into parts called wedges or sectors. The circle represents 100%, while each sector represents a part of 100%. This allows you to easily compare each sector to one another. Each percent corresponds to an equivalent number of degrees in the circle.

To construct a circle graph, follow these steps:

1. If necessary, convert the data into percents.
2. Calculate each percent as an angle in degrees.
3. Draw a circle.
4. Draw each of the angles using a protractor and straight edge.
5. Label the circle graph.

Example

The table shows Jolanda's movie rentals by category for the past three months.

Category	Number of Rentals
Drama	10
Comedy	7
Action	2
Horror	1

Construct a circle graph to represent this information.

Solution

Step 1

If necessary, convert the data into percents. Divide each part of the data by the total data. Then, multiply by 100 to get the percent for each activity.

The total number of movie rentals is 20.

Drama $= \dfrac{10}{20} \times 100\% = 50\%$

Comedy $= \dfrac{7}{20} \times 100\% = 35\%$

Action $= \dfrac{2}{20} \times 100\% = 10\%$

Horror $= \dfrac{1}{20} \times 100\% = 5\%$

The total percents should add up to 100.
$50 + 35 + 10 + 5 = 100$

Step 2

Calculate each percent as an angle in degrees. Divide the percent by 100. Then, multiply by 360°.

Drama = 50% ÷ 100 = 0.5 × 360° = 180°
Comedy = 35% ÷ 100 = 0.35 × 360° = 126°
Action = 10% ÷ 100 = 0.1 × 360° = 36°
Horror = 5% ÷ 100 = 0.05 × 360° = 18°

Step 3

Draw a circle.

Use a compass to make a circle large enough to label the sectors.

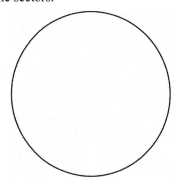

Step 4

Draw each of the angles.

Use a protractor to draw each of the angles or sectors. Start at the top of the circle graph, using the largest angle. Move in a clockwise direction until the smallest angle is drawn.

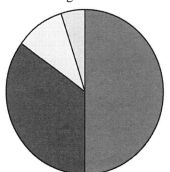

Step 5

Label the circle graph.

Include the category and percent for each sector. Give the graph a title.

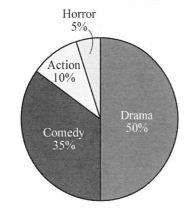

Jolanda's Movie Rentals

20S.1 Solve problems that involve creating and interpreting graphs, including: bar graphs; histograms; line graphs; and circle graphs.

READING AND INTERPRETING BAR GRAPHS

The first step to understanding the information in a graph is being able to read the information. In bar graphs, double bar graphs, and histograms, the height of the bar tells you the number of items in a category. You determine the height of the bar by reading the scale.

Example

Ashawna made a graph showing how students in her class get to school. The bar on the left shows how many students take the bus to school. The top of the bar is even with the number 12 on the scale. This means that 12 of the students in Ashawna's class take the bus.

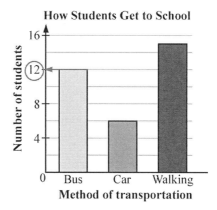

The line that the middle bar comes to is not even with a number on the scale. To find out how many students come to school by car, you need to find out what number that line represents.

Every other line on the scale has a number on it, and those numbers count up by 4s. Half of 4 is 2, so the lines count up by 2s. The first line is 2, the second one is 4, and the third one is 6. A total of 6 students go to school in a car.

How Students Get to School

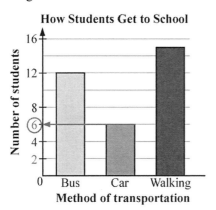

The bar on the right does not end at a line. Find out what number needs to go in the space to read how many students walk to school.

The lines count up by 2, which means that the line below the space is 14 and the line above it is 16. The number exactly between 16 and 14 is 15. There are 15 students who walk to school.

How Students Get to School

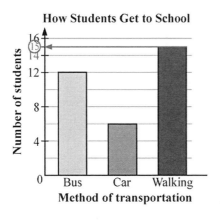

Once you have learned how to read a graph, you can interpret the information in it. You can make judgments about the kinds of things that are more or less popular. You can also compare the different amounts shown or find the total number of people surveyed.

Example

Amir works at a clothing store in the mall. Part of his job is to keep track of the kinds of items that are the most popular. At the end of a very busy week, he makes a bar graph to show the sales of some of the popular items.

Items Sold in One Week

How many more shoes were sold than jeans?

Solution

Step 1

Determine the number of jeans and the number of shoes sold.

The top bar shows how many jeans were sold. The end of the bar is even with 100 on the scale, so 100 people bought jeans.

The bottom bar shows how many pairs of shoes were sold. The end of the bar is not even with a number on the scale, so you need to find out what number that line represents.

The numbers on the scale count up by 50s, and you need to go up 5 lines to get from one number to the next. This means that each line represents $50 \div 5 = 10$ items. The bar comes to one line below 200, so 190 pairs of shoes were sold.

Step 2

Find the difference.

Subtract the number of people who bought jeans from the number of people who bought shoes. $190 - 100 = 90$

There were 90 more pairs of shoes sold than jeans.

20S.1 Solve problems that involve creating and interpreting graphs, including: bar graphs; histograms; line graphs; and circle graphs.

INTERPRETING DATA IN A HISTOGRAM

A histogram looks similar to a bar graph, but there are no gaps between the bars because the data is continuous.

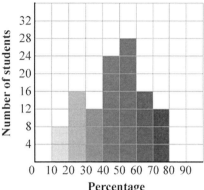

Percentage

In a histogram, each bar represents a range of data rather than a single category, as it would in a bar graph. In the given histogram, the lightly shaded bar on the far left shows that eight students scored between 10% and 20% on a test. With a histogram, you have no way of knowing the exact values. You do not know which of those eight students got 12% or 18%, only that they scored somewhere between 10% and 20%.

Interpreting data in a histogram is similar to interpreting data in a bar graph. Make sure you know which ranges are being shown, and then read up the vertical axis to see how many values fall into that range.

Example

At Aria's school, the Grade 6 math final exam was much too difficult, and many of the students failed. The teachers decided to change the passing grade to make sure that at least three-quarters of the students passed. The given histogram shows the breakdown of the marks received by the Grade 6 students.

Marks Received on the Final Exam

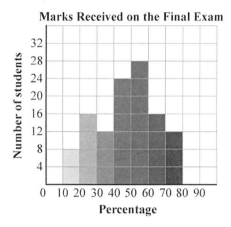

Percentage

What will be the new passing grade that ensures at least three-quarters of the students will pass the exam?

Solution

Step 1

Calculate how many students need to pass.
First, add up the number of students who got each range of marks.
8 + 16 + 12 + 24 + 28 + 16 + 12 = 116
Next, divide by 4 to find out how many students there are in one-quarter.
116 ÷ 4 = 29
Finally, multiply by 3 to find out how many students there are in three-quarters.
29 × 3 = 87
This means that at least 87 of the students need to pass the exam.

Step 2

Find out how many students pass if 50% is the passing grade.
Add up the number of students who got 50% or higher.
28 + 16 + 12 = 56
Fifty-six students pass if the passing grade is 50%. This is much fewer than three-quarters of the students. That means the passing grade has to be lower.

Step 3

Find out how many students pass if 40% is the passing grade.

Add up the number of students who got 40% or higher.

$24 + 28 + 16 + 12 = 80$

If the new passing grade is 40%, 80 students will pass. This is still fewer than three-quarters of the students.

Step 4

Find out how many students pass if 30% is the passing grade.

Add up the number of students who got 30% or higher.

$12 + 24 + 28 + 16 + 12 = 92$

Ninety-two students got 30% or higher. This is more than three-quarters of the students.

The teachers need to change the passing grade to 30% so that at least three-quarters of the students will pass.

20S.1 Solve problems that involve creating and interpreting graphs, including: bar graphs; histograms; line graphs; and circle graphs.

IDENTIFYING GRAPHS THAT MAY BE BIASED

Graphs are used for comparing data. Data can be quickly interpreted and conclusions can be formed based on information presented in graphs. However, graphs can be set up in ways that make results appear more or less profound than they actually are. Sometimes, whether intentionally or not, graphs are manipulated in ways that lead people toward making certain conclusions. For example, the title of a graph can be written in a way that suggests people should reach a particular conclusion about the data shown in the graph.

Example

The given graph shows gasoline prices from 1995 to 2005. Consider the titles "Rapid Price Increases of Gasoline" and "Gasoline Prices from 1995 to 2005." The first title sets the mind to look for a certain pattern in the data. The second title is neutral, leaving the viewer to draw his or her own conclusion. Titles should only indicate what the data is about and be free of any analysis and judgment.

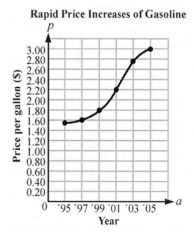

The scale of a graph can also be skewed to either enhance or minimize the apparent differences between variables. One way this can be done is to exclude a large portion of the range of a graph in order to make differences appear larger.

Example

For a school project, Jimmy surveyed the members of the graduating class at his school to find out each student's favourite burger joint. He asked the students to choose among the four fast-food places in the area. He used the results to create a bar graph.

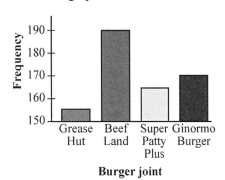

What is misleading about the bar graph Jimmy created?

Solution

The bar graph is omitting responses 0 to 150 for each restaurant. Based on the graph, it appears that Beef Land is significantly more popular than every other restaurant and that almost no one likes Grease Hut. If the values 0 to 150 are included in the graph, the results appear much more even.

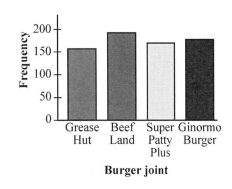

Another source of bias is found when graphs are illustrated with bars of different widths or pictures of different sizes.

Example

One of these graphs is misleading.

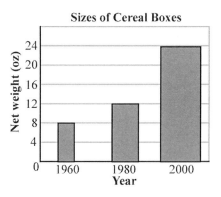

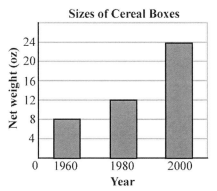

Identify the misleading graph, and explain what was done to it to mislead the reader.

Solution

In the first graph, the bars increase in width as the weight increases. This makes the weight increase appear more dramatic. This misleads the reader.

In the second graph, all the bars are equal in width. This makes the weight increase appear less dramatic, and does not mislead the reader.

A graph of the average number of goals scored per game by three soccer teams is given.

Identify what is misleading about the graph.

Solution

The diameter of each soccer ball is proportionally related to the number of goals per game. This means that the area of each successive soccer ball is increasing significantly faster than the diameter. The second ball has about 4 times the area of the first, and the third one has about 9 times the area. This makes higher-scoring teams appear to have significantly better averages.

_____

Use the following information to answer the next question.

A survey is conducted in a class of 55 students to determine their favourite flower. The given table shows the results.

Type of Flower	Number of Students
Rose	25
Lily	10
Tulip	15
Sunflower	5

1. Which of the following graphs represents the data correctly?

A.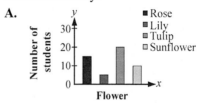

B.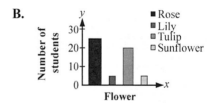

C.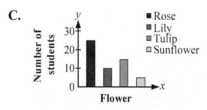

D.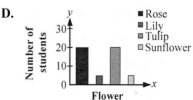

Use the following information to answer the next question.

Mr. Garcia made a circle graph to show the breakdown of each school day. First, he created a table to show how much of the day each activity takes up.

Activity	Percentage of School Day (%)
Breaks and lunch	25
Science	14
Math	17
Social studies	14
Language	20
Other	10

Then, he made a key to show which colour represents each activity in his circle graph.

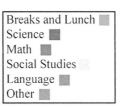

Breaks and Lunch
Science
Math
Social Studies
Language
Other

2. Which of the following circle graphs **best** represents Mr. Garcia's data?

A.
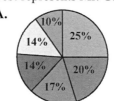
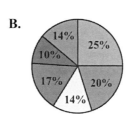

B.
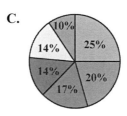

C.

D.

Use the following information to answer the next question.

Sophie conducted a probability experiment with two coins. She recorded her results in a tally chart. To make it easier to interpret, Sophie wants to create a bar graph from her recorded data. She was given the following steps.

1. Determine the number of outcomes.
2. Draw the *x*-axis and the *y*-axis.
3. Draw a bar for each outcome.
4. Label the *x*-axis and the *y*-axis.
5. Title the bar graph.

Sophie realized the steps she was given were not in the correct order.

Numerical Response

3. What is the correct order of the steps? (Record your answer as a five-digit number.) _____

Use the following information to answer the next question.

The given table shows the different types of footwear sold by a shoe store in an average week. Overall, 184 sales were made.

Footwear	Number of Sales
Sandals	36
Boots	28
Loafers	24
Sneakers	48
Slippers	20
Pumps	28

4. When a circle graph is used to present this information, how many degrees will be in the section representing loafers?
   - **A.** 13°
   - **B.** 24°
   - **C.** 47°
   - **D.** 86°

Use the following information to answer the next question.

An IQ test was given to 180 randomly selected students. The test results are shown in the given histogram.

Results of an IQ Test

5. Which of the following conclusions about the IQ scores is supported by the histogram?
   - **A.** The average IQ score of the students surveyed is 100.
   - **B.** Half of the students surveyed have an IQ score of 100 or greater.
   - **C.** The number of students with an IQ score between 85 and 95 is the same as between 95 and 100.
   - **D.** The number of students with an IQ score of 85 is greater than the number of students with an IQ score of 80.

Use the following information to answer the next question.

The data in the table shows the favourite activities of a group of middle school students.

Activity	Number of Students
Dancing	25
Painting	20
Reading	15
Sports	30
Music	25

6. The data in the table would **best** be represented by a

   A. line plot

   B. bar graph

   C. histogram

   D. stem-and-leaf plot

Use the following information to answer the next question.

This bar graph shows the amount of municipal waste produced by the top ten waste producers in 2000.

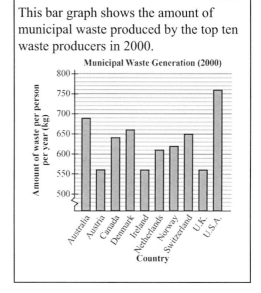

7. Which of the following statements about the information provided in the graph is **false**?

   A. Denmark produced 100 kg less waste per person than the United States.

   B. The United States produced more than twice as much waste as the United Kingdom.

   C. Austria, Ireland, and the United Kingdom all produced the same amount of waste per person.

   D. The Netherlands and Switzerland combined produced as much waste as Canada and Norway combined.

Use the following information to answer the next question.

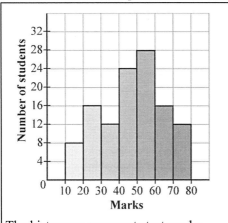

The histogram represents test marks received by 116 students.

8. Which of the following sets of numbers correctly displays the given data?

A.

Number of Students	Marks
12	10–20
16	20–30
8	30–40
24	40–50
22	50–60
12	60–70
16	70–80

B.

Number of Students	Marks
12	10–20
24	20–30
12	30–40
16	40–50
16	50–60
22	60–70
8	70–80

C.

Number of Students	Marks
8	10–20
12	20–30
12	30–40
16	40–50
16	50–60
22	60–70
24	70–80

D.

Number of Students	Marks
8	10–20
16	20–30
12	30–40
24	40–50
28	50–60
16	60–70
12	70–80

ANSWERS AND SOLUTIONS
STATISTICS

1. C	3. 52413	5. C	7. B
2. C	4. C	6. B	8. D

1. C

The bars on the graph will add up to the total number of students surveyed.

$25 + 10 + 15 + 5 = 55$

The bars should also all be the same width or else it is misleading. This graph correctly displays the favourite flowers of the students.

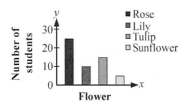

2. C

Use the given table and key to construct a circle graph of Mr. Garcia's data.

Step 1

Calculate each percentage as an angle in degrees. This will determine how much of the circle graph each activity should take up.

First, divide the percentage by 100. Then, multiply by 360°.

- Breaks and lunch:
  $25\% \div 100 = 0.25 \times 360° = 90°$
- Science: $14\% \div 100 = 0.14 \times 360° = 50.4°$
- Math: $17\% \div 100 = 0.17 \times 360° = 61.2°$
- Social studies:
  $14\% \div 100 = 0.14 \times 360° = 50.4°$
- Language: $20\% \div 100 = 0.20 \times 360° = 72°$
- Other: $10\% \div 100 = 0.10 \times 360° = 36°$

Step 2

Draw a circle using a compass, and add each sector using a protractor.

To show each activity, use the given key and the angle measures found in step 1.

Start at the top of the graph using the largest angle. This is 90° for "Breaks and Lunch."

Move clockwise until the smallest angle is drawn. This is 36° for the "Other" category.

The partially completed circle graph with angle measures is shown.

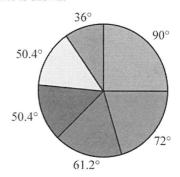

Step 3

Label the circle graph using the percentages from the table.

3. **52413**

The correct order of steps is given.

- Title the bar graph. It is important to determine the title first because it will help keep the data organized.
- Draw the x-axis and the y-axis. The next step should be to create the graph.
- Label the x-axis and the y-axis. It is important to label your axes before the number of outcomes is determined. This makes it easier to input the data into the bar graph.
- Determine the number of outcomes. Sophie should have two outcomes, one for heads and one for tails.
- Draw a bar for each outcome. The bar for heads should show how many times she flipped heads. The bar for tails should show how many times she flipped tails.

The correct order of steps is 5, 2, 4, 1, 3.

4. **C**

Step 1
Find the percentage of sales of loafers.

Divide the sales of loafers by the total number of shoe sales.

The total number of sales is 184.

The percentage of sales for loafers is
$\frac{24}{184} \times 100 \approx 13\%$.

Step 2
Determine how many degrees in the section represent loafers.

To convert the percentage to an angle, convert the percentage to a decimal and then multiply by 360°.
$\frac{13}{100} \times 360° \approx 47°$

The section in the circle graph representing loafers is approximately 47°.

5. **C**

Determine which conclusion is supported by the given histogram:

Step 1
Determine the average IQ score of the students surveyed.

The average score cannot be determined from the histogram because exact values are required to calculate mean. You cannot make the conclusion that the average IQ is 100.

Step 2
Determine if half of the students have an IQ score of 100 or greater.

First, find the number of students with IQ scores less than 100 by adding up the number of students in each bar from 80 to 100.
$5 + 20 + 20 + 40 = 85$
Then, find the number of students with IQ scores of 100 or greater.
$40 + 30 + 5 + 20 = 95$
Since 95 is more than half of the 180 students surveyed, you cannot conclude that half of the students have an IQ score of 100 or greater.

Step 3
Compare the number of students with an IQ score of 80 or 85.

The number of students with a particular score, such as 80 or 85, cannot be determined from a histogram. Histograms only show data in ranges, so exact values are not given.

Therefore, you cannot conclude that more students had an IQ score of 85 than 80.

Step 4
Compare the number of students with IQ scores between 85 and 95 to those with scores between 95 and 100.

- Between 85 and 95, there are $20 + 20 = 40$ students.
- Between 95 and 100, there are 40 students.

You can conclude that the number of students with an IQ score between 85 and 95 is the same as the number of students between 95 and 100.

Therefore, the only conclusion supported by the graph is that the number of students with an IQ score between 85 and 95 is the same as between 95 and 100.

6. B

The data is divided into categories. The best choice of graph to display categorical data is a bar graph.

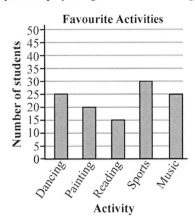

Number of students who participate in after-school activities

7. B

The United Kingdom produced 560 kg of waste per person in 2000. Twice as much as this amount is $560 \times 2 = 1\ 120$. The United States did not produce 1 120 kg of waste per person. The statement that the United States produced more than twice as much waste as the United Kingdom is false.

Denmark produced 660 kg of waste per person, and the United States produced 760 kg of waste per person. Since $760 - 660 = 100$, the statement that Denmark produced 100 kg less waste per person than the United States is true.

The statement that Austria, Ireland, and the United Kingdom each produced 560 kg of waste per person is true.

The Netherlands produced 610 kg of waste per person, and Switzerland produced 650 kg of waste per person. Canada produced 640 kg of waste per person, and Norway produced 620 kg of waste per person. Since $610 + 650 = 1\ 260$ and $640 + 620 = 1\ 260$, the statement that the Netherlands and Switzerland combined produced as much waste as Canada and Norway combined is true.

8. D

The histogram displays the given information.

- 10–20→ 8 students
- 20–30→ 16 students
- 30–40→ 12 students
- 40–50→ 24 students
- 50–60→ 28 students
- 60–70→ 16 students
- 70–80→ 12 students

UNIT TEST — STATISTICS

Use the following information to answer the next question.

Sherry makes a frequency chart to show how the number of Grade 6 students attending her school has changed over five years. She uses the enrolment at the end of the second week of January for each of the five years.

Year	Frequency
2007	48
2006	43
2005	32
2004	37
2003	25

1. Which of the following histograms shows the changes in the Grade 6 population?

A.
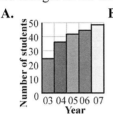

B.
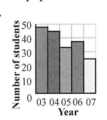

C.
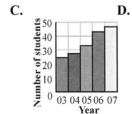

D.
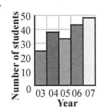

Use the following information to answer the next question.

The given table shows the change in population of a town over five years.

Year	2001	2002	2003	2004	2005
Population (thousands)	5	7	10	11	12

2. Which of the following line graphs correctly displays the information in the given table?

A.
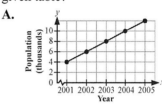

B.
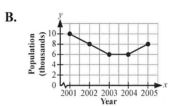

C.
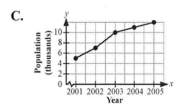

D.
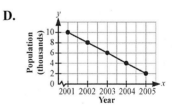

Use the following information to answer the next question.

Amounts of Rain in Three Canadian Cities

	Toronto	Montreal	Vancouver
Rain (mm)	800	1 125	1 125
Wet days	160	190	195

3. Based on the data in the table, which of the following graphs is misleading?

A.

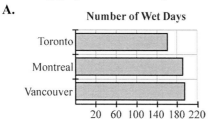

Number of Wet Days

B.

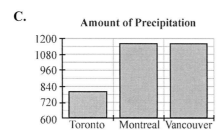

Number of Wet Days

C.

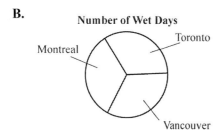

Amount of Precipitation

D.

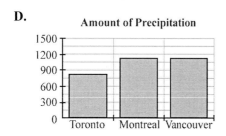

Amount of Precipitation

Use the following information to answer the next question.

To train for a race, Ahmad runs 10 metres every second after a 2 second start.

4. Which of the following graphs describes the distance that Ahmad ran in each second of his training run?

A.

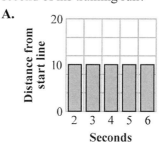

B.

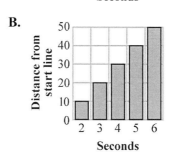

C.

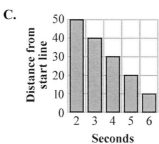

D.

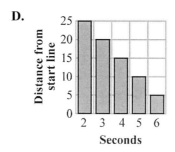

Use the following information to answer the next question.

This given circle graph shows the world's consumption of energy sources.

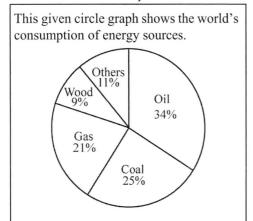

5. Rounded to the nearest degree, how many degrees of the circle represents Gas?

   A. 21°   **B.** 46°

   C. 76°   **D.** 90°

Use the following information to answer the next question.

Neil surveys 30 students on the playground to see how many siblings they have. He records the data in a frequency table.

Number of Siblings	Frequency
0	⦀⦀
1	⦀⦀ ⦀⦀ ||
2	⦀⦀ ||
3	|||
4	||
5	
6	|

6. Which of the following graphs is **most appropriate** to display this data?

   A. Line plot

   B. Bar graph

   C. Histogram

   D. Stem-and-leaf plot

Use the following information to answer the next question.

Mrs. Henry makes a histogram of the math marks on the final exam.

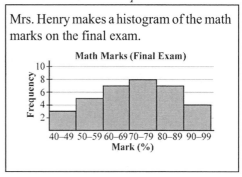

Numerical Response

7. According to her histogram, how many students scored a mark of 80% or higher? _____

Use the following information to answer the next question.

Mariah surveyed the students in her grade who own pets to determine the type of pet each student has.

Pet	Number of Students
Snake	3
Dog	15
Cat	25
Fish	10
Bird	5

Written Response

8. Construct a circle graph to represent this information.

ANSWERS AND SOLUTIONS — UNIT TEST

1. D	3. C	5. C	7. 11
2. C	4. B	6. A	8. WR

1. D

The correct histogram must show the given information.

- 2003 must reach a height of 25.
- 2004 must reach a height of 37.
- 2005 must reach a height of 32.
- 2006 must reach a height of 43.
- 2007 must reach a height of 48.

This histogram shows the changes in the Grade 6 population.

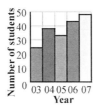

2. C

The information in the table shows that the population of the town increases over five years. Graphs A and C are the only graphs that show a constant increase in population.

Graph A shows that the population in 2001 was 4 000. This value does not match the information in the table.

In graph C, as shown, all of the values match the information given in the table.

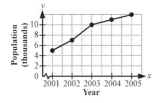

3. C

Check for the ways in which a graph can be misleading.

The data can be represented in a graph in three misleading ways:

- Not including labels on the axes
- Beginning the dependent axis at a point greater than zero
- Increasing the axes by uneven increments

The y-axis in the graph C does not start at zero. Therefore, the graph is misleading.

4. B

Reading a bar graph is very similar to reading a line graph. Start with the x-axis and follow the bar to the top. Then, read across to the y-axis to find the value that the bar reaches. An increase of 10 metres from the start line for every second of Ahmad's run is shown in B.

5. C

To calculate the degrees in a circle graph that are required to represent Gas, follow these steps:

Step 1: Determine the percentage of the circle graph that Gas represents and convert the percentage into a decimal number.

$$21\% = \frac{21}{100} = 21 \div 100 = 0.21$$

Step 2: Multiply the decimal by 360°, the sum of the central angles in a circle.
$$0.21 \times 360° = 75.6°$$

Rounded to the nearest degree, the section of the circle graph that represents Gas measures 76°.

6. **A**

This is discrete data, so the best choices would be either a line plot or a stem-and-leaf plot. Because there are only 30 values and the range of the values is quite small, a line plot is a better choice.

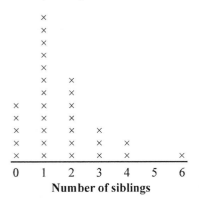

Number of siblings

7. **11**

Step 1

Read the data in the histogram.

Find the number of students who scored a mark of 80% or higher. This data is shown in the two bars on the right side of the graph.

In total, 7 students scored a mark between 80% and 89%, and 4 students scored a mark between 90% and 99%.

Step 2

Add the total number of students in each grade range that is higher than 80%.

$7 + 4 = 11$

A total of 11 students scored higher than 80% on the math final exam.

8. **WR**

Step 1

Convert the data into percentages.

Divide each part of the data by the total data, and multiply by 100 to get the percentage for each activity. The total number of pets is
$3 + 15 + 25 + 10 + 5 = 58$.

- Snake: $\frac{3}{58} \times 100\% \approx 5\%$

- Dog: $\frac{15}{58} \times 100\% \approx 26\%$

- Cat: $\frac{25}{58} \times 100\% \approx 43\%$

- Fish: $\frac{10}{58} \times 100\% \approx 17\%$

- Bird: $\frac{5}{58} \times 100\% \approx 9\%$

The total percentages should add up to 100.
$5 + 26 + 43 + 17 + 9 = 100$

Step 2

Calculate each percentage as an angle in degrees.
Divide the percentage by 100, and multiply by 360°.

- Snake: $\frac{5}{100} \times 360° = 18°$

- Dog: $\frac{26}{100} \times 360° = 94°$

- Cat: $\frac{43}{100} \times 360° = 155°$

- Fish: $\frac{17}{100} \times 360° = 61°$

- Bird: $\frac{9}{100} \times 360° = 32°$

The total of the measures of the angles should add up to 360.
$18 + 94 + 155 + 61 + 32 = 360$

Step 3

Draw a circle.

Use a compass to make a circle large enough to label the sectors.

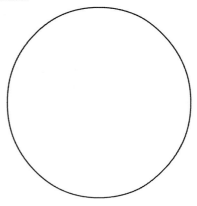

Step 4

Draw each of the angles.

Use a protractor to draw each of the angles or sectors. Start at the top of the circle graph, and use the largest angle. Move in a clockwise direction until the smallest angle is drawn.

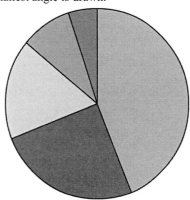

Step 5

Label the circle graph.

Include the category and percentage for each sector. Give the graph a title.

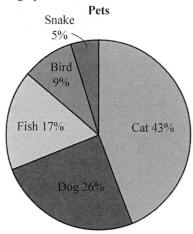

KEY Strategies for Success on Tests

KEY STRATEGIES FOR SUCCESS ON TESTS

This section is all about the skills and strategies you need to be successful on tests. It is designed for you to use together with your classroom learning and assignments.

FINDING OUT ABOUT THE TESTS

Here are some questions you may wish to discuss with your teacher to help you prepare for quizzes and tests:

- What will this test assess, or cover?

- How much time do I have to write the test?

- How important is this test to my final grade?

- Are there any materials provided for the test?

- What materials do I need to bring to write the test?

- What kind of questions are on the test? Will they be multiple choice? Short answer?

Having a good understanding of effective test-taking skills can help you do well on tests. Being familiar with different types of questions may also help you.

THINGS TO CONSIDER WHEN TAKING A TEST

It is normal to feel anxious before you write a test. You can manage this anxiety by using the following strategies:

- Think positive thoughts. Imagine yourself doing well on the test.

- Make a conscious effort to relax by taking several slow, deep, controlled breaths. Concentrate on the air going in and out of your body.

- Before you begin the test, ask questions if you are unsure of anything.

- Jot down key words or phrases from any instructions your teacher gives you.

- Look over the entire test to find out the number and kinds of questions on the test.

- Read each question closely, and reread if necessary.

- Pay close attention to key vocabulary words. Sometimes, these words are **bolded** or *italicized*, and they are usually important words in the question.

- If you are putting your answers on an answer sheet, mark your answers carefully. Always print clearly. If you wish to change an answer, erase the mark completely, and ensure that your final answer is darker than the one you have erased.

- Use highlighting to note directions, key words, and vocabulary that you find confusing or that are important to answering the question.

- Double-check to make sure you have answered everything before handing in your test.

- When taking tests, students often overlook the easy words. Failure to pay close attention to these words can result in an incorrect answer. One way to avoid this is to be aware of these words and to underline, circle, or highlight them while you are taking the test.

- Even though some words are easy to understand, they can change the meaning of the entire question, so it is important that you pay attention to them. Here are some examples.

all	always	most likely	probably	best	not
difference	usually	except	most	unlikely	likely

Example

1. Which of the following equations is incorrect?

    A. $3 + 2 = 5$

    B. $4 - 3 = 1$

    C. $5 \times 4 = 15$

    D. $6 \times 3 = 18$

HELPFUL STRATEGIES FOR ANSWERING MULTIPLE-CHOICE QUESTIONS

A multiple-choice question gives you some information and then asks you to select an answer from four choices. Each question has one correct answer. The other choices are distractors, which are incorrect.

The following strategies can help you when answering multiple-choice questions:

- Quickly skim through the entire test. Find out how many questions there are, and plan your time accordingly.

- Read and reread questions carefully. Underline key words, and try to think of an answer before looking at the choices.

- If there is a graphic, look at the graphic, read the question, and go back to the graphic. Then, you may want to underline the important information from the question.

- Carefully read the choices. Read the question first and then each choice that goes with it.

- When choosing an answer, try to eliminate those choices that are clearly wrong or do not make sense.

- Some questions may ask you to select the best answer. These questions will always include words like *best*, *most appropriate*, or *most likely*. All of the choices will be correct to some degree, but one of the choices will be better than the others in some way. Carefully read all four choices before choosing the answer you think is the best.

- If you do not know the answer, or if the question does not make sense to you, it is better to guess than to leave it blank.

- Do not spend too much time on any one question. Make a mark (*) beside a difficult question, and come back to it later. If you are leaving a question to come back to later, make sure you also leave the space on the answer sheet, if you are using one.

- Remember to go back to the difficult questions at the end of the test; sometimes, clues are given throughout the test that will provide you with answers.

- Note any negative words like *no* or *not*, and be sure your answer fits the question.

- Before changing an answer, be sure you have a very good reason to do so.

- Do not look for patterns on your answer sheet, if you are using one.

HELPFUL STRATEGIES FOR ANSWERING WRITTEN-RESPONSE QUESTIONS

A written response requires you to respond to a question or directive indicated by words such as *explain*, *predict*, *list*, *describe*, *show your work*, *solve*, or *calculate*. The following strategies can help you when answering written-response questions:

- Read and reread the question carefully.

- Recognize and pay close attention to directing words such as *explain*, *show your work*, and *describe*.

- Underline key words and phrases that indicate what is required in your answer, such as *explain*, *estimate*, *answer*, *calculate*, or *show your work*.

- Write down rough, point-form notes regarding the information you want to include in your answer.

- Think about what you want to say, and organize information and ideas in a coherent and concise manner within the time limit you have for the question.

- Be sure to answer every part of the question that is asked.

- Include as much information as you can when you are asked to explain your thinking.

- Include a picture or diagram if it will help to explain your thinking.

- Try to put your final answer to a problem in a complete sentence to be sure it is reasonable.

- Reread your response to ensure you have answered the question.

- Ask yourself if your answer makes sense.

- Ask yourself if your answer sounds right.

- Use appropriate subject vocabulary and terms in your response.

ABOUT MATHEMATICS TESTS

WHAT YOU NEED TO KNOW ABOUT MATHEMATICS TESTS

To do well on a mathematics test, you need to understand and apply your knowledge of mathematical concepts. Reading skills can also make a difference in how well you perform. Reading skills can help you follow instructions and find key words, as well as read graphs, diagrams, and tables. They can also help you solve mathematics problems.

Mathematics tests usually have two types of questions: questions that ask for understanding of mathematics ideas and questions that test how well you can solve mathematics problems.

HOW YOU CAN PREPARE FOR MATHEMATICS TESTS

The following strategies are particular to preparing for and writing mathematics tests:

• Know how to use your calculator, and, if it is allowed, use your own for the test.

• Note taking is a good way to review and study important information from your class notes and textbook.

• Sketch a picture of the problem, procedure, or term. Drawing is helpful for learning and remembering concepts.

• Check your answer to practice questions by working backward to the beginning. You can find the beginning by going step by step in reverse order.

• Use the following steps when answering questions with graphics (pictures, diagrams, tables, or graphs):

  1. Read the title of the graphic and any key words.

  2. Read the test question carefully to figure out what information you need to find in the graphic.

  3. Go back to the graphic to find the information you need.

  4. Decide which operation is needed.

• Always pay close attention when pressing the keys on your calculator. Repeat the procedure a second time to be sure you pressed the correct keys.

TEST PREPARATION COUNTDOWN

If you develop a plan for studying and test preparation, you will perform well on tests.

Here is a general plan to follow seven days before you write a test.

COUNTDOWN: 7 DAYS BEFORE THE TEST

1. Create your own personal test preparation plan.

2. Review the following information:

   – Areas to be included on the test

   – Types of test items

   – General and specific test tips

3. Start preparing for the test at least seven days before the test. Develop your test preparation plan,
   and set time aside to prepare and study.

COUNTDOWN: 6, 5, 4, 3, 2 DAYS BEFORE THE TEST

1. Review old homework assignments, quizzes, and tests.

2. Rework problems on quizzes and tests to make sure you still know how to solve them.

3. Correct any errors made on quizzes and tests.

4. Review key concepts, processes, formulas, and vocabulary.

5. Create practice test questions for yourself, and answer them. Work out many sample problems.

COUNTDOWN: THE NIGHT BEFORE THE TEST

1. Use the night before the test for final preparation, which includes reviewing and gathering materials needed for the test before going to bed.

2. Most importantly, get a good night's rest, and know you have done everything possible to do well on the test.

TEST DAY

1. Eat a healthy and nutritious breakfast.

2. Ensure you have all the necessary materials.

3. Think positive thoughts, such as "I can do this," "I am ready," and "I know I can do well."

4. Arrive at your school early, so you are not rushing, which can cause you anxiety and stress.

SUMMARY OF HOW TO BE SUCCESSFUL DURING A TEST

You may find some of the following strategies useful for writing a test:

- Take two or three deep breaths to help you relax.

- Read the directions carefully, and underline, circle, or highlight any important words.

- Look over the entire test to understand what you will need to do.

- Budget your time.

- Begin with an easy question or a question you know you can answer correctly rather than follow the numerical question order of the test.

- If you cannot remember how to answer a question, try repeating the deep breathing and physical relaxation activities. Then, move on to visualization and positive self-talk to get yourself going.

- When answering questions with graphics (pictures, diagrams, tables, or graphs), look at the question carefully, and use the following steps:

  1. Read the title of the graphic and any key words.

  2. Read the test question carefully to figure out what information you need to find in the graphic.

  3. Go back to the graphic to find the information you need.

- Write down anything you remember about the subject on the reverse side of your test paper. This activity sometimes helps to remind you that you do know something and are capable of writing the test.

- Look over your test when you have finished, and double-check your answers to be sure you did not forget anything.

Practice Test

PRACTICE TEST

Use the following information to answer the next question.

Mr. Guerrero gives four different students two statements and asks each to reach an appropriate conclusion, if possible, from the two given statements. The student's names, statements, and conclusions are as shown.

Amber

1. If a triangle has two equal sides, then it is isosceles.
2. In $\triangle ABC$, $AB = AC$.

Amber concludes that $\triangle ABC$ is isosceles.

Annette

1. When two lines intersect, vertically opposite angles are equal in measure.
2. Lines l_1 and l_2 intersect, forming vertically opposite angles x and y.

Annette concludes that the measure of $\angle x$ is equal to the measure of $\angle y$.

Javier

1. If a triangle is a right triangle, then the side opposite the right angle is the hypotenuse.
2. In right triangle DEF, side d is opposite angle D.

Javier concludes that side d is the hypotenuse.

Milos

1. If two angles are acute, their sum is less than 180°.
2. The sum of the measures of $\angle A$ and $\angle B$ is less than 180°.

Milos concludes that $\angle A$ and $\angle B$ are acute angles.

1. Based on the two given statements that each student received, which of the following statements with respect to the conclusions reached by each of the students is **true**?

   A. The conclusion reached by each student follows from the two given statements.

   B. Only Milos and Javier have a conclusion that follows from the two given statements.

   C. Only Amber and Annette have a conclusion that follows from the two given statements.

   D. Only Amber, Annette and Milos have a conclusion that follows from the two given statements.

Use the following information to answer the next question.

Taylor, Sidney, Luca, and Morgan went to a Halloween party. They chose to go as Anthony, Cleopatra, Romeo, and Juliet.

- Taylor bought the Romeo and Cleopatra costumes, but not her own costume.
- Sidney helped the girl dressing as Juliet make her costume.
- Luca went as Anthony.
- Morgan drove two friends who were dressed as Anthony and Cleopatra to the Halloween party.

2. Which of the following charts matches each person with his or her Halloween costume?

A.

Name	Costume
Taylor	Juliet
Sidney	Cleopatra
Luca	Anthony
Morgan	Romeo

B.

Name	Costume
Taylor	Juliet
Sidney	Romeo
Luca	Anthony
Morgan	Cleopatra

C.

Name	Costume
Taylor	Cleopatra
Sidney	Juliet
Luca	Anthony
Morgan	Romeo

D.

Name	Costume
Taylor	Romeo
Sidney	Cleopatra
Luca	Anthony
Morgan	Juliet

Use the following information to answer the next question.

Christopher is given the first four numbers in a particular series: 2, 5, 7, and 12. He is then asked to find the fifth number. He identifies the pattern that a number is added to the previous one, and he finds the fifth number to be 19.

Numerical Response

3. If the pattern continues, the sixth number in the series will be _____.

Use the following information to answer the next question.

Jasmine has worked out the given circle graph for her personal budget of $5 400/month.

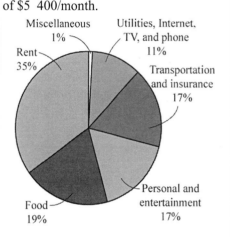

4. The amount of money that Jasmine has budgeted for her personal and entertainment expenses is
   A. $54.00   B. $594.00
   C. $918.00   D. $1 890.00

Use the following information to answer the next question.

Prior to beginning her college school year, Nikki budgets her monthly income of $1 800 as shown:

1	Food—25%
2	Clothing—15%
3	Tuition—15%
4	Childcare—15%
5	Travel—10%
6	Miscellaneous—5%
7	Entertainment—15%
8	Savings—0%

After Nikki's classes begin, she learns that she will receive a bursary of $200 per month from the college. She wants to allocate the same dollar amount from her previous budget for each item in her new budget and put the $200 toward savings.

5. Which of the following circle graphs shows Nikki's new budget, based on a monthly income of $2 000?

A.
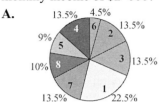

B.
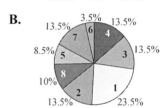

C.
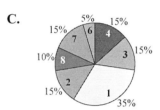

D.
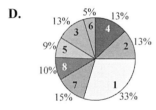

Use the following information to answer the next question.

The Tokarek family has set aside $5 000 for a family vacation. Their budget for transportation, food, accommodations, entertainment, and spending money is shown in the chart below.

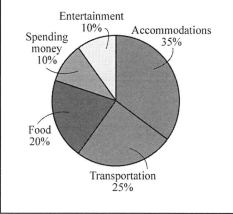

Use the following information to answer the next question.

Jonathon took out a loan for $5 550 with an interest rate of 6.5%/a, compounded weekly.

8. If Jonathan would like to pay off the loan at the end of 2.5 years, the number of compounding periods is

   A. 52   B. 104

   C. 130   D. 365

Use the following information to answer the next question.

A $68 400 investment was made. At the end of 12.7 years, it was worth $128 875.

Numerical Response

9. The amount of compound interest earned on the investment is $_____.

Use the following information to answer the next question.

Brenda's bank charges her $0.50 for each cheque that she writes, $0.40 for each ATM transaction that she makes, and a monthly $1.75 maintenance fee. In the month of August, Brenda wrote 17 cheques and made 11 ATM transactions.

10. What was the total amount in bank fees that Brenda paid in August?

    A. $2.65   B. $11.15

    C. $12.90   D. $14.65

Numerical Response

6. If 80% of the transportation budget is for airfare, then the amount of the transportation budget, to the nearest dollar, that the Tokareks have allotted for airline tickets is $_____.

7. Which of the following equations represents the value of a $500 investment with a simple interest rate of 6%/a over several years?

   A. $t_n = 30n$

   B. $t_n = 3\ 000n$

   C. $t_n = 500(1 + 6n)$

   D. $t_n = 500(1 + 0.06n)$

Use the following information to answer the next question.

This graph indicates the growth patterns for $1 000 invested in a simple interest account compared to the same amount invested in an account which compounds interest annually.

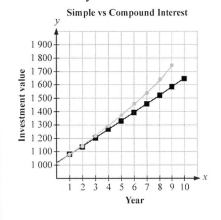

11. How many years does it take before the difference in the two investments is roughly $100?

A. 5 B. 6

C. 7 D. 8

Use the following information to answer the next question.

The diagram shows the dimensions of a box for a board game.

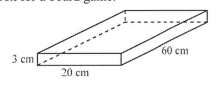

12. If 5 board games of this size can be packed into a crate, the minimum volume of the crate must be

A. 3 600 cm^3 B. 10 800 cm^3

C. 14 400 cm^3 D. 18 000 cm^3

Use the following information to answer the next question.

The following diagram represents the dimensions of a professional soccer field. The width of the field is $\frac{3}{4}$ the length and the radius of the centre circle is $\frac{1}{10}$ the width.

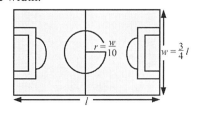

13. What are the dimensions of the soccer field, given that its perimeter is 420 m?

A. 152.7 m × 114.5

B. 120.0 m × 90.0 m

C. 85.4 m × 64.1 m

D. 60.0 m × 30.0 m

Use the following information to answer the next question.

The volume of this rectangular prism is 2 520 cm^3.

Numerical Response

14. If the height of the given prism is 15 cm and the width is 7 cm, then the length of the prism is _____ cm.

Use the following information to answer the next question.

> A glass box in a laboratory contains 150 fruit flies. After 25 days, the population of the fruit flies increases to 340.

15. The constant rate of change of the fruit fly population during this period is

   A. 7.6 flies/day   **B.** 8.6 flies/day

   C. 9.6 flies/day   **D.** 10.6 flies/day

Use the following information to answer the next question.

> Anjuli wanted to determine the perimeter of the given shape. Anjuli estimated the perimeter to be 72 yd. She used her stride as a referent, and each stride was about 1 yd.

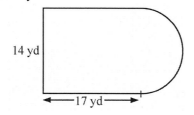

14 yd

←—— 17 yd ——→

16. Based on the actual perimeter of the shape, what was the error of Anjuli's estimation, in terms of stride lengths?

   A. 1 stride   **B.** 2 strides

   C. 3 strides   **D.** 4 strides

Use the following information to answer the next question.

> The area of a swimming pool is 350 m^2.

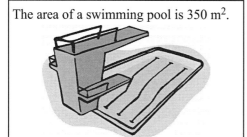

17. What is the area of the swimming pool expressed in square kilometres?

   A. 0.35 km^2 **B.** 0.035 km^2

   C. 0.0035 km^2 **D.** 0.000 35 km^2

Use the following information to answer the next question.

> Krista walks a total of 5.4 mi to get from her house to school and back again every day.

18. What is the distance Krista walks every day expressed in yards?

   A. 7 687 yd   **B.** 9 504 yd

   C. 540.22 yd   **D.** 28 512.4 yd

Use the following information to answer the next question.

> A shipping company rents a shipping container with a volume of 44 yd^3.

Numerical Response

19. The container is _____ ft^3.

Use the following information to answer the next question.

> This right triangular prism has a surface area of 42 m^2.

20. If the given prism increases in size by a scale factor of 3, then what will the surface area of the new prism be?

   A. 378 m^2 **B.** 336 m^2

   C. 252 m^2 **D.** 126 m^2

Use the following information to answer the next question.

> The area of a circle is 35 cm^2.

21. If the radius of the circle is increased by 2 cm, what is the area of the new circle, rounded to the nearest tenth of a centimetre?

   A. 73.8 cm^2 **B.** 89.5 cm^2

   C. 97.1 cm^2 **D.** 104.4 cm^2

Use the following information to answer the next question.

> When Rosalie visited her grandmother, she found a wooden block at the bottom of an old toy box. The block was shaped like a triangular prism, so Rosalie measured it and then calculated the surface area.

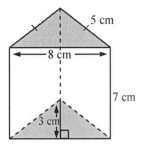

22. What is the surface area of the wooden block Rosalie found?
A. 192 cm^2 B. 180 cm^2
C. 150 cm^2 D. 136 cm^2

Use the following information to answer the next question.

> Macy owns a rectangular plot of land that measures 15 m × 6.5 m. In order to plough the land, Macy digs down and evenly removes 0.75 m of dirt from the top portion of the plot.

23. By the time she finishes, how much dirt will Macy remove, rounded to the nearest hundredth?
A. 27.08 m^3 B. 52.34 m^3
C. 73.13 m^3 D. 94.25 m^3

Use the following information to answer the next question.

> The volume of a right cylinder is 1 056 cm^3.

24. What is the volume of a right cone with the same base and height?
A. 176 cm^3 B. 352 cm^3
C. 528 cm^3 D. 704 cm^3

Use the following information to answer the next question.

> Two types of cylindrical fence posts are available at a lumber yard. One type of fence post has a diameter of 9 cm and a height of 3 m. The second type of fence post has the same height as the first but twice the volume.

25. The diameter of the second type of fence post, to the nearest tenth, is
A. 12.7 cm   B. 14.0 cm
C. 16.8 cm   D. 18.0 cm

Use the following information to answer the next question.

> A five-pin bowling ball has a diameter of approximately 12.6 cm, and a ten-pin bowling ball has a diameter that is approximately 9.2 cm more than that of a five-pin bowling ball. Given these dimensions, prior to drilling the finger holes in a ten-pin bowling ball, its volume, using $\pi = 3.14$, is x cm^3 more than the volume of a five-pin bowling ball.

Numerical Response

26. To the nearest hundred, the value of x is
_____.

Use the following information to answer the next question.

> Matt spots an airplane flying at an angle of elevation of 42° from his position on the ground. The plane is flying at an altitude of 2.50 km.

27. The distance between Matt and the point on the ground directly below the plane is approximately
A. 1.67 km   B. 1.85 km
C. 2.25 km   D. 2.78 km

Use the following information to answer the next question.

From the top of a cliff that is 90 metres (m) high, an observer sees two boats, one directly behind the other, heading for shore. The angle of depression from the observer to the farther boat is 35°, while the angle of depression to the closer boat is 55°.

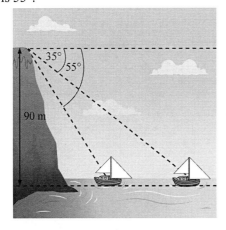

28. What is the distance between the two boats?

   A. 47 m   **B.** 66 m

   C. 119 m   **D.** 184 m

Use the following information to answer the next question.

The airport tower in Townsville is located 25.8 km from the closest edge of a nearby lake. At exactly 3:00, a plane is flying over the closest edge of the lake. The pilot measures the angle of depression to the airport tower in Townsville to be 22.5°.

Numerical Response

29. Expressed to the nearest tenth, the distance between the airplane and the airport tower at 3:00 is _____ km.

Use the following information to answer the next question.

A triangle is given.

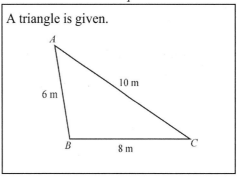

30. If a scale factor of 3:4 is applied to the given triangle, which of the following diagrams shows the resulting triangle?

   A.

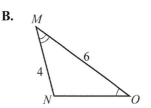

   B.

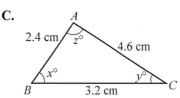

   C.

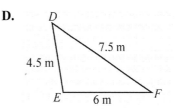

   D.

        D

              7.5 m

   4.5 m

       E   6 m   F

*Use the following information to
answer the next question.*

This map shows the distance between an
amusement park and a school. The map
scale is 1 in = 5 mi.

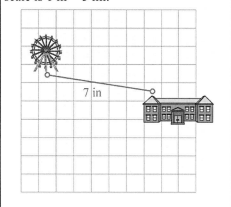

7 in

31. What is the actual distance between the
amusement park and the school?

  A. 25 mi   **B.** 30 mi

  C. 35 mi   **D.** 40 mi

*Use the following information to
answer the next question.*

The given table shows how three original
lengths were changed to their image
lengths. It also shows the scale factor used
for each change.

Original Length (cm)	Scale Factor	Image Length (cm)
8	x	16
y	$\frac{1}{8}$	56
10	0.2	z

32. What are the values for x, y, and z that
correctly complete the given table?

  A. $x = \frac{1}{2}$, $y = 7$, and $z = 2$

  B. $x = 2$, $y = 7$, and $z = 50$

  C. $x = 2$, $y = 448$, and $z = 2$

  D. $x = \frac{1}{2}$, $y = 448$, and $z = 50$

*Use the following information to
answer the next question.*

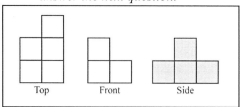

Top   Front   Side

33. Which of the following groups of blocks
is **best** represented by the given
diagrams?

  A.   **B.**

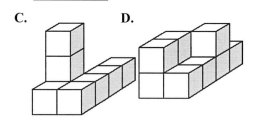

  C.   **D.**

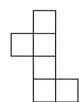

*Use the following information to
answer the next question.*

A three-dimensional solid can be created
by using a net with a two-dimensional
pattern.

34. Which of the following nets **cannot**
make a cube?

  A.   **B.**

  C.   **D.**

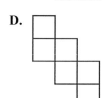

Use the following information to answer the next question.

Rachel stacked some cube-shaped boxes in her garage. Three points of view of the stack of boxes and its base are shown.

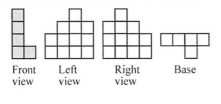

Front view   Left view   Right view   Base

35. Which of the following 3-D diagrams represents the stack of boxes?

A.

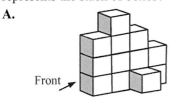

Front

B.

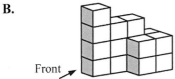

Front

C.

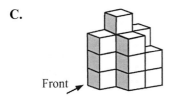

Front

D.

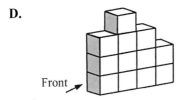

Front

Use the following information to answer the next question.

Casey checked the outdoor temperature at 11:00 A.M. for six days in a row. He recorded the temperatures in the given table.

Day	1	2	3	4	5	6
Temperature (°C)	18	19	15	19	18	20

36. Which of the following broken-line graphs displays the data recorded in Casey's table?

A.

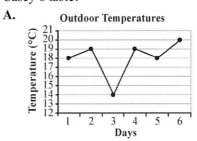

B.

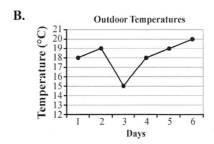

C.

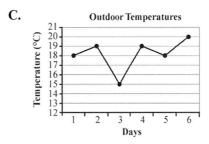

D.

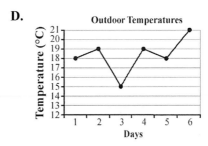

Use the following information to answer the next question.

This graph represents the estimated population growth of California.

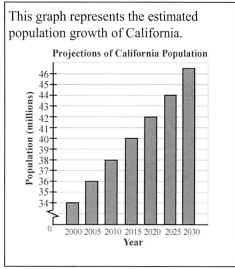

37. The trend in the graph suggests that as

A. time goes on, the population of California will increase

B. time goes on, the population of California will decrease

C. the population of California goes up, the time will increase

D. the population of California goes down, the time will decrease

Use the following information to answer the next question.

The given circle graph illustrates the percentage of votes obtained by each of five different candidates who ran in an election.

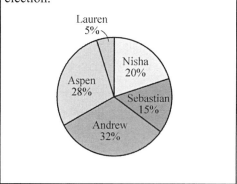

38. If a total of 1 200 votes were cast, the number of votes that Andrew received was

A. 320   B. 384

C. 420   D. 516

Use the following information to answer the next question.

Gwen recorded the weather in Lethbridge for a 30-day period and wants to use a circle graph to display the results.

☀	Sunny	12 days
🌬	Windy	3 days
☁	Cloudy	9 days
🌧	Rainy	6 days

Numerical Response

39. When drawing the circle graph, how many degrees will Gwen use to represent the sunny days? _____°

Use the following information to answer the next multipart question.

40. John bought 3 bottles of pop for $3.75.
Stan bought 5 bottles of pop for $6.25.
Chung bought 7 bottles of pop for $8.75.

What is the rate of change for this linear relation?

A. $0.50 / bottle

B. $0.75 / bottle

C. $1.25 / bottle

D. $1.75 / bottle

ANSWERS AND SOLUTIONS — PRACTICE TEST

1. C	9. 60475	17. D	25. A	33. B
2. A	10. D	18. B	26. 4400	34. C
3. 31	11. C	19. 1188	27. D	35. A
4. C	12. D	20. A	28. B	36. C
5. A	13. B	21. B	29. 27.9	37. A
6. 1000	14. 24 cm	22. C	30. D	38. B
7. D	15. A	23. C	31. C	39. 144
8. C	16. B	24. B	32. C	40. C

1. C

Amber's and Annette's conclusions are correct.

Javier's conclusion is incorrect. His second statement does not say that angle D is the right angle.

Milos' conclusion is incorrect. His second statement does not say that angles A and B are acute. It is possible that angle A could equal 150° and angle B could equal 20°.

2. A

Set up a chart similar to the following chart, and determine an individual's possible costume from the given information.

	Anthony	Cleopatra	Romeo	Juliet
Taylor				
Sidney				
Luca				
Morgan				

It is known that Taylor is not Romeo or Cleopatra, Sidney is not Juliet, Luca is Anthony, and Morgan is not Anthony or Cleopatra.

	Anthony	Cleopatra	Romeo	Juliet
Taylor		✗	✗	
Sidney				✗
Luca	✓			
Morgan	✗	✗		

Since Luca is Anthony, no one else can be Anthony and Luca can be no one else.

	Anthony	Cleopatra	Romeo	Juliet
Taylor	✗	✗	✗	
Sidney	✗			✗
Luca	✓	✗	✗	✗
Morgan	✗	✗		

By the process of elimination, Taylor must be Juliet.

	Anthony	Cleopatra	Romeo	Juliet
Taylor	✗	✗	✗	✓
Sidney	✗			✗
Luca	✓	✗	✗	✗
Morgan	✗	✗		✗

By the process of elimination, Morgan must be Romeo, and Sidney must be Cleopatra.

	Anthony	Cleopatra	Romeo	Juliet
Taylor	✗	✗	✗	✓
Sidney	✗	✓	✗	✗
Luca	✓	✗	✗	✗
Morgan	✗	✗	✓	✗

Therefore, Taylor went as Juliet, Sidney went as Cleopatra, Luca went as Anthony, and Morgan went as Romeo.

3. 31

Step 1
Identify the pattern in the given series.
Starting after the second number, 5, it appears that the next number in the series is the sum of the previous two terms.
$2 + 5 = 7$
$5 + 7 = 12$
$7 + 12 = 19$

Step 2
Determine the sixth number in the series.
The sixth number in the series would be
$12 + 19 = 31$.

4. C

The circle graph shows that Jasmine budgeted 17% of her monthly income for her personal and entertainment expenses.

Calculate 17% of Jasmine's monthly income.

Jasmine's monthly income is $5 400, so 17% of her monthly income is equal to 0.17 × 5 400 = 918.

Therefore, the amount of money Jasmine has budgeted for her personal and entertainment expenses is $918.00.

5. A

Nikki's new budget consists of $2 000 per month, but the dollar amount for each item is the same as her previous budget. The dollar amount for each item can be calculated by multiplying $1 800 (Nikki's previous monthly income) by each percentage, as set out in her budget.

Category	Budget ($)
Food	0.25 × 1 800 = 450
Clothing	0.15 × 1 800 = 270
Tuition	0.15 × 1 800 = 270
Childcare	0.15 × 1 800 = 270
Travel	0.10 × 1 800 = 180
Miscellaneous	0.05 × 1 800 = 90
Entertainment	0.15 × 1 800 = 270

Determine the new percentages in Nikki's revised budget. Divide the dollar amount allocated to each category by $2 000, and multiply the result by 100 to calculate the percentage.

Category	Budget (%)
Food	$\frac{\$450}{\$2\ 000} = 0.225$ $= 22.5\%$
Clothing	$\frac{\$270}{\$2\ 000} = 0.135$ $= 13.5\%$
Tuition	$\frac{\$270}{\$2\ 000} = 0.135$ $= 13.5\%$
Childcare	$\frac{\$270}{\$2\ 000} = 0.135$ $= 13.5\%$
Travel	$\frac{\$180}{\$2\ 000} = 0.09$ $= 9\%$
Miscellaneous	$\frac{\$90}{\$2\ 000} = 0.045$ $= 4.5\%$
Entertainment	$\frac{\$270}{\$2\ 000} = 0.135$ $= 13.5\%$
Savings	$\frac{\$200}{\$2\ 000} = 0.1$ $= 10\%$

These amounts are reflected in circle graph A.

6. 1000

From the circle graph, we can see that 25% of the Tokarek's $5 000 budget is allocated for transportation, which is equal to $5 000 × 0.25 = $1 250.

Since airfare constitutes 80% of their travel allowance, the cost of airfare should be 80% of $1 250.

80% of $1 250 = $1 250 × 0.80 = $1 000.

The airfare for the Tokarek family should be $1 000.

7. D

Step 1
Calculate the interest earned each year.
$I = Prt$
$= (500)(0.06)(1)$
$= \$30$

Step 2

Determine the sequence.

The value of the investment at the end of each year would form the arithmetic sequence $530, $560, $590,... with a common difference of $30.

Step 3

Determine the general term equation using the formula $t_n = a + (n-1)d$.

Substitute 530 for a and 30 for d.

$t_n = a + (n-1)d$
$\quad = 530 + (n-1)(30)$
$\quad = 500 + 30n$
$\quad = 500(1 + 0.06n)$

8. **C**

To calculate the number of compounding periods, n, over the total time of the investment, multiply the number of years by the frequency of compounding periods in one year.

The total time of the investment is 2.5 years, and the interest is compounded weekly, which is 52 times a year.

Multiply 2.5 by 52.
$2.5 \times 52 = 130$

The number of compounding periods at the end of 2.5 years is 130.

9. **60475**

Apply the formula $CI = FV - PV$ to calculate the amount of compound interest earned on the investment.

Substitute 128 875 for the final value, FV, and 68 400 for the present value, PV.

$CI = FV - PV$
$CI = 128\ 875 - 68\ 400$
$CI = \$60\ 475$

The investment made $60 475 in compound interest.

10. **D**

Step 1

Determine the amount charged for 17 cheques.

For 1 cheque, the bank charges $0.50, so multiply by 17.

$17 \times 0.5 = 8.5$

The charge for 17 cheques is $8.50.

Step 2

Determine the amount charged for 11 ATM transactions.

For 1 transaction, the bank charges $0.40, so multiply by 11.

$11 \times 0.40 = 4.40$

The charge for 11 transactions is $4.40.

Step 3

Determine the total amount in bank fees that Brenda paid.

Add the charge for 17 cheques, 11 transactions, and the maintenance fee.

$= 8.5 + 4.40 + 1.75$
$= 14.65$

Brenda paid $14.65 in bank fees in August.

11. **C**

The vertical axis increases in increments of $100. Thus 1 square represents $100.00. Look for a time where the vertical difference between the 2 points on the graph is closest to 1 square. At 6 years it is half of 1 square, and at 8 it is clearly more than 1 square. While it is hard to tell if it is exactly 1 square it is close at year 7.

12. **D**

Step 1

First, determine the volume of one board game by multiplying the length (20 cm) by the width (60 cm) by the height (3 cm).

$V = l \times w \times h$

$V = 20 \times 60 \times 3 = 3\ 600\ \text{cm}^3$

Step 2

To determine the minimum volume of a crate that can hold 5 board games, multiply the volume of one game by 5.

$3\ 600 \times 5 = 18\ 000\ \text{cm}^3$

The minimum volume of the crate would be $18\ 000\ \text{cm}^3$.

13. **B**

The perimeter of the rectangular soccer field is 420 m, and its width is $\frac{3}{4}$ its length. The perimeter of a rectangle $= 2l + 2w$.

Substitute $w = \frac{3}{4}l$ for w.

$$420 = \quad 2l + 2w$$
$$= 2l + 2\left(\frac{3}{4}l\right)$$

Create equivalent fractions and simplify.

$$420 = \quad \frac{8}{4}l + \frac{6}{4}l$$
$$= \quad \frac{14}{4}l$$
$$= \quad \frac{7}{2}l$$

Multiply both sides by the inverse fractional coefficient of $\frac{7}{2}$ to isolate l.

$$\frac{2}{7} \times 420 = \frac{2}{7} \times \frac{7}{2}l$$
$$120 = l$$

Therefore, the length of the soccer field is 120 m.

Substituting in 120 m, you can calculate the value of w as follows:

$$w = \frac{3}{4}l$$
$$= \frac{3}{4}(120)$$
$$= 90 \text{ m}$$

Therefore, the width of the soccer field is 90 m.

Thus, the dimensions of the soccer field are 120.0 m × 90.0 m.

14. 24 cm

To determine the length, use the formula for volume. Substitute the appropriate numbers for the volume (2 520 cm³), the width (7 cm), and the height (15 cm).

$$V = l \times w \times h$$
$$2\ 520 = l \times 7 \times 15$$
$$2\ 520 = l \times 105$$
$$2\ 520 \div 105 = l$$
$$24 \text{ cm} = l$$

The length of the prism is 24 cm.

15. A

Let p represent the population and t the time.
Constant rate of change

$$= \frac{\Delta p}{\Delta t}$$
$$= \frac{340 - 150}{25 - 0}$$
$$= \frac{190}{25}$$
$$= 7.6 \text{ flies/day}$$

16. B

Determine the perimeter, P, of the shape. This consists of three sides of a rectangle and the circumference of a semicircle. Compare it to Anjuli's estimated perimeter.

Step 1
Calculate the perimeter of the shape using the formula $C = \pi d$ for the circumference of a circle.

$$P_{shape} = P_{rectangle\ (sides)} + P_{semicircle}$$
$$= l + l + w + \frac{\pi d}{2}$$
$$= 17 + 17 + 14 + \frac{\pi(14)}{2}$$
$$= 48 + 7\pi$$
$$\approx 48 + 21.991\ 15$$
$$\approx 70.0 \text{ yd}$$

Step 2
Compare the actual perimeter to the estimated perimeter of the shape.

$$P_{difference} = P_{estimate} - P_{actual}$$
$$= 72 \text{ yd} - 70 \text{ yd}$$
$$= 2 \text{ yd}$$

Since 1 yd = 1 stride, the error in Anjuli's estimation is about 2 strides.

17. D

The horizontal conversion chart for area is given as shown.

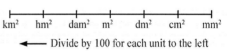

To convert from square meters to square kilometers, move three places to the left. Divide the distance by 100 for each step.

$$\frac{350}{100 \times 100 \times 100} = \frac{350}{1\ 000\ 000}$$
$$= 0.000\ 35$$
$$350 \text{ m}^2 = 0.000\ 35 \text{km}^2$$

The area of the swimming pool is 0.000 35 km².

18. B

Step 1
Choose the correct conversion ratio.
1 mi:1 760 yd

Step 2
Use the ratio to convert the distance into yards.
Multiply the given distance in miles (5.4) by the number of yards per mile (1 760).
$5.4 \times 1\ 760 = 9\ 504$
Krista walks 9 504 yd every day on her way to and from school.

19. 1188

Step 1

Determine the relationship between the units.

3 ft = 1 yd

To find the relationship between cubic feet and cubic yards, find the cube of 3.

$$1 \text{ yd}^3 = 3 \times 3 \times 3 \text{ ft}^3$$
$$= 27 \text{ ft}^3$$

Step 2

Perform the conversion.

You are going from a larger unit to a smaller unit, so you need to multiply.

$$44 \times 27 = 1\ 188 \text{ ft}^3$$

20. A

Step 1

Determine the scale factor.

The scale factor is given as 3.

Step 2

Apply the scale factor to determine the surface area of the new prism.

Since the surface area of the original object is given as 42 m^2 and the scale factor is 3, the surface area of the new prism can be calculated using the formula

$SA_{\text{proportional object}} = SA_{\text{original object}} \times$ scale factor^2.

In other words, $SA_2 = SA_1 \times$ scale factor^2.

$$SA_2 = SA_1 \times \text{scale factor}^2$$
$$SA_2 = 42 \times (3)^2$$
$$SA_2 = 42 \times 9$$
$$SA_2 = 378 \text{ m}^2$$

Therefore, the surface area of the new prism will be 378 m^2.

21. B

Step 1

Calculate the radius of the original circle.

$$A_1 = \pi(r_1)^2$$
$$35 = (3.14)(r_1)^2$$
$$(r_1)^2 = \frac{35}{3.14}$$
$$r_1 = \sqrt{\frac{35}{3.14}}$$
$$r_1 = 3.3386$$

Step 2

Make the required change to the dimensions of the circle.

$$r_2 = r_1 + 2$$
$$= 3.3386 + 2$$
$$= 5.3386$$

Step 3

Calculate the new area of the circle.

$$A_2 = \pi(r_2)^2$$
$$= (3.14)(5.3386)^2$$
$$= (3.14)(28.5)$$
$$= 89.49$$
$$\approx 89.5 \text{ cm}^2$$

The new area of the circle is 89.5 cm^2.

22. C

Step 1

Calculate the area of the triangular base.

Substitute the length of the base of the triangle (8 cm) and the height of the triangle (3 cm) into the area formula.

$$A = \frac{b \times h}{2}$$
$$A = \frac{8 \times 3}{2}$$
$$A = \frac{24}{2} = 12 \text{ cm}^2$$

Since there are two congruent bases, multiply the area by 2.

$$12 \text{ cm}^2 \times 2 = 24 \text{ cm}^2$$

Step 2

Calculate the area of each of the rectangular faces using the area formula $A = l \times w$.

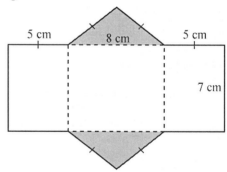

- One rectangular base has a length of 8 cm and a width of 7 cm.

  $$7 \times 8 = 56 \text{ cm}^2$$

- Two congruent bases have a length of 7 cm and a width of 5 cm, so multiply the area by 2.

  $$A = 2(7 \times 5)$$
  $$A = 2 \times 35 = 70 \text{ cm}^2$$

Step 3

Calculate the surface area.

Add the areas of the two triangular bases, the one rectangular base, and the two congruent rectangular bases.

$$\begin{array}{r} 24 \\ 56 \\ +70 \\ \hline 150 \end{array}$$

The surface area of the wooden block Rosalie found is 150 cm^2.

23. C

The dirt that is removed from the land is in the shape of a rectangular prism.

To calculate the volume of the rectangular prism, substitute the given values into the volume formula.

$$V_{\text{rectangular prism}} = A_{\text{base}} \times h$$
$$\begin{aligned} V_{\text{rectangular prism}} &= A_{\text{rectangle}} \times h \\ &= (l \times w) \times h \\ &= 15 \times 6.5 \times 0.75 \\ &= 73.125 \text{ m}^3 \end{aligned}$$

Round 73.125 to the nearest hundredth.
73.13

Macy will remove 73.13 m^3 of dirt by the time she is finished plowing the land.

24. B

The volume of a right cone is one-third the volume of a right cylinder that has the same base and height.

Divide the volume of the cylinder by 3.

$$\frac{1\ 056}{3} = 352$$

The volume of the cone is 352 cm^3.

25. A

Step 1

Determine the volume in terms of π for the first type of fence post by applying the formula for the volume of a cylinder.

The diameter of the first type of fence post is 9 cm; therefore, the radius is 9 ÷ 2 = 4.5 cm. Substitute 4.5 for r and 3 m = 300 cm for the height, h, and then solve for V.

$$\begin{aligned} V &= \pi r^2 h \\ V &= \pi \times 4.5^2 \times 300 \\ V &= \pi \times 20.25 \times 300 \\ V &= 6\ 075\pi \text{ cm}^3 \end{aligned}$$

Step 2

Determine the volume of the second type of fence post in terms of π.

Since the volume of the second type of fence post is twice the volume of the first type, it follows that the volume of the second type is

6 075π × 2 = 12 150π cm^3.

Step 3

Determine the radius of the second type of fence post by applying the formula for the volume of a cylinder.

Substitute 12 150π for V and 300 for h, and then solve for r.

$$\begin{aligned} V &= \pi r^2 h \\ 12\ 150\pi &= \pi r^2 (300) \\ 12\ 150\pi &= 300\pi r^2 \\ \frac{12\ 150\pi}{300\pi} &= r^2 \\ 40.5 &= r^2 \\ \sqrt{40.5} &= r \\ 6.36 &\approx r \end{aligned}$$

The radius of the second type of fence post is approximately 6.36 cm.

Step 4

Determine the diameter of the second type of fence post.

Since the diameter is twice the length of the radius, it follows that the diameter of the second type of fence post is approximately 6.36 cm × 2 ≈ 12.7 cm.

26. 4400

Step 1

Determine the volume of a five-pin bowling ball, V_1, by applying the formula for the volume of a sphere.

The diameter of a five-pin bowling ball is 12.6 cm, so its radius is 12.6 ÷ 2 = 6.3 cm.

Substitute 3.14 for π and 6.3 for r_1 in the formula $V = \frac{4}{3}\pi r^3$, and then solve for V_1.

$$\begin{aligned} V_1 &= \frac{4}{3}\pi r_1^3 \\ &\approx \frac{4}{3} \times 3.14 \times 6.3^3 \\ &\approx \frac{4 \times 3.14 \times 250.047}{3} \\ &\approx 1\ 046.86 \text{ cm}^3 \end{aligned}$$

Step 2

Determine the radius of a ten-pin bowling ball.
Since the diameter of a ten-pin bowling ball is
9.2 cm more than the diameter of a five-pin bowling
ball, it follows that the diameter of a ten-pin bowling
ball is 12.6 + 9.2 = 21.8 cm. Therefore, the radius
of a ten-pin bowling ball is 21.8 ÷ 2 = 10.9 cm.

Step 3

Determine the volume of a ten-pin bowling ball,
V_2, by applying the formula for the volume of
a sphere.

Substitute 3.14 for π and 10.9 for r_2 in the formula
$V = \frac{4}{3}\pi r^3$, and then solve for V_2.

$$V_2 = \frac{4}{3}\pi r_2^3$$
$$\approx \frac{4}{3} \times 3.14 \times 10.9^3$$
$$\approx \frac{4 \times 3.14 \times 1\ 295.029}{3}$$
$$\approx 5\ 421.85 \text{ cm}^3$$

Step 4

Determine the value of x.

Since the volume of a five-pin bowling ball is
approximately 1 046.86 cm³ and the volume of a
ten-pin bowling ball is approximately
5 421.85 cm³, it follows that the volume of a ten-pin
bowling ball is approximately
5 421.85 cm³ – 1 046.86 cm³ ≈ 4 374.99 cm³
more than the volume of a five-pin bowling ball.
To the nearest hundred, the value of x is 4 400.

27. D

Step 1

Draw a diagram to represent the given information.

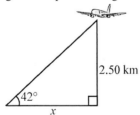

2.50 km

42°

x

Step 2

Identify the trigonometric ratio to use to solve for x
in the diagram, which represents the distance
between Matt and the point on the ground directly
below the plane.

The height 2.50 km is the side opposite the angle of
elevation. The side adjacent to the angle of elevation
is shown as x. This is the distance between Matt and
the point on the ground directly below the plane.
Since the opposite side and the adjacent side are
involved, the tangent ratio should be used.

$$\tan \theta = \frac{O}{A}$$

Step 3

Substitute the variables into the equation, and solve
for x.

$$\tan 42° = \frac{2.50}{x}$$
$$x\tan 42° = 2.50$$
$$x = \frac{2.50}{\tan 42°}$$
$$x \approx 2.78$$

The distance between Matt and the point on the
ground directly below the plane is approximately
2.78 km.

28. B

Step 1

Determine the distance to the farther boat, d_f, from
the base of the cliff using the tangent ratio.

$$\tan 35° = \frac{90}{d_f}$$
$$d_f = \frac{90}{\tan 35°}$$
$$d_f \approx 128.533$$

Step 2

Determine the distance to the closer boat, d_c, from
the base of the cliff using the tangent ratio.

$$\tan 55° = \frac{90}{d_c}$$
$$d_c = \frac{90}{\tan 55°}$$
$$d_c \approx 63.0187$$

Step 3

Determine the distance between the two boats by subtracting the distances from the cliff.

$$d_f - d_c \approx 128.533 - 63.0187$$

$$d_f - d_c \approx 65.5143$$

$$d_f - d_c \approx 66$$

To the nearest metre, the distance between the two boats is 66 m.

29. 27.9

Step 1

Draw a diagram to represent the given information. The angle of depression from the airplane to the tower is equal to the angle of elevation from the tower to the airplane, since both angles are measured from the horizontal. Let x represent the distance of the airplane from the tower.

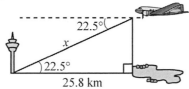

Step 2

Identify which trigonometric ratio to use to solve for x.

The unknown side, x, is the hypotenuse, and the 25.8 km side is adjacent to the 22.5° angle. Since the adjacent side and the hypotenuse are involved, the cosine ratio should be used.

$$\cos \theta = \frac{A}{H}$$

Step 3

Substitute the variables into the equation, and solve for x.

$$\cos 22.5° = \frac{25.8}{x}$$

$$x \cos 22.5° = 25.8$$

$$x = \frac{25.8}{\cos 22.5°}$$

$$x \approx 27.9$$

At 3:00, the distance of the airplane from the tower is approximately 27.9 km.

30. D

Use the formula for scale factor to determine the new side lengths of the triangle.

The scale factor can be written as the fraction $\frac{3}{4}$.

Set up the proportions.

Side AC is calculated as follows:

$$\text{scale factor} = \frac{\text{image length}}{\text{original length}}$$

$$\frac{3}{4} = \frac{x}{10}$$

$$\frac{30}{4} = x$$

$$7.5 = x$$

Side AB is calculated as follows:

$$\text{scale factor} = \frac{\text{image length}}{\text{original length}}$$

$$\frac{3}{4} = \frac{x}{6}$$

$$\frac{18}{4} = x$$

$$4.5 = x$$

Side BC is calculated as follows:

$$\text{scale factor} = \frac{\text{image length}}{\text{original length}}$$

$$\frac{3}{4} = \frac{x}{8}$$

$$\frac{24}{4} = x$$

$$6 = x$$

Therefore, the resulting triangle would have side measurements of 7.5 m, 4.5 m, and 6 m.

31. C

According to the map scale, 1 in = 5 mi. On the map, the distance between the amusement park and the school is 7 in. To find the actual distance, multiply by 5.

$$7 \times 5 \text{ mi} = 35 \text{ mi}$$

The actual distance between the amusement park and the school is 35 mi.

32. C

Determine the missing values from the table by using the scale factor formula for the values in each row of the table. Substitute the known values into the formula, and solve for the unknown value.

Step 1

Solve for x.

$$\text{scale factor} = \frac{\text{image length}}{\text{original length}}$$

$$x = \frac{16}{8}$$

$$= 2$$

Step 2

Solve for y.

$$\text{scale factor} = \frac{\text{image length}}{\text{original length}}$$

$$\frac{1}{8} = \frac{56}{y}$$

$$y = 8(56)$$

$$= 448$$

Step 3

Solve for z.

$$\text{scale factor} = \frac{\text{image length}}{\text{original length}}$$

$$0.2 = \frac{z}{10}$$

$$0.2(10) = \left(\frac{z}{10}\right)(10)$$

$$z = 2$$

Therefore, $x = 2$, $y = 448$, and $z = 2$.

33. B

Step 1

Determine the height of the front and side views.
Label each of the front squares with the number of blocks tall the shape can be as indicated by the front view. Label each of the right side views with the number of blocks tall the shape can be as indicated by the right side view.

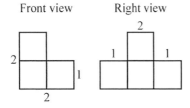

Step 2

Draw the three dimensional figure.

Cross reference the number from the front view and the right side view. If the two numbers are the same, that is the height of the object in that square of the plan view.

34. C

Step 1

Determine the shape and number of faces in a cube. A cube has 6 square faces.

Step 2

Although the nets may be different, each must have 6 square faces. In order to form a closed net, there must be square flaps on each side of the net.
While the following net has 6 square faces, the 2 projected square flaps are on the same side of the net and will overlap each other.

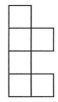

35. A

Step 1

Determine the height of each view.
Label each of the front squares with the height of the blocks as indicated by the front view. Label each of the left side views with the height of the blocks as indicated by the left side view. Label each of the right side views with the height of the blocks as indicated by the right side view.

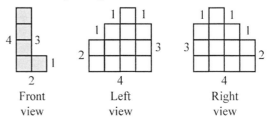

Step 2

Draw the three-dimensional view.

Cross-reference the number from the front view, left side view, and the right side view. If the two numbers are the same, that is the height of the object in that square of the plan view.

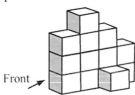

36. C

Step 1

Read each graph to determine which graph correctly displays the given data.

- Day 1: All four graphs correctly plot 18°. Continue reading the four graphs.
- Day 2: All four graphs correctly plot 19°. Continue reading the four graphs.
- Day 3: Graphs *B*, *C*, and *D* correctly plot 15°. Continue reading these three graphs.
- Day 4: Graphs *C* and *D* correctly plot 19°. Continue reading these two graphs.
- Day 5: Graphs *C* and *D* correctly plot 18°. Continue reading these two graphs.
- Day 6: Graph *C* correctly plots 20°.

Step 2

Identify the graph that correctly plotted all the given temperatures.

This broken-line graph correctly displays the data recorded in Casey's table.

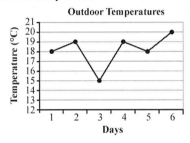

37. A

Generally, the height of the bars gets larger each year, so the trend is upward or positive, meaning the population of California is increasing as time goes on.

38. B

Step 1

Convert the percentage of votes cast for Andrew to a decimal number.

Divide the percentage of votes by 100.
$32 \div 100 = 0.32$

Step 2

Multiply the decimal number by the total number of votes cast.

$$\text{Votes cast for Andrew} = 0.32 \times 1\ 200$$
$$= 384$$

Andrew received 384 votes.

39. 144

Step 1: Determine the decimal that represents the portion of sunny days in June.

$$\frac{\text{sunny days}}{\text{total days}} = \frac{12}{30} = 12 \div 30 = 0.40$$

Step 2: Calculate 0.40 of 360°.
$0.40 \times 360° = 144°$

Thus, the degrees of the circle used to represent the sunny days is 144°.

40. C

In a linear relation, the rate of change remains constant, no matter which points are chosen.

$$\text{rate of change} = \frac{\Delta\ \text{cost(\$)}}{\Delta\ \text{bottles}}$$
$$= \frac{8.75 - 3.75}{7 - 3} = \$1.25 \Big/ \text{bottle}$$
$$\text{rate of change} = \frac{\Delta\ \text{cost(\$)}}{\Delta\ \text{bottles}}$$
$$= \frac{8.75 - 6.25}{7 - 5} = \$1.25 \Big/ \text{bottle}$$

Therefore, the rate of change for this linear relation is \$1.25/bottle.

NOTES

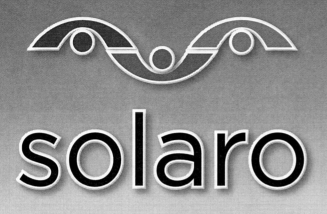

BOOK ORDERING INFORMATION

SENIOR HIGH SCHOOL TITLES

Castle Rock Research offers the following resources to support Alberta students. You can order any of these materials online at:

www.castlerockresearch.com/store

SOLARO.com - Study Online		The KEY		SNAP	Prob Solved	Class Notes
$29.95 ea.*		$29.95 ea.*		$29.95 ea.*	$19.95 ea.*	$19.95 ea.*
Biology 30	Mathematics 30-1	Biology 30	Mathematics 30-1	Biology 20	Biology 20	Biology 20
Biology 20	Mathematics 30-2	Biology 20	Mathematics 30-2	Chemistry 30	Chemistry 30	Chemistry 30
Chemistry 30	Mathematics 30-3	Chemistry 30	Mathematics 30-3	Chemistry 20	Chemistry 20	Chemistry 20
Chemistry 20	Mathematics 20-1	Chemistry 20	Mathematics 20-1	Mathematics 30-1	Mathematics 30-1	Mathematics 30-1
Physics 30	Mathematics 20-2	English 30-1	Mathematics 20-2	Mathematics 30-2	Mathematics 30-2	Mathematics 30-2
Physics 20	Mathematics 20-3	English 30-2	Mathematics 20-3	Mathematics 31	Mathematics 31	Mathematics 31
Science 30	Mathematics 20-4	English 20-1	Mathematics 20-4	Mathematics 20-1	Mathematics 20-1	Mathematics 20-1
Science 20	Mathematics 10 C	English 10-1	Mathematics 10 C	Mathematics 10 C	Mathematics 10 C	Mathematics 10 C
Science 10	Mathematics 10-3	Physics 30	Mathematics 10-3	Physics 30	Physics 30	Physics 30
English 30-1	Mathematics 10-4	Physics 20	Mathematics 10-4	Physics 20	Physics 20	Physics 20
English 30-2	Social Studies 30-1	Science 30	Social Studies 30-1	Science 10	Science 10	Science 10
English 20-1	Social Studies 30-2	Science 20	Social Studies 30-2			
English 20-2	Social Studies 20-1	Science 10	Social Studies 20-1			
English 10-1	Social Studies 10-1		Social Studies 10-1			
English 10-2						

Prices do not include taxes or shipping.

Study online using **SOLARO,** with access to multiple courses available by either a monthly or an annual subscription.

The KEY Study Guide is specifically designed to assist students in preparing for unit tests, final exams, and provincial examinations.

The **Student Notes and Problems (SNAP) Workbook** contains complete explanations of curriculum concepts, examples, and exercise questions.

The **Problem Solved** contains exercise questions and complete solutions.

The **Class Notes** contains complete explanations of curriculum concepts.

If you would like to order Castle Rock resources for your school, please visit our school ordering page:

www.castlerockresearch.com/school-orders/